Locating the
Industrial
Revolution

Inducement and Response

Locating the Industrial Revolution

Inducement and Response

Eric L Jones
La Trobe University, Australia

 World Scientific

NEW JERSEY · LONDON · SINGAPORE · BEIJING · SHANGHAI · HONG KONG · TAIPEI · CHENNAI

Published by

World Scientific Publishing Co. Pte. Ltd.

5 Toh Tuck Link, Singapore 596224

USA office: 27 Warren Street, Suite 401-402, Hackensack, NJ 07601

UK office: 57 Shelton Street, Covent Garden, London WC2H 9HE

Library of Congress Cataloging-in-Publication Data
Jones, E. L. (Eric Lionel)
    Locating the industrial revolution : inducement and response / by Eric L. Jones.
      p. cm.
    ISBN-13: 978-9814295253
    ISBN-10: 9814295256
    1. Industrialization--England--History. 2. Economic development--England--History.
3. England, Northern--Economic conditions--Regional disparities. 4. England, Southern--Economic
conditions--Regional disparities. I. Title.
    HC253.J66 2010
    330.942'08--dc22

                                                                        2010013919

British Library Cataloguing-in-Publication Data
A catalogue record for this book is available from the British Library.

In-house Editor: Juliet Lee Ley Chin

Photo image: Crofton Pumping House, Wiltshire, housing a Boulton & Watt beam engine of 1812.

Typeset by Stallion Press
Email: enquiries@stallionpress.com

Printed in Singapore.

For My Granddaughter Laura Caroline Cassell

CONTENTS

INTRODUCTION

National aggregates always hide more than they tell and this is the case even in England's relatively integrated and (by the eighteenth century) modernising society and economy.

Peter Clark, 1995

All the best social science is autobiographical, so it is said. If this is true, the present book may qualify, since it arose out of my experiences as a schoolboy in the south of England. Having attended evening classes on regional history taught by a Southampton University extra-mural tutor who held me fascinated with Hampshire's past, I was disappointed on going north to university at Nottingham to hear less than nothing about the south. My professor, David Chambers, was a regional historian par excellence, but to him that meant the Vale of Trent, Jedediah Strutt, and the stirrings of industrialisation in Nottingham and Derby.

Chambers dismissed southerners as 'supine peasants'. Although he omitted to acknowledge that many chose 'exit' rather than 'voice' and left for London or the colonies, there was something in what he said.[1] But I did not admire his corollary of ignoring what happened to those who stayed. What was it that had led their environment, once full of independent farmers and dotted with small manufacturers, to become exclusive to rich landowners, over-bearing farmers and under-valued farm workers?

This question had something to do with my choice of southern agricultural history for research at Oxford over the next nine years. During that time I made one attempt to right the glaring geographical imbalance in economic history, by writing a paper on the de-industrialisation of the south.[2] Subsequent circumstances and changing interests took me away from England and into the stratosphere of comparative and world history. This book is a

1

return to my roots — roots which unexpectedly tunnel towards a fresh conception of northern industrialisation.

Causes of the Industrial Revolution

Explanations of crucial episodes in the past are hotly disputed, a classic example being the explosion of life forms in the Cambrian Age between 365 and 325 million years ago. The explosive growth of output during the industrial revolution is an economic history parallel. What was involved? Rick Szostak sets the scene for us: regional specialisation, the emergence of new industries, an increased scale of production, and a dramatic increase in the rate of technological innovation.[3] Although 100 years ago J. H. Clapham described the industrial revolution as a 'thrice-squeezed orange', and innumerable pressings have been made since then, the complex of changes retains much of its mystery. Is there any unfamiliar approach left to try?

Perhaps there is. We enter the future backwards, said the poet Paul Valery. This book enters the past backwards by dealing first and foremost with the half of England that did not experience industrial revolution. The decay of manufacturing across the south of England is a 'control' against which to judge growth in the north, and a better one than the more distant experience of other countries. Institutional arrangements among English regions were closely similar, prompting us to look for less obvious factors.

Framing the issue around declining regions does not mean placing them in simple opposition to the ones that were growing; it exposes, instead, the forces affecting both sets. Industrialisation ceases to appear as a barely explicable upwelling of technology — you invent it and we will use it — but is seen to result from political and ideological changes bearing on investment markets. These changes were regionally expressed, which gives us our entrée into the process. As Szostak remarks, technological advance was partly a function of regional specialisation.

Some economists stigmatise the inclusion of early periods as succumbing to the historian's disease of origins. The comparative advantage of the economist does not lie in history, but the value of a broad and long analysis is unaffected by this limitation. Industrialisation's enormous consequences are not one whit diminished by considering the long run, while the causes become clearer. The argument is that it is not enough to concentrate on the accelerating rate of invention: the character of the economy encouraging this and willing to install the results in the productive system must be given its weight. Without a receptive economy the intellectual currents of the 18th century may still have inspired inventors but the social utility of their work would have been harder to realise.

Early histories, especially of Asia and the Middle East, provide ample evidence of technological advance. Some phases were remarkable but were less fruitful than industrialisation proper. The emphasis was on weaponry, luxury goods and massive buildings which reflected and reinforced traditional distributions of political power. Less was offered by way of goods for the mass market, and the prices of everyday consumables were seldom brought down. Economic energy was present but rent-seeking by the holders of power confined it to narrow channels. Economic expansion there may have been but rarely *intensive* economic growth.

The industrial revolution was novel because expansion and technological change occurred jointly. Expansion came first; the stellar inventions of the industrial revolution tended to emerge, however indirectly, in response to greater opportunities created by a widening of the market. This does not mean placing the weight of change on autonomous developments in demand. The emphasis remains on the supply side, on the sources and under-rated effects of rising competitiveness. Innovation, not just invention, and a more secure arena for investment, are what cry out for attention. Why did the changes occur first in England? Why did industrial locations shift so much within the country and what can this tell us about industrialisation in general?

During the late Middle Ages and early modern period the south had been the industrial half of the country, and the inversion produced by its decline was a 'Venetian Twilight', drawn out over the period from the 17th to the 19th centuries. Southern industries were starting to be eliminated well before the application of coal-fired steam engines to manufacturing in the north. How significant at first, then, was northern coal? Unlike most of his predecessors, a modern geographer recognises that the connection between industry and the coalfields was actually loose: 'the link between early industry and the occurrence of coal was no more than a tenuous relationship between areas of upland relief, poor soils, Paleozoic rocks and associated coal, water power and either timber for charcoal or pasture for sheep'.[4] More ordinary forms of increased competition reshaped the economy before coal had a general effect.

Underpinning wider regional competition lay freer and bolder investment in modes of communication. The investment was beginning under the early Stuarts, was apparent during the Commonwealth and Restoration periods, and was strongly encouraged by the 'elite settlement' of 1688. Throughout these tumultuous passages, the English elite were coming more decisively to embrace market ideology. Precisely how and why this was so remains unclear. Despite the obscurity, the consequences were two-fold: a reduction of rent-seeking and an acceptance of intra-elite competition as an everyday state of affairs.

Anyone who can recall school geometry may be reminded of the *pons asinorum*; if one cannot cross the bridge of asses, further progress in the subject is blocked. The *pons asinorum* of the economy was the bridge to competition among the elite; they had to cross it and relinquish 'feudal' rent-seeking. Switching the imagery to arithmetic, we should pay attention to subtraction as well as addition: we should examine the dismantling of old barriers as well as the creation of the new techniques so dear to industrial historians.

Industrialisation lay at the intersection of multiple factors, influences or forces, however they may be defined. Multi-factorial explanations are hard to fit together, but monocausal explanations are even less satisfactory because they require everything else to be poised waiting for the vital spark. With so much changing simultaneously there has always been scope for students of every corner of the economy, society and polity to emphasise or over-emphasise their specialities. Comparisons with overseas industrialisation are little help because England had already set the tone. Imitation is not the same as initiation. I agree with Cuenca Esteban that the English industrial revolution was a unique historical conjuncture rather than a fully determinate process.[5] Nevertheless, we cannot leave it at that. We have to see how far we can circumscribe the role of chance, until only an irreducible core of happenstance remains.

Historiography

About 1960 Rostow dramatised late 18th-century industrialisation as abrupt, calling it a take-off into sustained growth. Gradualism was out, the great aeronautical discontinuity was in. Belief in rapid industrialisation was congenial to economists, development economists in particular. They found it convenient to think that the first industrial revolution came about overnight, because this meant they did not need to wrestle with early periods that lacked aggregate statistical series. The further comforting implication was that industrialisation could be replicated fast. This cavalier attitude to time is part of the *deformation professionelle* of the economist, as exemplified for instance in the banking collapse of 2008–2009, when 'mathematical models were based on economic events in a very narrow window of time, *as short as ten years*'.[6]

For some economists of the Rostovian era any hint of interest in times as far back as the 17th century was especially suspect, as if this must involve Marxist interpretations of the Civil Wars: the Cold War atmosphere had paranoia lurking in it. It was neither economists nor economic historians as commonly understood, therefore, who discovered the significance of the domestic by-employments ('proto-industrialisation') of the early modern period that ironically became a cottage industry for academics during the 1960s and 1970s. Nor did they pay systematic attention to institutions; only later did economists turn to these.

A generation or more passed during which mainstream economic historians interested in English industrialisation concentrated on measuring magnitudes. The abiding residue of their labours was to bring the weight of change forward from the 18th into the 19th century, something already anticipated by Phyllis Deane and H. J. Habakkuk.[7] Subsequent quantitative work ignored or denied the significance, at times even the existence, of a lead-in period: if something were not conspicuous in the numbers, it cannot have mattered. Birth was assumed to take place without gestation.

My reading for this book reveals what seems, from a middle-of-the-road position, both undershoot and overshoot as regards the use of economic logic in history. Examples of any methodological position may of course be found, given the enormous number of books and articles, but certain tendencies are central to the work of historians and others central to economists. The former often strikes me as a little lacking in structure and sometimes too crudely hostile to what is called, but seldom specified in an operational way, capitalism. What must in retrospect seem transient, though undeniably monstrous, cruelties towards labour are over-generalised; and contemporary protests against mechanisation are taken at face value, even though nothing has been more beneficial to the working classes. Coleridge wrote to Shelley about the terrible task of casting anchors in Portsmouth dockyard, how badly the work aged the men, just as rope-making did.[8] Yet, he said, men resisted the introduction of machines. This was more understandable than Coleridge recognised but in general he was right.

Economists have some of the opposite blemishes: too casual a regard for human dignity, too great a willingness to accept dubious data as proxies for the real thing, and too much of a preference for neat solutions. Oddly, some of the difficulty comes from focussing on new technology. This did raise productivity, most definitely, but it is a sort of intermediate good, the invention and innovation of which has to be understood in the context of the whole society. Leading economic historians of technology, such as Joel Mokyr, understand this full well, but I am speaking of a surprising modal tendency to advance technological rather than economic explanations.

Deeper problems arise from assuming that institutions must evolve towards best practice, as if inefficient ones are automatically eliminated in the course of competition. Compared with trying to grasp how institutions and behaviour really may become encysted in the economy, such a position is rather uninteresting. A similar mistake is to believe that changes in relative prices will be met by automatic responses, whereas market failures and impediments along the way are more intriguing. Lapses such as this are finally attracting critical attention within economics, suffering as the subject is from bitter accusations about the efficient markets hypothesis and quantitative financial analysis.[9]

The reductionism that marks economics as well as other subjects has been aptly criticised by a mathematician who says the hope had been that grasping how the components behave would make sense of the ensemble. He observes that, 'only rarely has the dream come to fruition, and in too many cases reductionism became an end in itself … the real challenge is to master the process of reassembling the pieces, in ways that faithfully reflect the inevitable interactions among them'.[10] Like it or not (and it threatens investments in graduate-level economics), this steers back someway towards general history — though no two people will agree how far.

Statistics are often first collected after a new institutional form has been established, generating new reasons and opportunities for collecting numbers. This means that rising levels of activity may be picked up only when they have already been driving upwards for some time. As a result we find observation biases in the literature stemming from an excessive, sometimes exclusive, reliance on pre-formed bodies of data. In addition there is a tendency to devote space to more rather than less recent changes, as if they must necessarily be more formative.[11] With respect to institutional and political changes this is by no means guaranteed because old arrangements may persist for a long time.

Stuart Jones has pointed out that as late as 1860 the non-modernising sectors still contributed a shade more to national productivity growth than did the modernising sectors.[12] In 1860 the average person produced two-and-a-half times the output of his grandfather in 1780, which is a measure of the significance of the period. But the traditional sectors had contributed two-thirds of the rise in income per head, which is a measure of the persisting significance of old methods.

Eventually it dawned on economic historians that trying to compute aggregates from a weak statistical base was producing diminishing returns. It was not possible to span unbridgeable gaps or allow for insuperable defects in the surviving macro-series; national income accounting was neither a possible nor an appropriate framework for the 18th century, as Julian Hoppit forcefully pointed out in 1990.[13] After a discreet interval, institutionalism began to reappear. An interest in the political causes of growth returned. Early in the 21st century, without much warning and acting more or less independently, leading scholars began once more to ponder the sources of industrialisation. This might be called the causal turn. It began in 2004 with a book edited by Leandro Prados de la Escosura, achieved a blaze of publicity in 2006 with a best-seller by Greg Clark, and was followed in 2008 by Jan de Vries's thoughtful *Industrious Revolution*.[14] Other works are in the pipeline.

Spatial Aspects

Standard accounts skip over the role of inter-regional competition during the 17th and 18th centuries. They refer to the localisation of heavy and factory industries in the north — they could hardly do otherwise — but let the matter rest there. Only a few claim an explanatory role for the region, among them Sidney Pollard, who recognised the 'shifting kaleidoscope of industrial specialization before 1750'.[15] He wrote that, 'the national statistics which are normally used to illustrate economic growth cannot bear the enormous weight which is usually placed on them'. Regional fortunes were widely dispersed about the national mean, raising questions about the causes. Pollard's interest inspired the phase during the 1980s when a handful of

English scholars did attend to the regional nature of industrialisation, at least descriptively, though interest soon faded. Historians of districts or counties do continue to record what happened in them but they commonly assert the interest of their chosen patches without elaborating on the broader implications.

The South's failure to share in the classic industrial revolution, and its actual de-industrialisation, is surprising. The region was the old industrial heartland and shared the national features of culture, law and so forth. Policy with respect to overseas trade was a matter for the national government. Culture, in the sense of bourgeois values, has not been shown to have differed systematically by region. The legal system was national: local magistrates presided over the courts but operated a common system of law. National-level factors such as these cannot account for regional divergences and it is inappropriate to discuss economic change exclusively in terms of national aggregates.

Was the south's problem genuinely regional? Was there not merely a congeries of difficulties that would be better studied industry by industry or firm by firm? After all, some sardonic fellow called the region a 'metaphysical concept used by geographers'. But this hardly seems fair and is certainly not helpful. The dieback of southern manufacturing, although slow, was so wide-spread as to imply a common process. The alternative would be to accept, case by case, the multitudinous individual explanations given in local histories. Possibly some of these explanations did account for the decline of this trade or that business but more often they were likely to have been secondary effects reinforcing an underlying difficulty. In due course we will examine suggested explanations *seriatim*. But it seems reasonable to hope to find a unifying cause or at any rate to be able to narrow the range of possibilities.

What subdivisions of England are best to work with? Studies by provincial historians are based on counties, which have limited use. They are ecological rag-bags, since geology and soils do not conform to county boundaries. Even for agriculture William Marshall preferred larger units, stating that 'the arbitrary lines of counties are to be wholly disregarded'.[16] Objections to ecological regions on the grounds that they are 'ahistorical' seem beside the point.[17] Other things being equal, economic activities are located so as to minimise costs. Ecological particularity implies different cost structures, meaning that while ecological units do not determine history they surely channel it.

Dividing England into three parts is a first approximation. The first comprises London and Bristol, the largest cities in the 18th century, with the economy of London in particular affecting everywhere else. These cities are best viewed as distinct from the landscape of market towns and countryside. This landscape is cloven into two by the divide of the Tees-Exe line, which (though by no means without exceptions) gives us the primary physiographic divisions of Highland and Lowland Zones. For convenience we shall call the Highland Zone the North and the Lowland Zone the South, the latter also being referred to as the English Plain.

The Highland Zone in the north and west contains the harder rocks, higher ground and poorer soils, receives more rainfall, and experiences lower average temperatures. Poor soil does not necessarily mean infertility in an absolute chemical sense. The differences are relative and exert their influence through comparative costs of production: in England, little of the Highland Zone has ever concentrated on the growing of grain for sale. Differences between the two zones can be traced far back before the Middle Ages into prehistory, reflecting the relative difficulty of growing cereals in the north. About 1820, a teacher at Alston in the northern Pennines said that only five boys in his school had ever seen wheat growing.[18]

The Lowland Zone, in the south and east, has softer rocks, lower terrain, better soils, less rainfall, higher temperatures and longer growing seasons. It is the long-standing arable region and, being a more desirable human habitat as well as more exposed to incursions from the continent, has always been subject to greater competition for land. It may be worth noting that my examples come largely from south-central England, where I grew up and have worked off and on over the years, and where I have paid many visits to historical sites of every description. I have also lived in Devon and Somerset for months at a time and explored the ground there too. These districts do not seem to constitute too restricted a sample of the Lowland Zone. As to the north, I make no equivalent claims, but I was an undergraduate at Nottingham, wrote half my doctoral thesis on an estate bought by the cotton-spinner, Richard Arkwright, and have been John Simon Professor at the University of Manchester.

Given limited technology and imperfect communications, all forms of production had to shape themselves to local resources and terrain. These were not the sole influences on costs — the approach here is not geographical determinism. All that is suggested is that terrain-based differences in production possibilities gave one zone comparative advantage in pastoral husbandry and the other in cereal growing. Dateable improvements in crop growing altered the balance between them, intensifying the difference. The concept of comparative advantage is a general one which does not explain everything but is valuable because it clarifies. Particularistic accounts proclaiming that the notion is anachronistic are self-defeating and disappear into what a reviewer called 'a thicket of causes'.[19] There may have been many additional influences but to retreat to what the same reviewer calls, 'a "shopping list approach" to historical causality' is simply not helpful.

Arrow pointed out that while the Discoveries were no doubt investment enterprises — we know they were — the actual outcome could not be predicted by theory, only by 'the brute, though unknown, facts of geography'.[20] The distribution and redistribution of manufacturing in England likewise shaped itself to the brute facts of geography. Production possibilities differed between the Highland and Lowland Zones. This was not unknown to early topographers but was scarcely grasped by the general populace, whose horizons were unavoidably limited and whose enterprises adapted sluggishly to the changing realities of the costs of production where they lived. In times when place of residence and place of work tended to be the same, and information did not circulate at once, the level of stimulus needed to dislodge people was high. Markets for enterprise and movements of the workforce responded slowly. The re-sorting of economic activities is plain enough with hindsight but the trend was hard to discern at the time.

The spatial division is a simplification. Highland zone and Lowland zone, north and south, were not hermetically sealed. To some degree raw materials and factors of production flowed between them; industrial products certainly did. Anyone can complicate matters by discussing the separate experience of localities or industries within each region or devising ever more elaborate regional breakdowns (distinguishing, for example, between solid and drift geology, between the belts of hard and soft rock that alternate across the English Plain, or re-distributing the Midlands in various ways). But our aim is to clarify the outlines.

As always, it is easier to tear down generalisations than build them up. Much the best informed denial of the existence of a significant North-South divide between the 16th and 18th centuries is by John Langton.[21] He assembles statistics in order to map wealth distributions and county populations, and in these he finds only faint north-south differences. Langton insists that the economy consisted of innumerable pockets of activity. This is what we would expect when market areas were expanding too slowly to wipe the slate instantly clean and better communications were only gradually dissolving local monopolies. As it stands, it misses both the dynamic at work and the usefulness of broad groupings for investigating the processes of change.

Yorkshire, for example, would normally be considered a northern county and for ordinary purposes I treat it as such. But this is a short-hand for contrasts between the industrial West Riding and southern counties. On the other hand, the East Riding may be viewed as an extension of the 'south', because it lies south-east of the Tees-Exe line and is correctly part of the Lowland Zone. It is a sort of bleaker Salisbury Plain. In its leading features it has been described as closely akin to Oxfordshire, Hampshire or Sussex, whereas 'between the E. Riding ... and Westmorland or Northumberland — even between the E. Riding ... and the rest of Yorkshire — the gulf is apparent and profound'.[22]

Langton's critique is limited because his discussion seems to conflate extractive industries (including timber production) and manufacturing ones. He does not account for the motley pattern he identifies nor trace the fate of manufacturing enterprises in the south. When Highland and Lowland Zones are contrasted a divide is surely to be seen; these great zones pick up functional differences, and north and south are convenient labels for them. The issue should not be about geographical formalism but the approximations most fruitful for understanding economic change.

Another author has derided what he calls an obsession about dividing the country into Highland and Lowland Zones, with their traditions supposedly eternal and unchanging.[23] He points out that the variety of building traditions was far greater than a two-fold division. His point about localisms is indeed obvious but simply plunges us into another thicket. In any case no such obsession exists among economic historians. Their failing is that of casually mentioning places without much explicit regionalisation. For the purposes of analysis, Highland and Lowland Zones (including London and Bristol) seem preferable to infinite subdivisions or none at all.

Historical Aspects

Pre-industrial society was not static. The anonymous author of *The Institucon of a Gentleman* (1555) claimed that England already contained many gentlemen who had risen by merit, 'wherby it should appear that virtue flour-isheth among us'.[24] Virtue was more than its own reward, though what constituted virtue was seldom economic endeavour as now understood — it meant marrying well and currying royal favour, preferably both. The rewards included higher social rank, sinecures of every kind, invitations to the hunt, and grants of land or the wherewithal to buy an estate. Acquiring an estate was vital for sealing social position, as well as for obtaining agricultural rents. Whether the land could be held for long, or retained by a man's descendants, was another matter.

A defining achievement of economic growth was to swing the balance of endeavour away from these archaic strivings towards contributing socially useful products or services. Once industrialists had succeeded in this respect, they sought however to burrow back into a version of the older world. They sought to buy estates and assimilate to the manners and ape the blood sports of the gentry, as they still do. Continuity therefore seems the perennial order of English society. Yet protective colouration notwithstanding, rising socially through favour, offices or corruption on the one hand, and supplying what people will willingly buy on the other, were crucially different. The return of industrial fortunes to the land is merely the compliment that affluence pays to sycophancy.

Leaving aside the blur of individual competence, prudence, and good or bad luck, a regional metabolism in estate ownership was evident in early modern times. Thomas Fuller, author of *The History of the Worthies of England* (1662), recognised a divide in the geographical prospects of the virtuous.[25] Proximity to London was the vital distinction. Fuller said that gentry near London, 'quickly strip and disrobe themselves of their estates and inheritance', adding that Berkshire estates in particular 'are skittish and often cast their owners'.

His most telling observation was that families of the northern gentry who moved to the south faded away in a few generations, whereas southerners who moved north, 'acquire a settlement in their estates with long continu-ance'. He did not think that a greater distance from London was the source of this advantage, which was the result of thrift and moderate expense. Given the opportunities that access to the capital gave for wasting one's substance, this probably came to much the same thing. Until the industrial revolution, London was not only the prime source of both market and non-market wealth but also the greatest sink of temptation to fritter or gamble it away.

With new men constantly rising, there was no shortage of purchasers of embarrassed estates in counties near London, such as Berkshire, and land there turned over more rapidly than in the north.

As Helen Jewell depicts it in a survey of medieval perceptions, the north-south division is an ancient one to which the industrial revolution gave a 'noticeable twist'.[26] From the late middle ages into the 16th century, the south was the more prosperous zone. Between the 17th and 19th centuries the north was catching up and overtaking, only to lose out again (relatively speaking) in the 20th century. Many studies disguise the earlier inversion by starting only at the industrial revolution, then skipping forwards to the modern imbalance of prosperity and political influence consequent on what Peter Scott calls 'the triumph of the south'.[27] Other works convey the impression that England was comprised of London and the north, ignoring the non-metropolitan south altogether. No doubt the south appears to their authors as it did to Murray in 1856: 'the annals of the counties during the last 180 years have been happily uneventful'.[28]

Sources

Despite the grand scale of the units with which we shall be working, investigations of change at the regional level require far more scrutiny of local sources than is current practice in mainstream economic history. Simply learning the names and locations of places over a wide area is a sizeable task. Events are often recorded only in obscure publications, many of which are hard even for scholars to find. Mathias once wrote, 'the economic historians have led an invasion into that twilight world of the county archaeological and antiquarian society journals, once full of flints and fossils'. I have been one of the invaders. But acknowledging every reference to such sources would overload the endnotes with fugitive mentions of single places or trades. I have been as sparing as possible with references, though there will still seem to be plenty, and have tried to ease entry into the literature by adding a guide to further reading.

To delve into these matters means relying on local studies whose authors have been the ones to examine the documentary or ground evidence. Only through their hard work can many examples of early economic activity be discovered. Sometimes, it is necessary to follow up by studying the lie of the land or industrial archaeological remains. As R. H. Tawney remarked, in a phrase so often used as the basis for examination questions that it would be otiose to give a reference, historians need to get their boots dirty. Nathan Rosenberg said something similar with respect to understanding the sources of invention: economists must be prepared to get their hands dirty.[29] Physical traces are clues about what to look for in the written sources and they drive home how tiny the scale of business was in the past. The latter point is easy to forget. It is easy to forget, too, how slow change was, since we telescope the past by speaking in decades while ourselves living through days.

David Chambers claimed for the regional historian some insight into the past 'by the proxy of his own ancestors'. I have taken this literally in Chap. 6 by making use of work on the history of my own ancestors, much of it done by distant relatives and some of it highly professional. A sense of authenticity may be gained through a connection with the land and the people who formerly worked it. Authenticity translates into the chance of recognising procedures and costs which may be overlooked or thought trivial by those of a presentist turn of mind, for whom economic history is a mere manoeuvring of abstractions.

Local knowledge also drives home another point often forgotten, which is how numerous, various and provincial the provinces were. Alan Everitt identified 40 country communities, over 700 urban communities, and 9,000 rural parishes, 'all distinct from one another, all consciously separate, and many surprisingly different'.[30] He was referring to the 17th century, but the variety did not vanish overnight; it was a proxy for different mixes of occupations and products and different costs of production. Everitt warned against reading modern spatial units and their modern coherence back into the past. He concluded one of his contributions, 'if the pattern outlined in this paper seems to complicate unduly the task of recreating that society, it should perhaps be remembered that it is from the perpetual interplay between these diverse economies ... that the vital spark of progress and originality in this country has often arisen'.[31]

This observation was based on a lifetime's detailed knowledge and, although it throws the balance too far back towards splitting rather than lumping, does hint at inter-regional competition. It bears on the scale of past economies, rates of change and differential responses to the market, aspects easily ignored in macro-historical or economic analyses, which assume them away rather than investigate them, full of certainty that in the long run the market will win. Of more interest are *deviations* from market expectations and deviations cannot be found if they are assumed away. Nor will unexpected elements in the past be uncovered if economic history is written as *histoire a these* — looking for confirmation or disconfirmation of strongly worded hypotheses, and striving to escape from what Patrick O'Brien stigmatises as the 'tyranny' of detail.[32]

There is no doubt that hypotheses are often left vague by general historians who are captivated by descriptions of the past and whose method is to work from authority to authority, with the primary aim of contradicting some previous writer. Traditional historians make real contributions, however, when they discover fresh patterns in the evidence. As Casson observes, history matters because it permits the testing of ideas where initial facts are verifiable and the outcomes are known: it gets us away from the 'stylised facts' so often relied on in economics.[33] Yet we cannot deal with every one of Everitt's myriad communities or the like. We need to choose operational groupings. The lumping of units can always be relaxed later for specific purposes. What is there left to say but the obvious — we should make judicious but not excessive use of economic logic and chart our course between the *a priori* and the infinitely descriptive. No two people will make the same choices.

The South of England

Southern England features the picturesque market towns, villages, pubs and cottages on which its tourist industry trades. They are part of the evidence about the past, but it should be understood they are the results of economic failure, not success. We have to discount the rural depression of the late 19th and early 20th centuries, which froze settlements and communities in shapes that more energetic commerce would have altered. When the economy of the south began to grow vigorously again during the second half of the 20th century, the fossilising process was ironically perpetuated by the planning system.[34] The poorest dwellings had vanished or been removed by rural slum clearance and the cramped living space in those that remained was obviated — for moneyed incomers — by throwing two or three cottages into one.

The archaic elements that persist in the landscape encourage us to view the 18th century and before as more static and less violent than the reality. Looking back tends to telescope the happenings of lifetimes into passing mentions in the textbooks. This creates the impression that past events moved faster than contemporaries can have thought. De Vries wryly comments that, 'economists can hope that their accumulated knowledge will make posterity better off than it otherwise would be, but only economic historians can make our ancestors better off than they ever knew they were'.[35] By modern standards life was hard and change was gradual. Investigating the reasons for this will help pinpoint the self-restricting aspects of past economic life.

Acknowledgements

A paper introducing the topic appeared as Eric Jones, 'Missing out on industrial revolution', *World Econ.* **9**(4): 101–128, 2008, versions having been presented to the Japan Social and Economic History Society, Tokyo, in June 2008 and the Economic History seminar at the University of the West of England in December 2008. Chapter 6 is developed from a paper, 'Family history and bourgeois values: is the Clark thesis correct?' presented to the Family and Community History group at the University of Exeter in November 2008. Another paper, 'Environmental effects of blood sports in Lowland England since 1750', which is drawn on in Chap. 7, appeared in *Rural Hist.* **20**(1): 51–66, 2009, having been presented to the History seminar at the University of Exeter, Cornwall campus, in May 2008. I am grateful to the organisers and members of these seminars.

Most of the materials used here have been gathered over many years. Some are highly obscure, though others are now available on the Internet. I have been able, in recent times, to use the libraries of the Royal Agricultural College, Cirencester, the Business Enterprise Heritage Trust, and above all the superb library service of the Netherlands Institute for Advanced Study. The last mentioned is my main academic debt. I am grateful to the Rector, Professor Wim Blockmans, for the invitation to spend three months there in 2009 and to the staff for making the stay so memorable. Among the fellows-in-residence. I had outstandingly useful talks with two of the philosophers, Diana Stanciu and Tamas Demeter.

Beyond these debts, the number of people who have helped me is far, far too large and diverse to name them all. The list would be as long as the book. In a volume that in some wise began as a paper written for a conference in 1965, this is unsurprising. It makes my gratitude no less. For practical reasons, therefore, I shall confine my thanks to my wife, Sylvia (who edited the whole book for me), son Christopher, and daughter Deborah, and to those who have helped me regularly — the repeaters so to speak — Alan and Stephanie Albery, John Anderson (who read the whole draft), Brian Clist, Patrick Dillon, Shaun Kenaelly, the late Lew Lewis, John Lyons, Michael Tarrant, and the late Colin Tubbs. The book is dedicated to Laura, a most welcome addition to my family.

Endnotes

1. Compare the difference between northern miners and those they called 'Essex peasants' before the war, when there was 'no bridge across the north-south divide'. Hugh Barratt, *A Good Living* (Ipswich: Old Pond Publishing, 2000), pp. 54–55.

2. E. L. Jones, The constraints on economic growth in southern England, 1650–1850, *Contributions*, V, *Third International Conference of Economic History*, Munich, 1965 (Paris: Mouton, 1974), pp. 423–430.

3. R. Szostak, *The Role of Transportation in the Industrial Revolution: A Comparison of England and France* (Montreal and Kingston: McGill-Queen's University Press, 1991), p. 3.

4. C. T. Smith, *An Historical Geography of Western Europe before 1800* (London: Longmans, 1967), p. 579.

5. In Leandro Prados de la Escosura (ed.), *Exceptionalism and Industrialisation: Britain and Its European Rivals, 1688–1815* (Cambridge: Cambridge University Press, 2004), p. 57.

6. *Financial Times*, 14 February 2009 [italics added].

7. P. Deane and H. J. Habakkuk, The take-off in Britain, in W. W. Rostow (ed.), *The Economics of Take-Off into Sustained Growth* (London: Macmillan, 1963).

8. H. Jennings, *Pandaemonium 1660–1886: The Coming of the Machine as Seen by Contemporary Observers* (London: Andre Deutsch, 1985), p. 122.

9. P. Triana, *Lecturing Birds on Flying: Can Mathematical Theories Destroy the Financial Markets?* (Hoboken, N.J.: John Wiley, 2009); S. Broadberry, Recent Developments in the Theory of Very Long Run Growth: A Historical Appraisal, Warwick University Research Papers, Department of Economics, No. 818 (2007).

10. S. Strogatz, *International Herald Tribune*, 18 June 2009.

11. R. Taagepera and B. N. Colby, Growth of Western civilization: epicyclical or exponential? *Am. Anthropol.* **81**: 907–912, 1979.

12. F. Stuart Jones, The new economic history and the industrial revolution, *S. Afr. J. Econ.* **52**: 128, 1984.

13. J. Hoppit, Counting the industrial revolution, *Econ. Hist. Rev.* N.S. **43**(2): 173–193, 1990.

14. Prados de la Escoscura (ed.), *Exceptionalism and Industrialisation*; G. Clark, *A Farewell to Alms* (Princeton: Princeton University Press, 2006); and J. de Vries, *The Industrious Revolution* (Cambridge: Cambridge University Press, 2008).

15. S. Pollard, *Peaceful Conquest: The Industrialization of Europe 1760–1970* (Oxford: Oxford University Press, 1981), p. 10.

16. W. Marshall, *A Review of the Reports to the Board of Agriculture: from the Northern Department of England* (York, 1808), p. xxviii.

17. C. Husbands, Regional change in a pre-industrial economy: wealth and population in England in the sixteenth and seventeenth centuries, *J. Hist. Geogr.* **13**(4): 346, 1987.

18. J. Uglow, *Nature's Engraver: A Life of Thomas Bewick* (London: Faber and Faber, 2006), p. 131.

19. C. K. Hyde, in a review, *J. Econ. Hist.* **XLVI**: 527–528, 1986.

20. K. Arrow, Classificatory notes on the production and transmission of technological knowledge, *Amer. Econ. Rev., Pap. & Proc.* **59**: 35, 1969.

21. J. Langton, South, north and nation, 1550–1750, in R. Alan, H. Baker and M. Billinge (eds.), *Geographies of England: The North-South Divide, Material and Imagined* (Cambridge: Cambridge University Press, 2004), pp. 118–133.

22. Quoted in D. Neave, The identity of the east riding of Yorkshire, in E. Royle (ed.), *Issues of Regional Identity: In honour of John Marshall* (Manchester: Manchester University Press, 1998), p. 190.

23. E. Mercer, cited in P. S. Barnwell and M. Palmer (eds.), *Post-Medieval Landscapes* (Macclesfield: Windgather Press, 2007), p. 24.

24. Quoted by J. P. Cooper (G. E. Aylmer and J. S. Morrill, eds.), *Land, Men and Beliefs: Studies in Early-Modern History* (London: The Hambledon Press, 1983), p. 55.

25. Quoted by Anthony Wagner, *Pedigree and Progress: Essays in the Genealogical Interpretation of History* (London: Phillimore, 1975), p. 99.

26. H. M. Jewell, *The North-South Divide: The Origins of Northern Consciousness in England* (Manchester: Manchester University Press, 1994).

27. P. M. Scott, *Triumph of the South: Regional Development in the Twentieth Century* (Aldershot: Ashgate Publishing, 2007).

28. *Handbook for Travellers in Wiltshire, Dorsetshire, and Somersetshire* (London: John Murray, 1882 [first edition, 1856]), p. xix.

29. N. Rosenberg, *Perspectives in Technology* (Cambridge: Cambridge University Press, 1976), p. 2.

30. A. Everitt, *Change in the Provinces: the Seventeenth Century* (Leicester: Leicester University Press, 1969), p. 6.

31. A. Everitt, Country, county and town: patterns of regional evolution in England, in Peter Borsay (ed.), *The Eighteenth-Century Town: A Reader in English Urban History 1688–1820* (London: Longman, 1990), p. 113.

32. P. O'Brien, Provincializing the first industrial revolution, *Work. Pap. Glob. Econ. Hist. Netw.* **17**: pp. 1–43, 2006.

33. M. Casson, *The Regulation of the Victorian Railway System: A Theoretical Perspective* (University of Reading: typescript, May 2008).

34. A. Laws, *Understanding Small Period Houses* (Ramsbury: The Crowood Press, 2003), p. 9.

35. D. Vries, *The Industrious Revolution*, p. 86, n. 22.

CHAPTER 1

THE VIEW FROM LITTLE ENGLAND

It is endogenous development that determined which societies were able to take advantage of exogenous opportunities.

Xue Yong, 2007

World historians depict economic growth as a horse-race. A popular view is that Europe lacked an early start but leapt ahead of the rest of the world by means of borrowing and plundering or the fluke of having accessible deposits of coal.[1] Among European countries, England is presented as either the first of the criminal states or the first lucky country. A related interpretation is that England would not have achieved growth without immigration from continental Europe, the expansion of international trade, or both. Do externalist approaches such as these really account for Europe's ascent? Was England's particular rise merely an epiphenomenon of European history?

Much is to be learned from a comparative perspective, which has now become a familiar scholarly approach.[2] Global and international comparisons have, however, unfortunately attracted those whose *a priori* aim is to deny Europe or England special features or prolonged sequences of development; this volume offers some corrective. This opening chapter considers, first, what advantages Europe as a whole may have had and, second, how unusual England was among European countries. The remainder of the book concentrates on the latter aspect: English responsiveness to internal economic opportunity. Material exclusively about England thus starts with Chap. 2.

The Eurasian Context

The insistence that international trade, not to mention greed, explains the Fate of the East and Rise of the West has been exploded by Tirthankar Roy.[3] He casts icy water on the notion that the outward-oriented sectors of unwieldy units such as Europe and Asia were large enough to determine their development, either individually or through interacting. He notes that continents have different resource endowments, reinforced by different population histories. In short, Roy demonstrates that to understand the way each continent developed, we need chiefly to assess its internal evolution.

Conclusions, which in the circumstances it may seem ironic to call similar, were reached by Joseph Bryant, who coined the term 'Similarity School' for those who emphasise the comparability of societies across the whole of Eurasia.[4] Bryant urges that this position must be incomplete because it marginalises institutions and occupational structure. One of his most telling suggestions is that the proportion of merchants, lawyers and bureaucrats — and, no doubt, artisans — slowly came to differ among societies. Assertions that societies across Eurasia marched in lockstep neglect this important fact: even were standards of living closely comparable, development was unlikely to have been determined by income averages.

At a general level, the expression of inventive potential was determined by the different proportions of bourgeoisie. An example may be the onset of printing, the technical requisites for which were available in China, Japan and Korea without giving rise to anything like Europe's mass production of printed books.[5] East Asian countries could print books yet did so only on the smallest scale, for reasons that are often called cultural but were actually institutional, political and economic: tiny elite demand and restrictive practices on the part of their literati. In Italy, on the other hand, merchants' and lawyers' demand was growing rapidly during the first half of the 15th century, when texts were still hand-written by companies of manuscript copyists. Gutenberg and Caxton responded to this felt need, which arose within several European countries.

Europe, including England, did borrow from the East, acquiring, for instance, Arabic numerals. On the church at Chedworth in the Cotswolds, there are dates of the 1490s carved in the Arabic form, probably having been introduced by Italian merchants who came there to buy wool. Mechanical fulling, the horizontal loom, the spinning wheel and the practice of carding constituted a textile revolution in 12th- and 13th-century England, having originated from India and China, while knitting arrived from the Arab world.[6] As a peripheral part of Eurasia, England thus did share many distant developments, yet the broad brush of Eurasian similarity only weakly explains its singular performance. What have to be taken into account are

Europe's innate differences from Asia and England's extreme difference. As far as the industrial revolution was concerned, Asian developments were parts of the background, maybe necessary but not sufficient.

Wide areas may have exhibited similar developments, but this does not demonstrate that novelties always arose by diffusion. Areas of the world in virtual isolation from one another achieved approximately similar solutions. The point is illustrated by Tokugawa Japan. The Shogunate that ruled the country from 1600 to 1868 was not utterly absolutist and shared a measure of power with the daimyo, the lords. The daimyos' wings had been clipped after the Tokugawa victory at Sekigahara in 1600 but they retained authority over their own domains, having come to terms with the shogun via a form of elite settlement. Left to develop as they might within an increasingly integrated market, the domains began to specialise in different mixes of products. Inter-regional trade and competition followed. This created a pallid version of the regional differentiation of late pre-industrial England, which as we shall see was partly the outcome of another elite settlement, that between William III and the Whig lords and London merchants.[7]

The key to change lies in the response to inducements. Response cannot be anticipated; it is merely a simplifying device on the part of economists to assume that every opportunity represented by differences in relative prices will be seized. This is the 'vasty deep' problem, named after a passage in Shakespeare's Henry IV Part 1, where Glendower boasts, 'I can call spirits from the vasty deep', only to have Hotspur reply, 'Why, so can I, or so can any man; But will they come when you do call for them?' Response was always 'the crucial question' according to Carlo Cipolla, when he denied that necessity, the so-called the mother of invention, explains anything at all.[8]

In the wide Eurasian scheme, comparable developments in political and military spheres are intriguing and it is not to be denied they deserve investigation. According to Lieberman, who has produced the most detailed description (but whose aim is to cut Europe down to size), the similarities amount to synchronised demographic fluctuations, the loosely equivalent consolidation of small political units in peripheral Eurasia between 1450 and 1830 and greater state regulation of religion.[9] At this level of abstraction he admits no East-West dichotomy, despite hinting at special European vigour. Other authors find no systematic differences in the standard of living between East and West before the industrial revolution, though it should be reiterated that average living standards are unlikely to pinpoint the ingredients of economic growth.[10] Equally, no indications about subsequent growth are provided by the finding that the level of urbanisation in the world long hovered about 9 to 11 per cent.[11] This is said to have been the maximum possible in the framework of traditional societies and would persist until there was a step-change in productivity. In itself the long-standing level of urbanisation offers few clues as to the nature of that change.

Some changes were nevertheless creeping forwards. Rein Taagepera, who has measured very long-run trends in the area and population of empires, identifies an upward break in the size of empires about AD 1600.[12] Although he calls the subsequent period the Russo-British or European era, he treats the world as a single political system, despite the fact that major polities interacted only very, very slowly. Taagepera cites the invention of light cavalry as an example of interaction. This was already influencing the size of political units in the Middle East about 600 BC but took 400 years to reach China, 'but reach it did, eventually'. Such a lag was too protracted to account for anything as specific as industrialisation and Taagepera makes no such claim. Nor does it seem credible that processes such as these can be explained, as many world historians believe, by adventitious factors like luck over resource endowments or the laser-beam miracles of new technology.

The history of technology is a puzzle. Historians and archaeologists continually push the earliest dates of inventions further and further back in time. In many cases actual innovation did ensue, though sustained rises in real per-capita income seldom followed. Narrowly based despotic or author-itarian regimes did not necessarily discourage invention and innovation but channelled them in socially unrewarding ways. The interests of rulers or ruling groups lay primarily in military, palatial and monumental equipment and structures, as is evident in archaeological remains. Although the dura-bility of structures may seem to bias the record in the direction of fixed capital, other indications confirm that rulers really had little interest in consumer goods that might have raised living standards. The products of early technology were distant in more ways than one from the mass-produced goods of the industrial revolution.

Whatever long-term political uniformity there may have been, certain large regions of the world were recurrently the hearths of technological invention and adoption.[13] The irregular distribution of new technology may reflect non-political variables, in which respect culture is often cited.[14] Culture is taken to imply values, meaning a generalised morality. Attempts to explain history in these terms are rarely convincing, since there are serious definitional and measurement difficulties.[15] Culture is sometimes made to include institutions, which are a different matter since they reflect political choices in ways that inherited values do not. Nor is it often stipulated how far culture influences the economy rather than vice versa. At one stage, authors held that Confucian culture blocked Asian growth whereas now they argue it is actively growth promoting. The divergent experience of countries with supposedly equivalent cultures at the same period casts doubt on the entire line of reasoning.[16]

Cultural values that promote economic activity are said to be characteristic of areas which in the distant past somehow escaped rule by despots. The driving force would therefore seem to have been political history after all. The stability of the divergent distributional patterns remains hard to demonstrate. Multiple equilibria such as these may be what economists expect but highly general assumptions about government and culture may be being substituted for actual documentation. Twentieth-century experiments at suppressing personal enterprise and expunging associated values in the Communist bloc were too brief to provide useful tests of effects that are represented as lasting for hundreds of years. Cem Karayalcin observes that over the long run there were major switches between progressive and conservative values and these, he urges, 'are hard to square with any explanation other than one that sees cultures as ultimately endogenous'.[17]

Taking as his criteria less ephemeral matters than culture, that is to say property rights, market integration and factor markets, Jan Luiten van Zanden finds that South and South-East Asia failed to develop institutions which were effective for commercial exchange.[18] Japan and China did so during the 17th and 18th centuries but by then Western Europe had a headstart of some hundreds of years. With respect to low interest rates and the efficiency of capital markets, 'the leading position of Western Europe went completely unchallenged'. (p. 350). Stephen Broadberry and Bishnupriya Gupta had already calculated that between 1500 and 1800 the prosperous parts of Asia were at the income level only of the stagnating southern, central and eastern parts of Europe, not that of north-western Europe.[19] Differences within Europe and between the continent and other civilisations were apparent well before 1800.

Which of its features created Europe's advantage? A leading candidate — not suggested as the sole cause — is the fragmentation thesis, of which a convenient summary is to be found in the article by Karayalcin.[20] His paper usefully disposes of three of the commonest alternative explanations: cultural differences; supposedly chance events such as Europe's discovery of coal and invention of the steam engine; and windfall gains such as grabbing American resources. He sums up Europe's good fortune instead as 'the political circumstances that had prepared on the ground a 'stock of institutions' enabling its inhabitants ... to take advantage of the windfall' (p. 993).

The kernel of the fragmentation thesis is that political competition within the European states-system prevented rulers from expropriating as much wealth as could the rulers of vast consolidated Eastern polities. European rulers offered relatively better public services to their subjects, who might otherwise have absconded to more generous states that lay close by. In Asia the consolidation of larger political units reduced or even closed the exit option and, as Karayalcin puts it, 'removed a structural barrier to high levels of expropriation' (p. 993).

Karayalcin recognises that the East–West distinction was not absolute or timeless by pointing to occasional phases when Asian rulers did happen to meet competition. On occasions like that they expropriated less and could not prevent their subjects from creating 'golden periods'. These less consolidated episodes are discussed in a book edited by Peter Bernholz and Roland Vaubel.[21] Nevertheless such promising episodes were not the norm in Asian history.

A corollary of the fragmentation thesis is that Asian rulers were not usually pressed to spend their proportionately large tax-take on growth-promoting policies. In the case of the Ottoman Empire and its predecessors in the Middle East, it has been shown that the rulers faced a type of agency problem. They were afraid of threats arising from those to whom they had delegated the task of collecting taxes in the countryside and as a result they capped the overall tax take.[22] This held down their own revenues and restricted them to inefficient, minimalist policies. In Europe, on the other hand, the privileges available to subjects enabled them to accumulate capital and invest it productively for themselves, with less fear of expropriation. The advantage remained intact long enough for growth and industrialisation to take place.

A fashionable variant of the 'Asia first' theme is offered by the Sinological School. Much recent work has strived to elevate the economic performance of Ming and Qing China nearly to the levels of Europe or England in

1800 — sometimes even beyond them. In principle this research is to the good, since those of us who are not China specialists were previously obliged to piece together accounts of Chinese history from very limited sources. Few such sources were directly concerned with economic affairs and others down-played China's achievements because they relied on scornful reports by early travellers. The scholarly vacuum has now been filled and the China-Europe welfare record evened up. Yet revisionism has over-stepped the mark, which returns us to Bryant's point: whether or not standards of living really were comparable, income averages tell us next to nothing about institutions and little about all-round growth potential.

Despite the efforts of first-generation revisionists, the horse-race (to use the prejudicial metaphor) was not won by China. We now know, for instance, that China did develop a plethora of informal rules which cut trans-actions costs, curbed moral hazard and facilitated commercialisation.[23] Yet China's legal codes were not designed for dispute resolution; they were acts of moralising conciliation rather than legal adjudication. No professional legal class of the type so influential in the West emerged in China. Clearly the economy could operate and expand on a less formal basis, but only subject to limitations. Debin Ma ends his study of the topic by questioning whether China's traditional belief system and political bureaucracy were capable of generating institutions that could make contracts secure and facilitate system-wide impersonal exchange.

Narrower contrasts concerning agricultural performance are drawn between the Yangtze delta during Qing times and England in the 18th century. They are not persuasive since they contain misconceptions such as a tenfold exaggeration of imports of bean-cake fertiliser to Jiangnan, which is the southern part of the Yangtze delta.[24] As Chinese economic history enters a more mature phase, we find a scholar such as Yong Xue concluding that, 'what sets apart the English case is the homegrown ingredient that enabled it to exploit its exogenous opportunity. Jiangnan was not simply an unlucky England — it was no England at all' (p. 222).

Like those who homogenise space, other scholars homogenise time. Some treat all periods prior to (sudden, late) industrial change in England as if they were one and the same. No significant prior processes are acknowledged; the aeons of time before the industrial revolution become the *terra nullius* of chronology. The usual method by which this is supported is projecting back real income per capita from modern levels. A graph of GDP per capita in constant dollars between the present day and AD 1 drops down fast as time recedes. It soon threatens to fall below the *x*-axis. Since this is impossible, because everyone would have starved, income is assumed to have run back through the centuries and millennia only just above the axis, implying a world of perpetual poverty and economic stasis. Alternatively the few verifiable data points may be joined up. Either approach eliminates possible fluctuations and conveys the impression of a long, flat, dull historical landscape.[25]

In similar vein a hypothetical graph of world population is extremely popular. It shows the enormously steep demographic growth of the 19th and 20th centuries and is almost always so generalised that earlier fluctuations are ironed right out. The Black Death, for example, is squashed out of the record. Applied to pre-industrial times, the underlying logic, which is that most income and population growth has been modern, distracts us from searching for previous episodes of change. Early economic history becomes a zero-sum game.

This approach appeals to the generalising mind. By selecting the right intervals, the late Colin Clark was able to characterise the effects of the First World War as 'slight and temporary', lasting only until the early 1920s; likewise it has been urged that the bombing of Japan and Vietnam had no long-term effects.[26] On interpretations such as these nothing ever happened in history. The facts in the textbooks can only describe a ceaseless treading of water: conflicts over resources were as purposeless as Milton's battles of kites and crows. The presentist mood in economics reinforces this attitude. It assumes that previous fluctuations, if indeed they occurred, must have been minor and transient, and can hold no useful message for students of growth.

On the contrary something may be learned from passing episodes of pre-industrial growth and especially from what checked them. It used to be rare for this to be acknowledged. Nevertheless Broadberry, after observing that economists and economist-economic historians have rarely taken periods before the industrial revolution seriously, now accepts that there were several bursts of technological change, though each was followed by stagnation.[27] Daron Acemoglu and Gabrizio Zilibotti, taking their cue from Fernand Braudel, had already picked out three 'failed takeoffs' in European city states: Florence in the 14th century, Genoa in the late 16th century, and Amsterdam in the 18th century.[28] They noted that economies in the early stages of development are dependent on agriculture, and hence on the weather, and that in the days when industry relied on farm-produced inputs, bad harvests immediately reduced output. English economic historians have always known this.[29]

On a broader canvas, the *Growth Recurring* model identifies major growth phases in Song China (10th through 13th centuries AD) and Tokugawa Japan (the 17th-century segment), as well as in Europe, and anticipates that other examples may be found.[30] These episodes lack warrantable aggregate statistics (not that those for the early industrial period in England are anything but shaky) but do reveal combined structural and technological change, rising living standards and rising population. The organisation and material equipment of early economies were certainly fragile, and real incomes were vulnerable to weather-induced fluctuations and occasional upturns in population, but what kept growth episodes so few was mainly excessive rent-seeking on the part of the holders of political power. Few or not, the existence of any early growth at all refutes the notion that before the industrial revolution economic history was uniformly bleak. Sustained growth and industrialisation needed, however, something more: a means of resisting the constraints and shocks that reversed promising early episodes.

Although it is becoming slightly old fashioned, some authors still proclaim that Europe deviated early from a common civilisational trend — long before the point at which, to employ Patricia Crone's terms, it capped its deviance by inventing industry.[31] Crone is amusingly acerbic about the manner in which Western scholars greet medieval Europe's acquisition of the 'commonplace appurtenances of civilized societies', as if they were self-evident stepping stones to modernity. All they implied, she remarks, was that Europe had 'finally joined the club'. As a member of the traditional society club, though, it was a failure, dismantling its feudal institutions and displaying a disturbing facility for inventing technologies as early as the 13th century. What could replace traditionalism in Europe? Her answer, echoing the fragmentation thesis, was a pluralist political society and more than one variant of Christianity. The elite were not sufficiently united to keep society in its place. Deviant success was underpinned by ecological riches. Crone's external perspective (she is an Islamic specialist) is refreshing and stages the first act of the European play for us. But since England differed from the remainder of Europe, there are further acts to come.

At the opposite pole from those who conceive time as uniform until it was ruptured by industrialisation are therefore scholars who locate the sources of modern growth at some specific, very early, period. There is no agreement among competing authors about this but some of the suggestions are very ingenious. One of the boldest proposals is that Europe's distinctiveness descends from the early Christian selection of a cosmology congruent with attaining growth.[32] Beyond the usual problems with cultural explanations, such as showing that the pronouncements of religious officialdom were followed in practice, difficulties with path-dependent theses of this type include bridging the yawning gaps among observations. As with all mono-causal theories, far too much else has to be held constant.

Another danger is infinite regress. It can always be shown that processes had predecessors but sometimes the relevance of this may be little more than that of the most ambitious proclamations of the Similarity School — virtually amounting to the claim that a cupboard is not empty because it is full of air. The colligation problem (where to start) can be solved only in terms of the needs of a particular analysis. With respect to the industrial revolution little is to be gained by probing back before the 16th century. The Middle Ages are an insecure base from which to measure change, given that estimates of the population of England in 1300 range between four and six million![33]

Various aspects of medieval economic life have nevertheless been credited with formative roles. Agreed, the Middle Ages witnessed remarkable technological advance in Western Europe. Yet it is having one's cake and eating it to boast in the same breath that average earnings in medieval agriculture were as high as they were in the late 18th century. The technological energies of the high Middle Ages did not last and high real earnings in the latter part of the period were growth-by-disaster, resulting from a better land-labour ratio once the Black Death had killed a sizeable fraction of the population.

The European Context

Europe's ghost acreage — the equivalent of extra land and marine resources gained through venturing overseas — increased unimaginably once the Americas were appropriated. The potential increased first; there was a marked lag before large imports of resources actually arrived. Not only were the discoveries and establishment of colonies in America and the West Indies the results of 'no necessity', as Adam Smith famously declared, but this is a classic case where the relevance lay in the response: Spain and Portugal found the wealth of the Indies, or at least the precious metals which Mercantilist regimes thought were wealth, without developing much. It was the north-western quarter of Europe that exploited the real resources of the outer world effectively.

Europe's achievement may not have been a close derivative of Eurasia's, but was England's a derivative of Europe's? Medieval and early modern England was peripheral to the commercial and industrial parts of the continent. Insofar as it had an external trading sector, the country functioned as a resource colony, especially from the perspective of Italy. The Cotswolds were the Australia of the day, to which Italian merchants or their agents came to buy wool. Other developments also half relied on borrowed expertise. Medieval monarchs imported Lombards to introduce financial skills, while in the late 16th and 17th centuries, Dutchmen were brought in to practice advanced techniques of sea defence and land drainage. These immigrations and technology transfers, though widely spaced, do give the appearance of a backward region catching up.

Diasporas of Protestants fleeing from Roman Catholic persecution characterised the 16th and 17th centuries, and England received its share of them. The introduction of the New Draperies, enigmatic though the tale is, usually involved immigrants. Flemings, Walloons and Jews descended on Norwich. One quarter of the population of the city was 'Fleming' by 1580, and the statement that half of these were not textile workers implies the other half were.[34] Further 16th-century newcomers included Frenchmen brought in to expand the glass industry and Germans who came to mine copper.

Without doubt the Flemings boosted the economy of East Anglia and occasional places further west, just as the Huguenots brought additional business and technical skills in the late 17th century. But the Flemings came into conflict with existing elites and remained socially apart for an astonishingly long time — the last sermon in Dutch was not preached in Norwich until 1900.[35] (In Leiden, which also received immigrants from the southern Netherlands, there is still in 2009 a Walloon church where the services are held in French.)

Nevertheless, the role of immigrants can be overstated. Their economic relevance lay in the fact that they came from highly developed parts of Europe.[36] Yet they were not colonising a wilderness, instead moving to moderately developed areas already dense with traditions of the cloth industry. Moreover their minority status as confessional immigrants isolated them, reinforcing their tight-knit family groupings. In some respects this may have been a business advantage but it prolonged a separateness that must have restricted their influence. The suggestion that the native inhabitants of late medieval Norwich, say, would never have changed without the jolt administered by the immigrants is surely an exaggeration.[37]

The complicated processes of taking up or imitating different varieties of woollen cloth depended on whether the localities involved had hitherto specialised on relatively light fabrics, such as worsteds rather than heavier cloths, and possessed the requisite technical skills or task-specific human capital. Switching to serge-making in Devon, for example, proved straight-forward compared with the difficulties in a broadcloth area such as Suffolk. Devon serge-making was established without any significant immigrant contribution.[38]

Likewise the standard view that non-ferrous metal mining depended on the immigration of Germans during the 16th century seems wrong; the blast furnaces with which they worked were inadequate and they made no lasting impact.[39] Not until the adoption of the English reverberatory furnace at the end of the 17th century did smelting really change. The mining historian, Roger Burt, thinks that the reverberatory furnace may be, 'the great unsung innovation of the industrial revolution'.[40]

When industrialisation began, or began to intensify again, in the 15th and 16th centuries, Flanders already had two centuries of industry behind it and Holland was developing fast. Some of the Dutch development derived from Flanders, from which refugees had come, while Dutch farming had previously absorbed new crops from northern Italy. Migrations of artisans and transmissions of technique were nothing new; they were characteristic of sequential movements within the region that economists and geographers call, after the spatial shape noted by a French government report, the 'blue banana'.[41] The allusion is to the boomerang shape of the developed belt running from northern Italy to northern England.

What was unexpected was England's relatively quick rise to primacy. (The concept of primacy implies the inclusion of variables commonly, but not necessarily, associated with economic performance, such as military strength and soft power.)[42] In the later stages, when the country was securing eminence at the expense of the Dutch Republic, a non-market element was involved, that is to say military violence. The English aim was, 'to sweep the Dutch from the seas', take over their trade and capture their colonies. This was when New Amsterdam became New York. Not that the Dutch were

Simon-pure themselves: they had been fierce non-market operators during the eighty-year war by which the Dutch Republic won its independence from Spain. The Dutch closed the Scheldt and stifled the trade of Antwerp. Otherwise, give or take the standard mercantilist drives of the age, competition was commercial.

Viewed over a few centuries European economic history has been remarkably changeable. It is tempting to think that the sequence of economic and other forms of leadership, the decline of once-advanced zones and rise of others, must have been determined by a common process, but this is unlikely. Cardwell's Law, as Joel Mokyr expresses it, states that nowhere retains technological or industrial leadership for long. But as he says, this is an empirical regularity which does not bring with it a general explanation. Nor can the argument be sustained that what is to be seen is the working out of a 'first in, first out' law, whereby the disadvantages of technological leadership automatically accumulate, like genetic errors in the human body, eliminating each leader in turn.[43]

De-industrialisations along Western Europe's central belt may have followed analogous paths but this does not demonstrate a relationship. For better or worse, economic change was influenced by foreign affairs and trade policy, the outcomes of which seem to have been substantially contingent rather than internal to the economy or the result of calculation by diplomats. Instead, the sequence of declines implies a variety of errors arising because of perverse or inadequate responses to external competition. If this really was a pattern, it may suggest no more than that, when confronted by serious competitors, businesspeople tend to respond in much the same way. In any case the sequence is blurred because of the stickiness of financial centres, which failed to relocate until long after industry and trade had moved away.[44] This seems akin to 'Goldsmith's Puzzle', whereby financial institutions continue to elaborate despite decline in the economies around them.[45] As far as I know this curious feature has not been elucidated.

The perception of sequential decline may thus be misleading. If we take Venice, the first example, historians are nowadays inclined to suggest that changes on the Venetian mainland and in trading patterns offset the abandonment of woollen manufacturing within the city itself. For all that, the power and influence of the Venetian Republic within Europe and the Mediterranean basin did lose their former significance. As traditional historiography says, Venice was by-passed by economic, then political, competitors on the North Sea. Future struggles for primacy were to take place closer to England.

England's Exceptionalism

The industrial revolution made England unique. Admittedly claims of exceptionalism spring too readily to English lips, but they do to the lips of nationals of all countries. The issue is whether industrialisation was prefigured by developments found only in England. How likely was England *ex ante* to be the country that would generate industrial revolution? Care has to be taken not to exaggerate features that were preceded, shared or surpassed elsewhere. For instance, how unusual was the social structure? Not necessarily as much as appears. To refer to a small example, when Roy Porter praises coach travel for enabling English people of all classes to rub shoulders he is stretching a point. He is overlooking the fact that the Dutch stress the superiority of their passenger barge *trekschuit* to stage coaches because it really did mix the classes.[46] Coaches were far dearer and more exclusive and in this respect, England was more ordinarily European than were the Dutch. On his own ground of intellectual history, though, Porter is correct to say that during the first-third of the 18th century most Enlightenment thinking was English.[47] This upsurge of optimistic and practical curiosity nurtured economic advance.

Mention of the Dutch raises the question of whether England and Holland should be treated together, as constituting an anomalous North Sea commercial economy distinct from the remainder of agricultural Europe. Their joint deviation from European norms is being stylishly termed the Little Divergence (as opposed to the Great Divergence between China and Europe). The overlap between English and Dutch practices is being advanced as a fresh finding, though it has long been known.[48] While it is true that England borrowed much from Holland, sometimes the useful arts, sometimes merely aspects of decoration, the two countries also fought one another. Enthusiasm about transfers may obscure indigenous developments in England's more varied environment. The most formative divergence in the whole wide world remains the one whereby England became the first industrial nation.

The defining economic feature of 17th- and 18th-century England is widely agreed to have been the reduced percentage of the workforce engaged in farming. High labour productivity in agriculture was a feature of these two centuries and cannot be traced from the Middle Ages. The 18th and 19th centuries witnessed a further important alteration, though one whereby England became a more rather than less normal European country: its urban system moved from the lopsided, fragmented and localised pattern of previous times — 'typical of the peripheral countries of Europe' — to a rank-ordered network on the model of the mainland European core.[49]

A straw in a different wind is that the country lacked a real merchant marine and until Elizabeth's reign had to rely on other people's shipping. From the commercial standpoint, hiring foreign vessels may have made sense, almost foreshadowing the fluidity of the so-called Anglo-Saxon business model today. But strategically it was precarious and did not fit with a national bid for primacy. As to financial organisation, it may be possible with a degree of mischievous ingenuity to push back the turning point to the reforms of Henry VII and his Chancellor's Catch-22 criterion for taxation, Morton's Fork. An open-ended search for precursors would however run to infinite regress. Historical significance is more than chronological precedence.

1688 is a starting point that is coming back into vogue, in contrast to explanations which assign industrialisation no earlier date than the late 18th century and no causes other than material ones. The elite settlement that followed the accession of William III is felt to have ushered in a fresh era of security, with positive effects on willingness to take investment risks. The arbitrariness of Stuart rule was ended, as we shall have later occasion to remark. Anticipating that discussion, 1688 is more than a conventional turning point. Complete peace did not follow — the French bombarded Teignmouth in 1690 and warning beacons flared across the West Country — but fiscal exceptionalism did begin. England's fiscal-military state was secured, but subjected to parliamentary oversight. Its aggressive 18th-century ambitions were securely funded.

An alternative case would amount to saying that true change had come with the Civil War, described as originally a tax revolt.[50] During this conflict and the subsequent Interregnum, Customs and Excise evolved into effective public servants, collecting state revenues that rose more steeply than per-capita GDP. From 1641 a consensus about taxation was forged among the elite, whereas the citizens of England's rivals long continued to resist tax increases. This stretches the analysis back, but no further than the mid-17th century.

What is under consideration is not economic growth or industrialisation as such. It is economic primacy. The significance is debateable since it is not clear how England's bid for primacy conduced to industrialisation. A connection may exist but it remains curious that the high taxation needed to support external warfare, and taxation's regressive incidence, actually reduced spending in the mass market, notably during the Napoleonic wars. Industrialisation was surely hampered by this. An implication may be that domestic political stability was more influential via investment than any depressing effect that tax policy had on mass consumption. If so, it heightens the role of 1688.

A starting point even before the Civil War is to be found in an argument mentioned by Ron Harris, that the common law included a tradition of economic liberalism descended from Edward Coke in the early part of the 17th century.[51] When economic activities fell outside Parliament's purview, or Parliament deregulated them, the common law judges could free the market. The question is how much they really did so. The claim has been made that they sometimes reinforced existing regulations on the grounds that ancient common law justified socially desirable restrictions and was simply not open to repeal by statute. The judges claimed, for example, that the common law sanctioned controlling the grain market. Harris gives other examples of their conservative interventions and insists that these cannot be determined by adding up statutes or clauses in statutes; what actually happened in the courts needs to be discovered. Whatever the statute book may have said, it was no guarantor of enforcement. This weakens any interpretation that seeks to portray 1688 as promoting laissez-faire outright. It limits the easy notion that full parliamentary sovereignty was achieved.

Early examples of judicial actions that abolished restrictions and freed the market may of course be found. Overall the English elite came to accept market competition among their members, embracing what is called an open access order. But this is a very general proposition. The danger of invoking a tradition of market freedom lies in a tendency to join up the dots, so to speak, and present an incomplete set of parliamentary enactments and judicial decisions as moving smoothly to dominance after 1688. Reality was less one sided. English practice was not unfailingly conducive to market activity. The awkward conclusion may have to be that the industrial revolution took place as much despite the legal situation and tax policy as because of them.

Hypotheses in modern economic history often assume automatic responses to price incentives. Scholars in past generations came closer to the decisions and decision makers of the past than undiluted abstractions of this type. But scrutiny of one sphere after another makes generalisations old and new dissolve to the touch. Studies of the New Draperies, often held to have had a galvanising effect on backward English textile producers, but in truth ambiguous in their origins, illustrate the point. John Chartres's mild rebuke of a famous model of London's economic influence, that 'the specified relationships are harder to sustain when examined in greater depth', may stand for criticism of many a current orthodoxy.[52]

Accounts of the industrial revolution are described as having moved from emphases on military successes and associated trade expansions in favour of stressing its home-grown nature, with technology at the heart.[53] The proposed corrective is to reassert the role of international trade, making a calculation which piles assumption on assumption in order to conclude that income per head in Britain rose by 45 per cent between the 1760s and 1850s but would have risen only five per cent without foreign trade. Maybe: but by the latter decade, exports were featuring the products of the new technologies — and these had not been invented simply because of the opportunity to export them. The role of international trade is likely to be overdrawn because a major source of comparative data for the early modern period happens to concern it; the result is an observation bias.[54] If we consider London, it is merchants' papers that have survived, as against documentation — any documentation — for the numberless small manufacturing enterprises in the capital.[55]

The emphasis on trade usually leads authors to stress the role of London, which among its other functions was the prime trading city. The growth of population in London is seen as pulling up agricultural productivity. Bruce Campbell, who has written an authoritative study of the long period from 1300 to 1776, attributes the greater productivity of farm labour to changes in the structure and tenure of land holdings and consequent (but scarcely specified) changes in work practice.[56] Changes in cropping and husbandry methods are played down. His is a trade model of England's growth, incorporating the expansion of London as the stimulus and the application of human creativity to economic endeavour as one of the driving forces.

It is difficult to see how long demand for food could have preceded supply; to square the demotion of technical change in agriculture with the great increase of the horse population; to accept the weight placed on London, when as late as 1640 its population was less than that of Kent and Sussex combined; or to understand why the stream of creative individuals was manna falling on England alone. For a long while London's reach was greater than its grasp, which may be where some of the confusion lies. Alan Everitt showed that in 1640, London's population was barely seven per cent of the population of England and Wales.[57] Feeding the capital was, and increasingly became, a vital exercise but it was a special case of the task of supplying the growing proportion of the English population now coming to depend on the market rather than its own resources. Everitt cites the examples of thousands of workers as far apart as Somerset and Derbyshire who had to find in the marketplace food they could afford to buy.

Why was it England that responded so energetically to industrial opportunities; still more pertinently why did certain English localities respond but not others? Let us mention again the New Draperies. These have been portrayed as the crucial positive shock yet become ambiguous on examination.[58] Despite impressively detailed scholarship, the New Draperies are hard to isolate. We might unkindly quip that they represent the painstaking in pursuit of the indefinable but at least we can be sure they were not invariably continental transplants. Often enough the products were variants on English-made fabrics; 'bays' for instance may have been an old Essex product under a new name.[59]

It is almost as though, wherever one looks, the primary evidence casts doubt on efforts to construct generalisations. Still more surprising is that, despite all the works in which England's success has been read back into one or other seemingly propitious feature, the country appears to have been so ill-prepared in a number of ways. The paradox is acute. Max Weber saw England as possessing an irrational property system that was an unlikely support for the enclosure movement or industrialisation.[60] When entitlements were so uncertain, would-be developers must have found it difficult to assess the risks of investment.

The irrationality of the property system was what Weber thought of as his 'England Problem', an affront to the tidy continental mind. There was no land registry and clumsy means had to be adopted in order to pin down titles with precision: as we shall notice in a later chapter, a Wiltshire manor which my ancestors sold in 1625 was still being referred to as 'Stratton Jones' in the middle of the 18th century. The example was brought to mind by the observation that property rights were simply not specified in a way conducive to growth. However rapid the rate of growth may seem compared with what went before, a lack of clarity in the law may actually have been holding it back. As Harris remarks, offsetting expedients in the legal system did enable English exceptionalism to work because 'something in the mix did the trick'.[61] But this makes the process the more mysterious.

The Heart of the Matter

The heart of the matter was not the inducement for the English to get rich, whether by an industrial route or any other. Given the alternative of poverty, people always have an incentive to improve their lot. What is interesting is how England seized its opportunities. The output of manufactured goods soared, their real prices fell, and average real incomes soared too. All precedent was surpassed and everywhere else was outclassed. Yet there was an anomaly. Even before the north was growing fast, southern England was shedding its manufacturing industries.

Industrialisation in the north and the stripping away of industry from the south may look like Siamese twins, but this misses the point. The south's decline began too early for it to have been the straightforward victim of a superior north; only the later stages can have fallen prey to competition from coal and steam. The changes in both regions were instead responding, though in opposite directions, to common influences. Southern de-industrialisation, to which we will turn next, reveals the underlying forces at work. It puts economic growth and the industrial revolution into an unfamiliar but suggestive context.

Endnotes

1. K. Pomeranz, *The Great Divergence: China, Europe, and the Making of the Modern World Economy* (Princeton: Princeton University Press, 2000).

2. E. L. Jones, *The European Miracle: Environments, Economies and Geopolitics in the History of Europe and Asia* (Cambridge: Cambridge University Press, 1981 [third edition, 2003]).

3. T. Roy, Review: an Asian world economy? *Econ. Polit. Wkly* 36(31): (4 Aug 2001), 2937–2942. Doyne Dawson also disposes of many 'world history' propositions in The Assault On Eurocentric History, *J. Hist. Soc.* 3: 403–427, 2003.

4. J. M. Bryant, The west and the rest revisited: debating capitalist origins, European colonialism, and the advent of modernity, *Can. J. Sociol.* **31**(4): 403–444, 2006. J. M. Bryant, A new sociology for a new history? Further critical thoughts on the Eurasian similarity and great divergence theses, *Can. J. Sociol.* **33**(1): 149–167, 2008.

5. E. L. and S. B. Jones, Book industry: historical overview, in Joel Mokyr (ed.), *Oxford Encyclopedia of Economic History*, I (New York: Oxford University Press, 2003), pp. 273–277.

6. N. B. Harte (ed.), Introduction in *The New Draperies in the Low Countries and England, 1300–1800* (Oxford: Oxford University Press, 1997), p. 3.

7. E. Jones, Missing out on industrial revolution, *World Econ.* **9**(4): 101–128, 2008.

8. Quoted by J. Mokyr, in Philip Tetlock *et al.* (eds.), *Unmaking the West: "What-if" Scenarios That Rewrite Western History* (Ann Arbor: University of Michigan Press, 2006), p. 318 n. 63.

9. V. Lieberman, Transcending East–West dichotomies: state and culture formation in six ostensibly different areas, *Mod. Asian Stud.* **31**: 463–546, 1997.

10. See e.g. R. C. Allen, in R. C. Allen *et al.* (eds.), *Living Standards in the Past: New Perspectives on Well-being in Asia and Europe* (Oxford: Oxford University Press, 2005), p. 17.

11. P. Bairoch, *Economics and World History: Myths and Paradoxes* (New York: Harvester Wheatsheaf, 1993).

12. R. Taagepera, Expansion and contraction patterns of large polities: context for Russia, *Int. Stud. Q.* **41**(3): 475–504, 1997.

13. D. Comin, W. Easterly and E. Gong, Was the wealth of nations determined in 1000 B.C.? NBER Working Paper 12657 (2006).

14. G. Tabellini, *Institutions and Culture* (Bocconi University, draft MS, 2007, (on Google Scholar).

15. E. L. Jones, *Cultures Merging: A Historical and Economic Critique of Culture* (Princeton, N.J.: Princeton University Press, 2006).

16. P. H. Mo, Effective competition and economic development of imperial China, *Kyklos* **48**(1): 88, 1995.

17. C. Karayalcin, Divided we stand, united we fall: the Hume-North-Jones mechanism for the rise of Europe, *Int. Econ. Rev.* **49**(3): 992, 2008.

18. J. L. van Zanden, The road to the industrial revolution: hypotheses and conjectures about the medieval origins of the 'European Miracle', *J. Global Hist.* **3**: 337–359, 2008.

19. S. Broadberry and B. Gupta, The early modern great divergence: wages, prices and economic development in Europe and Asia, 1500–1800, *Econ. Hist. Rev.* **59**(1): 2–31, 2006.

20. Karayalcin, 'Divided We Stand'. Examples of small European polities that escaped consolidation and grew rich are given in B. S. Frey, Functional, overlapping, competing jurisdictions: redrawing the geographic borders of administration, *Eur. J. Law Reform* **V** (3 and 4): 543–555, 2005.

21. P. Bernholz and R. Vaubel (eds.), *Political Competition, Innovation and Growth in the History of Asian Civilizations* (Cheltenham: Edward Elgar, 2004).

22. K. K. Karaman, Decentralized coercion and self-restraint in provincial taxation: the Ottoman Empire, 15th–16th centuries', *J. Econ. Behav. Organ.* (2009), doi:10.1016/j.jebo.2009.03.001.

23. D. Ma, Growth, institutions and knowledge: a review and reflection on the historiography of eighteenth- and nineteenth century China', *Aust. Econ. Hist. Rev.* **44**(3): 259–277, 2004.

24. Y. Xue, A 'fertilizer revolution': a critical response to Pomeranz's theory of geographic luck, *Mod. China* **33**(2): 195–229, 2007.

25. K. Inwood, Economic growth and global inequality in long run perspective, *Rev. Income Wealth* **48**(4): 581–593, 2002.

26. C. Clark, *The Economics of 1960* (London: Macmillan, 1942), p. 2; N. Nunn, The importance of history for economic development, Harvard Economics Working Paper, October 2008, p. 15.

27. S. Broadberry, Recent developments in the theory of very long run growth: a historical appraisal, *Warwick Econ. Res. Pap.* **818**: 6, 2007.

28. D. Acemoglu and G. Zilibotti, Was Prometheus unbound by chance? Risk, diversification, and growth, *J. Polit. Econ.* **105**: 713, 1997.

29. E. L. Jones, *Seasons and Prices: The Role of the Weather in English Agricultural History* (London: George Allen & Unwin, 1964), pp. 21–27.

30. E. L. Jones, *Growth Recurring: Economic Change in World History* (Ann Arbor: University of Michigan Press, second edition, 2000).

31. P. Crone, *Pre-Industrial Societies: Anatomy of the Pre-Modern World* (Oxford: Basil Blackwell, 1989), Chap. The oddity of Europe.

32. D. Lal, *Unintended Consequences: The Impact of Factor Endowments, Culture, and Politics on Long-Run Economic Performance* (Cambridge, Mass.: The M.I.T. Press, 1998).

33. Broadberry, Recent developments, p. 9, citing J. Hatcher.

34. Harte, *New Draperies*, pp. 218, 233.

35. R. H. Mottram, *If Stones Could Speak* (London: Museum Press, 1953), p. 130.

36. H. Schilling, Innovation through migration: the settlements of calvinistic Netherlanders in sixteenth- and seventeenth-century central and western Europe, *Histoire Sociale — Soc. Hist.* **XVI**(31): 7–33, 1983.

37. Harte, *New Draperies*, p. 233.

38. D. C. Coleman, An innovation and its diffusion: the 'new draperies', *Econ. Hist. Rev.* N.S. **22**(3): 428, 1969.

39. R. Burt, The transformation of the non-ferrous metals industries in the seventeenth and eighteenth centuries, *Econ. Hist. Rev.* **XLVIII**(1): 23–45, 1995.

40. R. Burt, University of Exeter, personal communication.

41. K. Davids and J. Lucassen (eds.), *A Miracle Mirrored: The Dutch Republic in European Perspective* (Cambridge: Cambridge University Press, 1995), Introduction and Maps.

42. C. P. Kindleberger, *World Economic Primacy 1500–1990* (New York: Oxford University Press, 1996).

43. E. Ames and N. Rosenberg, Changing technological leadership and industrial growth, *Econ. J.* **LXXIII**(289): 13–31, 1963.

44. P. Spufford, *From Antwerp to London. The Decline of Financial Centres in Europe* (Ortelius Lecture No. 4, Wassenaar: NIAS, 2005), p. 34.

45. E. L. Jones, Review of Raymond W. Goldsmith, *Premodern Financial Systems Aust. Econ. Hist. Rev.* **29**: 85–86, 1989.

46. R. Porter, *Enlightenment: Britain and the Creation of the Modern World* (London: Allen Lane, The Penguin Press, 2000), p. 20.

47. Porter, *Enlightenment*, p. xviii.

48. For instance L. Jardine, *Going Dutch: How England Plundered Holland's Glory* (London: HarperCollins, 2008), does not give credit to earlier work like C. Wilson's elegant *Holland and Britain* (London: Collins, 1946).

49. P. Clark, *Small Towns in Early Modern Europe* (Cambridge: Cambridge University Press, 1995), pp. 118–119.

50. P. K. O'Brien, 'Fiscal exceptionalism: Great Britain and its European rivals from Civil War to triumph at Trafalgar and Waterloo', in D. Winch and P. K. O'Brien (eds.), *The Political Economy of British Historical Experience, 1688–1914* (Oxford: Oxford University Press/British Academy, 2002), pp. 245–246, 251.

51. R. Harris, Government and the economy, 1688–1850, in R. Floud and P. Johnson (eds.), *The Cambridge Economic History of Modern Britain* I: 204–237, 2004.

52. J. Chartres, Food consumption and internal trade, in A. L. Beier and R. Finlay (eds.), *London 1500–1700: The Making of the Metropolis* (London: Longman, 1986), p. 191.

53. G. Clark *et al.*, Made in America? The New World, the Old, and the industrial revolution, *Am. Econ. Rev. Pap. & Proc.* **98**(2): 523–528, 2008.

54. Roy, 'An Asian World Economy?'

55. A. L. Beier, Engine of manufacture: the trades of London, in A. L. Beier and R. Finlay (eds.), *London 1500–1700: The Making of the Metropolis* (London: Longman, 1986), p. 151.

56. B. M. S. Campbell, The uses and exploitation of human power, in *Economia e Energia Secc. XIII–XVIII*, Istituto Internazionale di Storia Economia 'F, Datini' Prato (Florence: Le Monnier, 2003), pp. 192–211.

57. A. Everitt, The marketing of agricultural produce, 1500–1640, in J. Chartres (ed.), *Agricultural Markets and Trade 1500–1750* (Cambridge: Cambridge University Press, 2003), pp. 63, 131 n. 2.

58. R. C. Allen, Britain's economic ascendancy in a European context, in Leandro Prados de la Escosura (ed.), *Exceptionalism and Industrialisation: Britain and Its European Rivals, 1688–1815* (Cambridge: Cambridge University Press, 2004), p. 30.

59. Harte, *New Draperies*, pp. 1–2.

60. J. Getzler, Theories of property and economic development, *J. Interdiscip. Hist.* **26**(4): 644–645, 1996.

61. Harris, *Government and the Economy*, p. 236.

PART I

DE-INDUSTRIALISATION: SOUTHERN ENGLAND

CHAPTER 2

THE ANOMALY OF THE SOUTH

The dramatic economic changes which we call an industrial revolution did not exhaust the economic experience of Britain. If one is really interested in the structure and course of the British economy in the early nineteenth century ... an understanding of the economic structure of declining or stable sectors and of the backwaters of southern England [is] ... almost as relevant to the history of the British economy as a whole as a grasp of the spectacular events in cotton textiles, in iron and coal, and in Lancashire, Yorkshire, and South Wales.

B. E. Supple, 1960

The north of England is the type specimen from which 19th- and 20th-century industrialisations derive. Few scholars question the convention that it was where industrialisation began. They typically point to the correspondence with the coal-fields. By contrast the non-coal-bearing south is passed over as sunk in rural sloth, with nothing to contribute to the history of industry or economic growth. Its experience is almost deleted from the mainstream historical record.

Approaching industrial revolution studies via the de-industrialisation of southern England may therefore seem elliptical, even perverse. This book will nevertheless take the contrary view and hope to show, not that southern de-industrialisation was initially a consequence of industrialisation in the north, but that both derived from a single, though very prolonged, reversal of comparative advantage. The emphasis must be on the fact of a shift, since the ecological settings were permanent.

As mentioned, the medievalist, Helen Jewell, shows that the north-south divide long predated the industrial revolution, which however solidified it.[1] She observes that the divide was based partly on physiographic differences leading to a poorer agriculture and lower population in the north, features that magnified the wider economic divergence which followed. Herbert Heaton noted that as machinery and steam power came in, northern manufacturing competition became more powerful, the implication being that this was a late phase in a centuries-long competitive process, rather than the origin of change.[2]

What wedged the two regions apart was, ironically enough, the merging of markets. This was an outcome of improvements in transport and communications resulting from heavier investment in projects with long gestation periods. When markets fused, latent advantages enabled this town or that to prevail over its neighbours, whole districts to maintain their industry but others to see theirs dwindle, and eventually entire regions — north and south — to follow opposite economic paths. On this showing, the late preindustrial economy appears more mutable and progressive than is portrayed in standard accounts, which depict the industrial revolution as a once-and-for-all emergence from darkness into light.

The south was the wide area to the north-east, west and south of London, corresponding approximately to the standard geographical zone of Lowland England. The 18th century saw this area becoming ever more a region of landed estates, while the middle-class quarters of its market towns housed the residences of professional gentlemen who serviced the needs of agriculture, besides affluent retirees and half-pay officers. Writing about Winchester a quarter of a century after Jane Austen had died there in 1817, Mudie observed that, 'it is in short not a place to make a fortune, but it is one in which time may be agreeably spent …'[3] Adam Smith pointed out that consumption is the end of all production. Consumption, too, deserves its economic history. It provides more than descriptive closure because it enables us to rebalance our understanding of economic change.

De-Industrialisation Considered

Spatial change is not the primary concern of economic historians but may be the best or only pointer to alterations in the structure of the economy for periods when truly appropriate data are scarce or absent. Groups of industries in different settings may have a life, or in the south's case death, of their own. The distinctive associations of demography, settlements, communications, local markets and so forth create the pattern of response to economic stimuli which Moses Abramovitz has called 'social capability'.[4] In respect of de-industrialisation a more appropriate term might be social incapacity. By Abramovitz's own admission his phrase is a black box of factors that influence responsiveness via the diffusion of knowledge, composition of output, and level of investment. Regional studies make sense only if factors such as these combine into a supra-industrial force.

Even in the hands of modern economists, de-industrialisation is ill-defined and it is not clear whether it extends to the more serious issue of a decline in total regional income.[5] The term seems aimed at industrial contractions which jeopardise the eventual power of a region or nation to pay for needed imports. 'Eventual' and 'needed' are elastic concepts, as are the 'socially acceptable' levels of output, employment and exchange rates referred to in other definitions. Whether declining employment rather than the trend of output is what should be measured is likewise not self-evident. To assume that this is the case ties national or regional interests uncritically to the fortunes of industrial workers or workers in certain industries rather than to the interests of all workers, much less all consumers. Employment may fall yet output be maintained or even rise. The costs of change may be highly visible in the form of job losses in one or other trade while compensating benefits are thinly spread and hard to detect.

Threatened industries can organise against their losses, which a myriad consumers cannot readily do. Students of de-industrialisation may be misled if they rely on partisan claims which dwell on negative aspects without noticing more diffuse contributions to growth. And partisan writings are what tend to survive. Provided alterations in employment and income are reason-ably gentle, regional de-industrialisation may be a small price to pay for the increase in overall productivity when some other area learns cheaper ways of manufacturing. The task is not to weep at each passing re-arrangement of historical geography but to discover why particular regions, faced with compe-tition, were unable to alter the mix of their activities without net loss.

Economists generally agree that once a region or country steps onto the slippery slope of decline, it is likely to go on sliding.[6] Cumulative processes are set in motion, downward Myrdalian spirals. The strong countervailing policies needed to reverse them were uncommon in earlier times; regionally specific policies were rare. The more usual responses were attempts to cling on to any remaining trade, keep out 'strangers', and share business among the existing producers. Articles of Agreement signed by over 130 cloth-workers at Newbury in the late 17th century banned reducing prices, accepting goods in payment instead of money, and having yarn spun more cheaply in rural areas outside the Borough.[7] These measures may have helped cloth-working to limp along but it continued to shrink and never again generated nationally known entrepreneurs like the town's earlier heroes, Jack O'Newbury and Thomas Dolman. Newbury downshifted to inferior products and after a decorous interval its splendid Cloth Hall became a museum.

In the early Middle Ages the array of trades in almost every town had been extensive, even comprehensive. By contrast with subsequent periods, needs were met locally and goods seldom carried far to market. Such a statement is always relative, of course, but Defoe, touring the country at the start of the 18th century, was aware that the situation had since changed and towns had often become specialised. A full economic history of the south would involve describing the concentration of trades during and after late medieval times in the hope of accounting for the distributions he saw.

The circumstances reported by Defoe were the result of a barely reported withering of industries in small places, as manufacturing withdrew into larger towns and favoured localities. Industrial mortality was not new in early modern and late pre-industrial times — the breadth of the chronology is appropriate — and these periods witnessed an intensification of the process to the point where some trades ceased to exist in the whole south. The present purpose does not require expounding on the entire saga. It aims at grasping the basic process whereby most manufacturing was stripped away while growing in the north, where it culminated in the industrial revolution.

Defoe was mesmerised by the late pre-industrial distribution of specialities. He thought them 'natural' outgrowths of local position and endowments, and offered no real explanation. If towns, 'are lately encreas'd in trade and navigation, wealth, and people, while their Neighbours Decay, it is because they have some particular Trade … which is a kind of nostrum to them, inseparable to the place, and which fixes there by the nature of the thing'.[8] Trades made the names of the towns specialising in them the equivalent of brand names, like the names of districts where delicacies and drink originate, though without the legalistic devices to suppress competition that now characterise Europe. In England some foods had already become associated with specific towns or districts, Cheddar and Stilton for example.

For branding of this type there were often good reasons rooted in local ecology, meaning resource endowments, but the business side is underestimated. Commercial competition had a greater effect on the contraction or relocation of trades. Given that Defoe was writing three centuries ago, complaints in later ages, including our own, that local variety has collapsed 'within living memory', are almost comical. They hark back now to the consolidation of locally owned repair or servicing firms and not to the cessation of manufactures, which mostly disappeared long since.

The most significant point about de-industrialisation is the one already made, that it reflects productivity growth elsewhere, in someone else's industries. The purpose of industrial death, one might say, is so that the economic future may be different from the past and on balance better for society as a whole. Lest this reinforce the idea that southern de-industrialisation was a straightforward and welcome response to the intensification of industry in the north, consider that the process was a prolonged one in which competition came first from neighbouring towns, eliminating trades in favour of some nearby alternative, and ascending only gradually to the Victorian crescendo when the north took over.

Although some businesses attempted to move towards higher-value products, it was commoner for them to sink to ones of lesser value, requiring less capital and less skill on the part of the workforce, or to abandon manufacturing entirely. It might be said, only a little melodramatically, that poverty came to stalk the backyards of the market towns, such as the notorious alleys of Tewkesbury. 'Market' used as an adjective indicates the function of these towns within their farming districts. In a fashion comparable to the descent of water mills from grinding wheat for bread to producing coarser food for animals and eventually out of business altogether, so the textiles woven in southern towns fell from broadcloth to worsteds (which cut out the fulling stage) and thence to coarse shalloons or sackcloth, before the final cessation of cloth-making.

De-Industrialisation Examined

The broad and long re-sorting of economic distributions is an indication of considerable underlying competitiveness in the economy of the 16th and 17th centuries. It was competitive enough to go beyond Defoe's haphazard rise and fall of individual towns and their trades, to start inverting the roles of entire regions. This has been overlooked for at least three reasons: the first is that the industrial revolution is a success story compared with which economic decline seems trivial or uninteresting. Praiseworthy exceptions exist, such as Clapham's old study of the transfer of the worsted industry from Norfolk to the West Riding, but they are exceptions.[9] In any case industries typically drained away where they stood rather than move to the north along the lines of Clapham's article, notwithstanding Joseph Townsend's opinion of 1780 that manufacturers were 'leaving the South Countries and travelling to the North'.[10] When Arthur Young declared in 1809 that the manufacture of coarse velvet around Banbury had 'travelled to the North' he did not mean that the trade had physically migrated as opposed to shrinking on the spot through northern competition.[11]

The second reason is how slow the process was, with each change gradually lapping over the next. Given the habit of scholars to specialise by period, changes spread over two or three centuries are readily missed: early modern and modern times generate different types of evidence, different questions, different analytical methods and different literatures. Sometimes the period between the Restoration and the mid-18th century falls into a black hole. During the 17th-century industries such as the making of woollens were already vanishing from some places, yet they usually formed again somewhere nearby. In Berkshire the woollen industry more or less quit the villages where it had formerly operated, only to concentrate in local towns.[12] Afterwards, industries were rarely replaced in the same vicinity. Declines began to accumulate, and less and less of anything resembling the original manufactures remained.

The twilight phase was a long one, stretching into Victoria's reign, by which time commentaries are more numerous than before and the formerly obscure process becomes more visible. Reports of decline are biased towards enterprises which managed to hang on into the 19th century. After trade depressions and strikes in 1828 and 1834 some moneyed locals, David Ricardo among them, paid for distressed weavers to emigrate from the Stroud valley.[13] Interestingly, they sent them to Australia rather than the north of England. But in the 1850s there were still scores of hand-loom weavers in the cottages, sad-faced middle-aged men earning very little and dressed pathetically in cast-off clothes.

This was the fate of all who would not or could not change trades, emigrate or at least leave for the cities. The hand-loom weaver problem is well known. One description refers to the village of Broughton Gifford, Wiltshire, where in 1860 the weaver's earnings were barely superior to the farm worker's, health was worse and prospects not reassuring. 'That he [the weaver] has so long held his own against the steam power-looms of the factory is a marvel to all observers'.[14] This tenacity was based on long hours and extra toil on the hand-loom, because employers doubted whether special looms and machinery for 'fancy stuffs' would pay, though the Yorkshire men had invested in them.

Why did the hand-loom weaver not become a farm labourer? Despite facile assumptions in the secondary literature, substitution was not easy. The townie's dismissal of agricultural labour is misplaced. Farm work was a harder-learned, all-round task than even many contemporaries supposed: 'in-door and out-door habits, the loom and the plough, the shuttle and the sickle, the soft hand and the hard hand, cannot be interchanged at pleasure'. Before the Poor Law Amendment Act, the ratepayers of Broughton Gifford used to pay twice what they were paying at the end of the 1850s to maintain weavers who were not able or willing to do the only out-door work available. In Gloucestershire the last few hand-looms were worked at Uley and Dursley as late as the 1880s, but only by old people.[15]

A third reason for neglect is that the fugitive nature of the sources evades the research techniques of economist-economic historians. Analysis requires more than national textbook categories or 'as if' computations. A wide scatter of tiny enterprises in multiple trades, fading away over decades, left scant trace, and virtually no quantitative trace at all, since they seem rarely to have kept accounts. Nor do minuscule and failing firms commission histories. Sometimes the evidence is nothing more than the rusting premises beloved of industrial archaeologists. But although dereliction may be picturesque, a concentration on physical remains prompts a bleak view and encourages the protectionist notion that the activities of any given era should be retained in perpetuity. As Peter Levi commented about the history of the English landscape, things generate excellent questions, but seldom offer reliable solutions.[16]

Investigating southern economic history means working through intensely local materials in order to unravel the difficulties that slowly over-whelmed the multiplicity of poorly recorded firms and industries. Only when obscure references are assembled from documents and local histories does the extent of the shift become apparent, though even this is an uncertain exercise and bound to remain incomplete. Whereas Dell could use leases to trace the decline of the clothing industry in Newbury through changes in the occupants of individual buildings, too many leases have since been sold as curiosities in antique shops and not systematically collected by the county record offices.[17]

Notwithstanding the varied mass, almost the morass, of detail that does survive, we shall find that we are observing facets of a single theme. There was a common thread and it was regional — we have previously stated that the problem was over-arching and not an ad hoc succession of industry-specific or firm-specific troubles. Industries closed down right across the south. Almost as telling was the fact that the region did not share in the growth of new industries and new technologies taking place in the north. National and international demand for manufactured goods was expanding but the south did not or could not hold its own in contributing to the supply.

As a small but characteristic example, consider the hat industry carried on in two villages in 19th-century Gloucestershire.[18] The procedure was to felt wool and cover it with rabbit fur but the trade began to decline with the introduction of silk hats in the 1840s. There was absolutely no thought of switching in that direction and local circumstances did not attract outside entrepreneurs. The population of one of the villages collapsed in the 1850s and by the 1871 census there were only 15 workers in the felt industry left in the whole county.

Contemporary and modern authors have put forward a range of explanations for the loss of energy. Whereas some refer only to one industry, one shire (regional histories are commonly arranged on a county basis) or just a single locality, many do acknowledge that the experiences were part of a larger phenomenon. Nevertheless few delve far into the common issues or allow for exceptions to the de-industrialising story, which is to say the means whereby a handful of firms managed to hang on. Commentators prefer to attribute change to over-mastering by coal and steam.

Counter-Movements

Some entrepreneurs did respond to competition or opportunity by rearranging their businesses and upgrading their premises.[19] The plush-weaving masters in the Banbury district set up weaving sheds long before the adoption of machinery. Woollen weavers in Wiltshire, Somerset and Gloucestershire were grouped in workshops where the looms could be supervised and in these counties purpose-built water-powered mills began to appear. Barrie Trinder presents these and other examples to give the impression, fostered by contemporaries, of a struggle to survive. To the more active of those involved at the time, they may have seemed ordinary modernisations, doomed or not. They are reminiscent of the 'sailing-ship syndrome' in which a spurt of innovations is prompted by greater external competition.

Occasional brand-new enterprises were established in the southern counties and a handful was transferred there, the most conspicuous being Heathcoat's removal of a 100 lace workers from the Midlands to set up business afresh in a disused cotton mill at Tiverton, Devon, in 1809. Another lace manufacturer, Oram, also moved from Leicestershire to Tiverton. Similarly, London silk-makers moved into the Dorset towns in search of cheap workers; lace-making came in to Lyme Regis to counter poverty (or exploit cheap labour); Yorkshire lace manufacturers moved down south to occupy former clothing factories in Chard, Somerset (exploiting cheap premises) and the Fox family built new woollen mills at Wellington, Somerset.[20]

Not all of these enterprises prospered greatly, since local labour was probably not cheap when its quality was taken into account. Spinning and lace-making and straw-hat making, established from the 1790s to soak up pauper labour, were not usually successful. They were exceptions to prove the regional rule but did not weigh heavily in terms of national industry. The significance of the outliers lies in demonstrating that blanket explanations are unlikely to cover the case. Single factor explanations are tricky, since decline involved so many industries over such a wide area and such a long time. Instead of models which refer to some single deficiency of the southern environment, explanations are called for that allow room for the few enterprising firms that trod water or even swam against the tide.

Two possibilities come to mind. One is that pockets of demand occasionally sustained the manufacture of consumer goods for a long time. An instance was the Woodstock steel industry, which meant metal jewellery, fabricated (like high-quality sporting guns in London) from the workable and easily polished wrought iron of nails from worn-out horse-shoes.[21] A great range of glittering decorations and ornaments were made, some of them discs to decorate the handbags whose manufacture was apparently a derivative of the Woodstock glove trade. The jewellery was already well regarded before the end of the 16th century. It depended on skill and ingenuity in coming up with new designs that could be sold at high prices to local aristocrats and others with money. The trade disappeared in the 1860s, however, as the result of the eventual extreme cheapness of similar wares made in Birmingham and Sheffield.

Since the Woodstock steel manufacture ultimately perished, the point about demand is perhaps more convincingly illustrated by the situation in

Bath. There, ample rich customers were on the spot, supporting a surprising range of trades, down to a leech and a cork-and-bottle dealer.[22] Cut-glass and brass works used steam, and in 1802 there was even a manufactory of steam engines. A second reason why Bath's industries persisted or were established afresh was that for many of them capital requirements for entry were low. The capital market in the city was in any case exceptional: in 1794 small luxury goods traders put up a total of £10,500 to establish a hotel and pleasure gardens, and the Bath Society helped several thousand men and women start businesses or keep them going by lending a total of £12,000 between 1805 and 1835. The failure rate among small semi-luxury producers was high, but if exit was easy, entry had been surprisingly easy too.

Further successful developments that went against the trend turned out producer goods for farming. Here and there blacksmiths evolved into agricultural implement manufacturers, among whom Plenty of Newbury, Taskers of Andover, Nalder and Nalder of Wantage and Wallis and Steevens (sic) of Basingstoke exported steam traction engines, diversified into lorry-building, and lasted until after the Second World War. The casting shops of market town ironmongers also evolved into engineering works long before 1850 and were at their peak during the second half of the 19th century.[23] One of these enterprises was Stothert and Pitt of Bath, which was however not entirely independent of the industrial revolution further north, as may be seen from the fact that George Stothert was an agent for the Coalbrookdale Company. The examples here did not add up to a re-industrialisation of the south but did constitute exceptions to most of the regression.

De-Industrialisation Described

As befitted the supplying of mainly local markets, industries in the south were varied and often repetitive. Textiles predominated, iron was made, salt was boiled, and a range of consumer goods was produced. The market for some of the consumer items was widest because they could be carried by hawkers or taken for sale at the big autumn fairs, and as a result a few localities specialised in boots or buttons. All this nevertheless took place in tiny production units scattered through the countryside. There were factories too. Strictly speaking, they were 'manufactories', powered by hand rather than machines, though there were some water-powered mills. The first water-powered textile mill was in Dorset and there were cotton (fustian) factories in Wiltshire and elsewhere.

Declines were staggered across the region. No comprehensive industrial data exist. Where figures were collected it was for miscellaneous, incidental purposes and local historians have usually been able to unearth only fragmentary numbers. It could be argued that the earlier declines were offset by regenerated or freshly established trades and that de-industrialisation became general only in the late 18th century, the main eliminations taking place in the following half-century. This implies a very broad dating bracket of *c.* 1750 to *c.* 1850, though some examples occurred much earlier and others far later. Alternatively a continuum of industrial decay may be thought of as steadily clearing the board, culminating in a rural area devoid of its former manufactures and buying from elsewhere such goods as could be afforded.

Newbury's famous cloth trade, for instance, positively collapsed as early as the third quarter of the 16th century, with the demise of the Antwerp market, competition from the rise of the 'New Draperies' elsewhere, and increased regulation.[24] But this was not the end of textile trades in the borough; they lasted for another two centuries and staggered on into the 19th century. Likewise the last glass furnace in the Weald closed as early as 1618, and whereas the district had housed 80 ironworks in 1660, in 1720 it contained only 30.[25] By the late 18th century the entire south had become an industrial Lilliput, relatively speaking, as is evident from the overwhelming concentration of Boulton and Watt steam engines in the north in the years 1775 to 1800.[26]

The distribution of wealth as reflected in property tax assessments was quite stable for centuries during and after the Middle Ages, but there was a big change in the 18th century. At that time the agricultural counties were overtaken by the industrial ones. In terms of wealth rank, the median rise in Derbyshire, Lancashire and Yorkshire was 16 places, while the median rank of seven southern counties fell 8 places. In 1660 eight of the ten largest provincial towns had lain in the south but by 1861 eight were in the north.[27]

The shift in distributions came during what may perhaps be called the 'long industrial revolution', though some of it occurred even before anything this label reasonably describes. At the end of the 18th century the furnaces of the new ironworks set in Midland or northern landscapes were thought suitable subjects for Joseph Wright's romantic night-time paintings. Within 60 or 70 years a mordant view was being taken of what had happened in the interim, as reflected in Mrs. Gaskell's novel of 1855, *North and South*. 'A nineteenth-century conflict between North and South was as much a leading theme of English as of American history', wrote Asa Briggs.[28] Notice that it was a conflict of the 19th century, conspicuous only then, despite the southern decline which had been progressing by degrees — regressing would be a better word — for over two centuries.

Southern plant being mostly small, what passed for equipment or machinery was small too. Nevertheless, the physical scale over-impresses, not being matched in productive capacity. An example is the Boulton & Watt beam engine erected at Crofton in 1812, in an engine-house nowadays open as a tourist attraction. It was installed to pump water back into the summit pound of the Kennet and Avon canal. The engine and an additional one of 1846 are substantial and the building that houses them is tall, at least when one comes on it suddenly out in the Wiltshire fields. By modern standards, however, the horse-power generated is more limited than the impressive volume of the cylinders suggests — though not too low to be brought into action in July 2009, to save the canal from drying up when the modern electric pump failed![29]

Mainstream work on the economic history of industry seldom mentions regional differences beyond alluding to the establishment of the cotton industry in Lancashire or reiterating that development came on the coal fields. Among histories of particular places, the bulk refers to northern towns or districts. Studies of the industrial revolution suffer because they feature areas of successful industrialisation so heavily and pay little or no attention to the two types of contrary case — areas where earlier 'pre-industrial industry' had declined or where there had never been manufacturing of any consequence. Such studies lack controls. Ignoring 'non-events' leads to the making of assertions about the correlates of industrialisation as if they necessarily explain it. This is especially so of the many accounts which state or imply that industry grew up on the coalfields because that was where the use of coal-fired steam power grew up.

De-industrialisation affected punctiform as well as cottage industries. Although by-employments were immensely widespread and highly significant — in 1600 the woollen trades alone probably occupied the spare hours of 25 per cent of the cottage-farming population in the whole country — it is a misapprehension to think that industry in the south was all rural domestic handicrafts.[30] The fact that every rural domestic trade did not transform itself into powered factory industry is a side issue or separate debate: the notion does not allow for certain trades, or the trades in some districts, being knocked out before any transition to powered factories was likely.

Even punctiform industries rarely moved into the factory stage *in situ*, Wealden iron, cloth and glass being illustrations. It was not just that, with hindsight, rural domestic industry seems a cul-de-sac alongside the route to modern growth; southern industries of most types proved a dead end. The heart of the matter was not the 'failure' of cottage industry but the 'failure' of southern industry.

Some industries are drawn to the sources of their raw materials or energy supplies. Others are mobile and factors beyond the physical environment determine why they are not promiscuously spread. Tanning is an interesting example and more important than it seems, the leather trade having been the fourth largest industry of all by value in 1851, ranking only after cotton, wool and iron, and employing 350,000 hands.[31] Individual tanneries survived in many small places during the 19th century and were not necessarily unprofitable: when Edmund Rudge, admittedly an aged miser, died in 1843 at 84 he left a fortune of £140,000 amassed as a tanner in Tewkesbury, Gloucestershire. Nevertheless the main story is one of progressive withdrawal from the region.

Little country tanneries were mostly unable to grow enough to supply wide areas. There was, for example, a shrinkage of tanning in the villages around the (then) Berkshire market town of Wantage, before the town's industry itself came to an end with the death of the last employer at 90 in 1825.[32] Wantage had been one of the largest tannery centres in the country, with one-quarter of its population employed in the trade. But its biggest tannery, though able to defeat rivals in surrounding villages and smaller towns, was unable to compete with those in London and Northampton. Details of the early phases of the competition are lost to the record, as is usual with trades where no large businesses survived to maintain interest.

Dubious ecological explanations of industrial location, as opposed to business reasons, are put forward for any number of trades. Thus the location of tanning is attributed to physical advantages, such as numbers of oak trees to provide bark, or water with special virtues, but this seems a rationalisation. It is more likely that the Wantage tanneries had what would now seem minor advantages of scale and their reach was extended by transport improvements. They undercut the village tanners, but themselves succumbed to the products of the larger and better-placed London tanneries. The implication is that as markets widened only tanneries of successively larger scales, with employers of personal energy at the right junctures, were capable of responding successfully.

Increasingly, the south specialised on farming and food processing to supply the region's own non-farm population, and more and more to provision the London food market. Some foodstuffs had reached London from the extremities of the country as early as the 16th century. That was by sea, but later the trade stimulated overland communications and inland navigation. Soils and climate were generally better than in the North, but the south's main superiority arose through being closer to the capital, which meant shorter distances to carry bulky foodstuffs. This, with the activities and professions associated with trade, accounted for the middle-class prosperity which — architecture being frozen history — is plain to this day in the many substantial Georgian houses of the market towns and villages.

While the decay of industry was regionally coordinated, it is less obviously a single phenomenon when considered over time. Profitable opportunities for doing business fluctuated through the years and the fortunes of different trades were not always in phase. Viewed chronologically the pattern was not a straightforward, progressive scraping of the board. A survey of Dorset illustrates this by comparing lists of the manufactures in the 17th and 18th centuries with those present during the first half of the 19th century.[33] Stained glass-making, for example, did not even persist from the 17th into the 18th century, whereas glass-making, silk-throwing and the making of band strings, articles of straw, stockings, ribbons and haberdashery (the last replacing the dwindling cloth trade of Sherborne) all came in. The preparing of parchment and a number of weaving trades in Dorset seem actually to have come and gone during the 19th century.

This warns us against taking every lament of the twilight years at face value: the trades lost were not an indefeasible heritage only then expunged. No single stock of industries existed in, say, 1600 or 1650 or 1700 to be whittled almost to nothing by the reign of Victoria; not all the trades which vanished were venerable, adjustments had occurred and experiments had been made. Of the many examples, a lace factory founded in Chipping Campden, Gloucestershire, in 1817 may be mentioned; it did not survive beyond 1850.[34] Other late bloomers went the same way. The fact that genuinely old and relatively new manufactures alike were evaporating strengthens the case for thinking that chronic disadvantages of the whole area were responsible.

County Illustrations

The record is both so voluminous and yet contains so many gaps that a comprehensive account is not possible. To make the task manageable, consider a sample of three counties, Kent in the east, Hampshire in the centre and Gloucestershire in the west. Separated from one another by intervening shires, they represent the region. They serve as proxies for the remaining shires, though, besides commonalities, they demonstrate differences reflecting relative proximity to London and access to the continent. In principle it would be possible to go on splitting until dealing with every firm in every industry in every town, but in practice that is neither possible nor a good method for finding the common elements in southern decline.

Further references to industries in the three sample counties and allusions to others from Oxfordshire to Devon will surface in later chapters, but neither this section nor the book as a whole will attempt a gazetteer. The East Anglian counties are not included for the practical reasons of limited space and lack of familiarity on my part. Their experience was comparable with that of the southern counties, however, and together these sub-regions constituted the Lowland England 'left behind' by the industrial revolution.

The places and trades mentioned in this chapter are often ones of which Victorian antiquaries happened to find traces. Thanks to their work, the *Victoria County Histories* and the proceedings of county archaeological magazines bulge with such an array of instances that to recount them all would grossly overload the text. The detail might fascinate local readers but would feel to others like ploughing through an encyclopaedia. We shall restrict ourselves to summary surveys of the three chosen counties.

First, take Kent, where industry in the Weald was nationally important in 1600.[35] The district was then the major producer of glass and iron (with 49 of the national total of 85 blast furnaces), and was also significant for dyed broadcloth. Admittedly, the distribution of the Wealden glass, iron and textiles industries overlapped spatially only at their peak, and their declines were not precisely in phase, nevertheless all three faltered by 1650, shrank during the late 17th century, were almost finished by 1700, and were dead by 1820. Glass-making vanished following prosecutions by a Stuart monopolist of Wealden producers using wood-burning furnaces rather than as a result of any industrial deficiency. The student of the district, Brian Short, cites complex causes and is adamant that until much later there was no switch to farming proper or to residence in the countryside for reasons of fashion and amenity. Only in the 19th century did landowners turn to their estates as refuges from industrialisation.

Another student of Kent, David Ormrod, places the emphasis on the offsetting growth of new industries on the northern edge of the county, in the Medway valley, and the towns of East Kent.[36] He makes much of the introduction of silk-making by Huguenot refugees, who nevertheless moved on in a generation from Canterbury to Spitalfields. By the mid-18th century, wool-combing, silk weaving and thread twisting were also sharply on the retreat.

Change in Kent, in Ormrod's view, was not de-industrialisation at all but reflected the trading and naval demands of the mercantilist state. The full force of this opinion is hard to understand, given the abandonment of the Weald by all of its manufactures, including ordnance production, and the decay of trades elsewhere in the county, yet it does indicate that part of what was taking place was an accommodation to changing patterns of demand. New industries grew up, or industries appeared in new locations, connected with military needs derived from the seat of government in London. Not every part of southern England was as well placed to capitalise on these imperatives.

But the second county, Hampshire, was also favoured by government contracts, here granted to Portsmouth dockyard and for a time to other coastal settlements, such as Buckler's Hard, where naval ships were built. These activities galvanised the economy of parts of the coast, sparking the Taylors' original mass production of interchangeable ships' blocks on the Itchen and Cort's all-transforming development of coke-smelted iron at Fontley, near Gosport. Military demand was fickle, certainly, and the Taylors, who had installed what was probably the first steam sawmill and second steam corn mill in the country, went bankrupt over the latter once war ended in 1783.[37] But although grass grew again in the streets of Portsmouth after the Napoleonic wars, the naval yard soon resumed its role as an advanced, internationally famous industrial plant. Nevertheless, this single achievement, remarkable though it was, could not preserve the other industries of Hampshire.

A broader view of the county is presented in T. W. Shore's *Hampshire Papers*, originally written in the 1880s and 1890s, with one paper entitled, 'Decayed Hampshire Manufactures'.[38] This report is emblematic of the south-central counties, in which textile trades especially were widespread, if only in penny packets. Shore's inventory is incomplete, there were too many tiny businesses for completeness, but even his level of detail is likely to mesmerise the general reader. The distillation below stands as a portrait, not a map, of the situation in the county and the counties around.

De-industrialisation is surely a pertinent term for what occurred in Hampshire and most other counties in the south: describing the process solely as an 'adjustment' from manufacturing to farming or rural residence cannot disguise the expunging of industry from the interior districts. Adjustment has two meanings. The first refers to the withdrawal of resources from industrial uses and their direct investment in the purchase of landed estates, farming operations or agricultural processing. There was some of this, perhaps most notably in respect of the Gentlemen Clothiers of Gloucestershire, though it is usually hard to demonstrate.

The second usage is less specific and records the coincidence of agricultural expansion at a time when industrial firms were closing down or paradoxically when new industrial enterprises were actually opening up, as in parts of Kent or with the movement of the lace industry into Devon. This time adjustment is the appropriate term because it does not assume an immediate substitution between the sectors, which would need to be shown from documentary sources. But it remains something of an abstraction through implying the unity of two partly separate processes. Chronological simultaneity may mislead.

Shore notes that at the start of the 19th century Hampshire's clothing trade was already decayed; it had gone from Winchester and was almost dead in Alresford and Andover. Yet, he adds, barragons, druggets, serges, Valentia tabinest and bombazines were then still made at Alton, together with silk and worsted tabbygreens which were exported to Philadelphia as the favourite summer wear for American gentlemen. Worsted yarn was spun in villages for 10 miles around Alton. Coarse woollens and fine linen had formerly been woven at Odiham, druggets and shalloons at Basingstoke and serges at Whitchurch. A 'factory' existed at Fordingbridge for spinning woollen yarn, Romsey at one time had 200 looms (partly moved on from Wareham, Dorset), and there were cloth-workers in Southampton.

All these activities were quite marginal by the early 19th century, the period Shore mostly discusses. He provides more information about the silk trade. One Winchester firm had employed 300 hands, its mills having been founded in 1792. The machinery was turned by hand, which makes it sound no mighty challenge to the silk producers of London and the Midlands, although in 1797 the establishments were moved to a site near Abbey Mills for the sake of water power. By 1807 more mills were at work in Winchester, with others in Hampshire's market towns and largest villages. The silk factory at Overton was recorded as existing from at least 1701 to 1850, employing most of the local womenfolk. But by 1890 only the mill at Whitchurch remained in use.

Corn mills had sometimes been converted to paper-making. By the end of the 18th century there was a solid group of paper mills in the Home Counties, with Hampshire conspicuous on the outer edge.[39] The most romantic success story, as it was called by Donald Coleman, was that of Portals. Henri de Portal, a Huguenot refugee who arrived hidden in a wine barrel, took the lease of a mill at Laverstoke in 1718 and in 1724 secured the monopoly of producing Bank of England notes. This was a licence to print money in two senses and soon enabled him to buy an estate nearby.

In the 1830s the number of paper mills began to contract. Coleman attributed this to economies of scale as the larger mills mechanised, which, together with better communications, made competition within the industry fiercer. The logic was concentration around major centres of demand, and while there was a spate of new establishments in the northern industrial counties, the Home Counties held firm and Hampshire too. Demand and transportation were the keys.

Shore scrapes around for vestiges of other trades, and finds a few, such as the making of glass as late as 1840 and a lace factory which employed 200 hands on the Isle of Wight in 1860. Totals of the workforce or the number of looms are the usual indicators of the size of firms and how reliable numbers such as '200 hands' may be is uncertain. It is rarely stated whether the figures refer to full- or part-time employees, males, females or children, or how often the looms were in use; they may be taken only as approximate measures of scale. Even then they may be exaggerations or at best maxima. Other measures, such as capital investment, are usually absent.

Shore mentions traces of an iron furnace at Bursledon (iron had also been made at Sowley Pond). In addition he noted that the manufacture of edge tools had once taken place at Wickham and persisted in 1890 at Conford and Bramshott. The tools were hand-made and much sought after locally, fetching a higher price than axe-heads, hooks and hoes from Sheffield. Yet none of these enterprises was expanding and none lasted much longer. Shore sums this up in true Victorian fashion by declaring that, in the steam era, Hampshire and the south were beaten by northern competition, because coal was cheaper in the north. Nevertheless he permits himself to speculate that inertia and old ways prevented adaptations that might have saved some of the industries. On reflection it is plain that inertia and clinging to old ways have to be explained.

A generation before Shore, another historian of Hampshire had addressed similar problems.[40] B. B. Woodward claimed that little by little the county had lost its woollen crafts to Yorkshire, because of improved machinery and (later) the adoption of steam in the 'coal country'. He gave the example of Romsey, which, when its clothing trade had gone, turned to making sacking, malting barley and converting its watermills to paper-making. None of these was able to guarantee a prosperous town.

Woodward began to contemplate a regenerative future for Hampshire as the haunt of consumers, an ultimate Victorian version of Jane Austen's England: 'the future prosperity of Romsey depends upon whether it can succeed in establishing itself as a pleasant place of residence. There is in the world a large class of English people who have small means and nothing to do. They chiefly affect certain cities in France, Belgium, and Germany, and the country towns of England...'[41] People like these required railway access to London and the sea-side, the men wanted a news-room, 'and other appliances for getting rid of the leisure of an idle man', and the women desired a church with, 'its general system in full activity' (a shrewd appreciation of the function of the Church of England as providing social centres for 'the Tory Party at prayer').

Romsey did not fulfil Woodward's hopes but there were villages that did, more and more of them as arable farming succumbed to overseas competition and released cottages to incomers. Coastal settlements were more popular still. His fairly accurate precognition of Hampshire's de-industrialised future had itself already been prefigured, not only by the Janeites but also by the sober neighbours of Bishop Shipley (died 1788) at Twyford, who looked with detestation on the Bishop's guests — English, French and American innovators, Benjamin Franklin among them. Local demand favoured producing food and drink and engaging in domestic, estate and farm service. By Woodward's day most manufactured goods were brought from elsewhere. Original thought, inventiveness and entrepreneurship were at discounts.

Like other southern counties, Hampshire was in course of reconstruction as a landscape for the landowner, the farmer and the retiree.

Our third and last case concerns the large and complex county of Gloucester. The Stroudwater valley, full of former woollen mills to this day, was the industrial heart of England — until the industrial revolution, that is — and its experience rounds out the eventual defeat of the southern manufacturer. As Urdank has pointed out, the woollen industry declined during the 19th century but ironically had not omitted to mechanise. It had previously undergone a transition to a factory system in which all the technological features associated with industrial revolution were to be found.[42]

The late survival of the Gloucestershire woollen industry, its mechanisation and its factories, was regionally anomalous. Urdank observes that with respect to adopting the steam engine, the industry had not lagged appreciably, sometimes not at all, behind Yorkshire. Its specific weakness in the face of competition is therefore hard to identify but seems ultimately to have stemmed from the high costs of operating steam away from the coalfields. This was not quite a late pre-industrial de-industrialisation in the form that affected so much of the south. Instead it was a case in which an industry that was modern enough in its day nevertheless succumbed to competition and descended into a rust-belt.

The woollen industry has understandably attracted most attention but it does not exhaust the history of Gloucestershire's industries. These were manifold, as they were everywhere when market areas were small. They included at least one case of early proto-factory development. As with the better-known examples at Malmesbury and Newbury, a Gloucester entrepreneur, Sir Thomas Bell, had founded a large manufactory in the 16th century. He bought a site called Black Friars, and turned the church into his mansion and the other surviving building into a workshop for 300 men making caps.[43]

The debate about why establishments of this type emerged anywhere has proved inconclusive, economies of scale, control of peculation and mechanisation all being cited without one clearly dominating the others. Bell's workshop was too early for there to have been any question of machinery. Neither scale economies nor the reduction of theft nor the two combined were sufficient to keep it going in the face of competition from cap-makers situated in London, the main centre of demand.

With pin-making, for which Gloucestershire was genuinely important —
by 1800 two-thirds of England's firms were in Gloucester and Bristol —
workshops were relatively large.[44] Nine factories were said to be employing
1,500 workers in Gloucester in 1809, supplying Spain and the United States
as well as the home market. Labour scarcity during the Napoleonic wars
inspired efforts at technological invention but this proved extraordinarily
difficult. The diffusion of new technology was far from costless or frictionless, although H. I. Dutton and S. R. H. Jones complain that other economic
historians assume this.[45]

The managerial failings of individual entrepreneurs seem responsible,
but whereas it might be thought that newcomers would come in to exploit
gaps in the market, they were not attracted even after machinery had
been introduced. The number of firms was few and one or two unfortunate
bankruptcies appear to have quashed the trade in Gloucester. It did however
start up in Stroud and a single water-powered mill at Painswick continued
to produce pins as late as 1982 (sic). Nevertheless, any expansion of
the industry took place in London and Birmingham. Decline in the
Gloucestershire Cotswolds was immensely prolonged but only a purist would
suggest that de-industrialisation is not a proper term for what happened
there.

A metal-working industry that required considerable skill was bell-
founding. There were early foundries in at least five Gloucestershire towns,
of which the most successful was the family firm of Rudhall, established in
Gloucester in the late 17th century. By the early years of the 18th century,
Rudhall had cast bells for seven cities, 36 market towns, four colleges, and
162 parishes in 13 counties, besides bells for gentlemen's seats, chapels and
shops. Between 1684 and 1830, 4,521 bells were cast.[46] They were sent to
churches up and down the Severn valley, since water transport was cheapest
and bells were heavy. Gloucester docks also enabled Rudhall to export bells
to Ireland, Jamaica and the American colonies, where a ring of eight cast in
1744 and rung by Paul Revere and his friends, is still hanging in Christ
Church, Boston.

In the early years of the 19th century, the firm was receiving enquiries
from western England from Cornwall to Lancashire, besides Wales, Ireland
and the Isle of Man. But during and after the Napoleonic wars, money
owed to it was hard to collect. The foundry passed to a daughter and, like
several southern firms, including the famous bell-foundry at Aldbourne,

Wiltshire, it was sold. Rudhall was bought in 1829 by the foundry at Whitechapel, London. Whitechapel was supposedly Britain's oldest manufacturing company, founded in 1570 and is perhaps traceable even earlier, to an unbroken line of bell-founders from 1420. In the early 19th century, Whitechapel was buying small foundries all over the country and closing them down. The aim was not to acquire property but to suppress provincial competition.

Bell-founding is not the first occupation to spring to the industrial historian's mind, but as our *tour d'horizon* of de-industrialisation demonstrates, the range of trades affected was thoroughly diverse. The length of time many of them took to fade away was prolonged. The explanations put forward for these phenomena are as varied as the businesses involved. While they touch on the problems of individual industries, they do not however comprehend every case, as we shall see in the following chapters. We therefore turn to discussing the commonest suggestion: that the south was deficient in natural resources.

Endnotes

1. H. M. Jewell, *The North–South Divide: The Origins of Northern Consciousness in England* (Manchester: Manchester University Press, 1994).
2. H. Heaton, *The Yorkshire Woollen and Worsted Industries: From the Earliest Times up to the Industrial Revolution* (Oxford: Clarendon Press, 1920), p. 279.
3. R. Mudie, *Hampshire: Its Past and Present Condition, and Future Prospects* (Winchester, n.d. [1839]), I, p. 77.
4. M. Abramovitz, Catching up, forging ahead, and falling behind, *J. Econ. Hist.* **XLVI**: 385–406, 1986.
5. F. Blackaby (ed.), *De-industrialisation* (London: Heinemann Educational Books, 1978), especially the chapter by Alec Cairncross, 'What is de-industrialisation?' The discussion here follows E. L. Jones, La deindustrializzazione come forma di aggiustamento economico: Il Caso Dell'Inghilterra Sud-Occidentale, *Quaderni Storici* N.S. **73**: 247–268, 1990.
6. F. Blackaby, *De-industrialisation*, p. 266.
7. R. F. Dell, The decline of the clothing industry in Berkshire, *Transactions of the Newbury District Field Club* **X**(2): 56, 1954.
8. D. Defoe, *A Tour through England and Wales* (London: J. M. Dent and Sons, 1928), I, p. 43.
9. J. H. Clapham, The transference of the worsted industry from Norfolk to the West Riding, *Econ. J.* **XX**: 195–210, 1910.

10. Quoted by E. A. L. Moir, The gentlemen clothiers: a study of the organization of the Gloucestershire cloth industry, 1750–1835, in H. P. R. Finberg (ed.), *Gloucestershire Studies* (Leicester: Leicester University Press, 1957), p. 260.

11. Quoted by A. M. Taylor, *Gilletts Bankers at Banbury and Oxford: A Study in Local Economic History* (Oxford: Clarendon Press, 1964), p. 76.

12. Dell, 'Berkshire'.

13. W. H. Marling, The woollen industry of Gloucestershire: a retrospect, *Transac. Bristol Gloucestershire Archaeol. Soc.* **36**: 320, 329, 1913.

14. J. Wilkinson, History of Broughton Gifford, *Wiltshire Archaeol. Mag.* **VI**: 36–38, 1860.

15. Victoria County History, *Gloucestershire* **II**: 197, 1907.

16. P. Levi, *The Flutes of Autumn* (London: Arena, 1983), p. 138.

17. Dell, 'Berkshire'.

18. Victoria County History, *Gloucestershire* **II**: 192, 1907.

19. B. Trinder, *The Making of the Industrial Landscape* (Gloucester: Alan Sutton, 1987 edition), p. 108.

20. Jones, 'La Deindustrializzazione'.

21. E. Marshall, *The Early History of Woodstock Manor* (Oxford, 1873), pp. 167, 265; A. James, Woodstock steel, *Country Fair* (March 1965), pp. 47–48.

22. R. S. Neale, The industries of the City of Bath in the first half of the nineteenth century, *Proc. Somerset Archaeol. Nat. Hist. Soc.* **108**: 132–144, 1964.

23. Trinder, *Industrial Landscape*, pp. 210–212.

24. D. Peacock, Jack of Newbury or the Winchcombe family and the woollen industry in sixteenth-century Newbury (Ph.D. Thesis, Reading University, 2003), p. 186.

25. Trinder, *Industrial Landscape*, p. 24. It is not stated whether they were a similar size at both dates.

26. W. Smith, *An Economic Geography of Great Britain* (London: Methuen, 1953 edition), pp. 96–97, 110.

27. E. L. Jones, The constraints on economic growth in southern England, 1650–1850, *Contributions* V, *Third International Conference of Economic History*, Munich, 1965 (Paris: Mouton, 1974), pp. 433–430.

28. Quoted by D. Daiches and J. Flower, *Literary Landscapes of the British Isles* (London: Bell & Hyman, second edition, 1981), p. 172.

29. *Newbury Weekly News*, 9 July 2009.

30. A. Everitt, *The Agrarian History of England and Wales* (Cambridge: Cambridge University Press, 1967), IV, p. 425.

31. J. Yeats, *The Natural History of the Raw Materials of Commerce* (London: Cassell, Petter, and Galpin, second edition [1871]), p. 298.

32. Ex inform Mr. John F. Parrott, who is writing the history of tanning in Wantage.

33. F. C. Warren, Dorset industries in the Past, *Proc. Dorset Nat. Hist. Archaeol. Soc.* **59**: 32–46, 1938.

34. Victoria County History, *Gloucestershire* **II**: 191, 1907.

35. B. Short, The de-industrialisation process: a case study of the Weald, 1600–1850, in P. Hudson (ed.), *Regions and Industries: A Perspective on the Industrial Revolution in Britain* (Cambridge: Cambridge University Press, 1989), pp. 156–174.

36. D. Ormrod, Industry 1640–1800, in A. Armstrong (ed.), *The Economy of Kent 1640–1914* (Woodbridge: Boydell and Kent County Council, 1995), pp. 85–109.

37. R. A. Pelham, The industrial revolution in Hampshire, *Wessex Geographer* **6**: 36, 1965.

38. T. W. Shore, *Hampshire Papers* (Hampshire Field Club, 1908–1911). In my estimation many of Shore's examples were brought together, unacknowledged, from the *General Views* of Hampshire agriculture during the Napoleonic period.

39. D. C. Coleman, *The British Paper Industry 1495–1860* (Oxford: Clarendon Press, 1958), pp. 147, 159, 219–220.

40. B. B. Woodward *et al.*, *A General History of Hampshire* (London, n.d. [1862] three volumes).

41. *Ibid.*, I, p. 361.

42. A. M. Urdank, Economic decline in the English industrial revolution: the Gloucester wool trade, 1800–1840, *J. Econ. Hist.* **XLV**: 427–433, 1985.

43. J. Johnson, *Tudor Gloucestershire* (Gloucester: Alan Sutton, 1985), p. 89.

44. E. Moir, *Local Government in Gloucestershire 1775–1800* [Tewkesbury] Bristol & Gloucestershire Archaeological Society Record Section **VIII**: 1969.

45. H. I. Dutton and S. R. H. Jones, Invention and innovation in the British pin industry, 1790–1850, *Business Hist. Rev.* **LVII**(2): 175–193, 1983.

46. M. Bliss and F. Sharpe, *Church Bells of Gloucestershire* (Gloucester: Alan Sutton, 1986), p. 69; M. Bliss, The last years of John Rudhall, bellfounder of Gloucester, 1828–1835, *Trans. Bristol & Gloucestershire Archaeol. Soc.* **121**: 11–22, 2003.

CHAPTER 3

SCARCE RESOURCES?

Traditionally the success of making Stroudwater scarlets and Uley blues lay
in the softness of the water. This is in no way borne out by the analysis of the
spring water of the west Cotswolds. The story was a complete hoax to outwit
any who would come from 'foreign parts' to learn the mysteries of the art.
The real secret lay in the preparation and blending of the raw wool and yarn.

Lionel F. J. Walrond, 1973

Explanations of southern industrial decline typically claim that the flaw was
a lack of natural resources, above all the absence of coal. That the high price
of coal eventually became a major competitive disadvantage is clear, but this
did not become insuperable until heavy industry based on coal-fired steam
engines was in full command of the north. That came to pass surprisingly
late; measured by horse-power applied to manufacturing, the truly weighty
period of industrial history arrived only with the third quarter of the 19th
century. What, then, explains the decline of southern industry long before
that time, including the decay of trades that never required significant appli-
cations of heat or power? In this chapter we will deal first with the possibility
that raw materials were cripplingly scarce or altogether absent, and secondly
with the much-touted inadequacy of energy supplies.

Raw Materials

The south was not an absolute resource desert. As the following details show,
this is readily demonstrated. More northerly areas, and occasionally even
France, drew on southern raw materials. During the 16th century firewood
was being shipped across the Channel from Sussex and Kent, the supply
coming from up to 10 miles inland.[1] In the late 17th century, Andrew
Yarranton noted that charcoal was made in the New Forest, 'and Shipt away

to *Cornwall* and other parts'.[2] The iron forge at Bringewood on the Shropshire-Herefordshire border made use of what were described as 'Sussex castings', possibly scrap from a Wealden ironworks.[3] Until late Victorian times, clay for pottery making, white sand and chalk beach boulders for making glass and iron ore from several spots were all exported as far away from the south as Glamorganshire, Staffordshire and Lancashire. Rather than a desert, it might almost be said that the south became a little resource colony of the north.

Since the early 18th century, diggings for clay had been expanding near Corfe Castle, Dorset, although the main expansion came in mid-century, following the arrival of William Pike, a Devon merchant.[4] Pike undertook to supply Josiah Wedgwood's factory in the Staffordshire Potteries. In 1791 Wedgwood entered into a five-year agreement for the exclusive use of clay from Pike's pits. He was to receive 1,200 tons of good clay and as part of the bargain Pike undertook to 'use his best endeavour in searching for, discovering and engaging' further deposits. Wedgwood also bought clay from a Poole man who leased land near Corfe and drew some from pits at Stoborough.

The clay was cut by hand, stacked in balls for weathering, then loaded into barges on the River Frome. The barges were towed to the Port of Poole for transhipment to vessels sailing for the Mersey. Thence the clay was carried to the Potteries by packhorse and later by canal. Some was taken directly to London by sailing barge. In 1806 a light railway for the trade was built from Corfe to Poole harbour. Estimates of the scale of export vary from 10,000 to 20,000 tons per annum. Potters' clay was also worked at Cowes on the Isle of Wight.[5] If it seems that carrying southern clay towards Midlands coal may simply have been cheaper than the other way round, coal scarcely enters into it: the pottery workshops of the 18th century had no power-using machinery.[6]

As for iron, it can be made to seem immensely scarce in the 18th century. Scrap was eagerly sought. The great ironmaster, Henry Cort, re-used old cannon and shells from the Admiralty yard at Portsmouth.[7] Nails were brought to Berkshire forges for re-pointing. They would have been large hand-made ones such as 10-inch blacksmiths' nails, which may make the fact of re-pointing seem a little less remarkable, but still testifies to the high value of iron. This is confirmed by the fact that the shore of the Solent in Hampshire was sometimes thronged with people scrabbling along the surf for pieces of sea-washed iron to sell to the ironworks at Sowley.[8] In Victorian times iron ore was shipped to South Wales from Hengistbury Head (Hampshire, now Dorset), where ironstone boulders called doggers were removed from the beach, as well as being dredged from inshore waters. Finally, we may note that iron was taken to South Wales from Seend, Wiltshire, during the 19th century, and on a larger scale from quarries near Banbury, Oxfordshire, which have been opened again in modern times.[9]

These exports show that it was not strictly an absence of raw material that prevented the development of an iron industry in the south, though individual deposits were small. A field geologist who studied the industry in the Surrey and Sussex Weald concluded that the sources of ore were used up.[10] Even there, however, the example may be one of the false positive natural resource explanations which attach themselves like limpets to the history of southern decline. A reason to suspect this is that the geologist notes how the lease of a furnace at Petworth in 1641 forbade the lessee to dig pits deeper than 30 feet. The dwindling of *output* which he reports is thus not certain evidence that local resource *inputs* had become unavailable.

A Resources Barrier?

None of this explains how the south of England became rural. Surely its raw materials might have kept the region at least minimally industrial? The industrial tide, as there is ample occasion to note, might have lifted all boats. Yet the straightforward fact is that the south had always been rural, its industries set in the countryside where no worker dwelt far from green fields and farming was still the main occupation.

Southern industry is neglected and agriculture's contribution has not received its full due. E. A. Wrigley has pointed out how scholars have concentrated on the supply of foodstuffs and overlooked agriculture's additional production of industrial raw materials and energy for use outside the farm sector.[11] He calculates that the land's contribution of products other than food rose six-fold between 1300 and 1800, mostly after 1600. The supply of non-food products was between two and three times greater than the growth of population.[12] Greater productivity per head also released agricultural labour to industry, and the industrial exports these workers produced would have been sufficient to pay for imports of food and raw materials. In reality England's only substantial raw material import at the start of the 19th century was cotton.

Wrigley was attempting to counter the striking thesis about comparative world history put forward by Kenneth Pomeranz in *The Great Divergence*.[13] Pomeranz urges that in 1800, Europe, including England, possessed scarcely any developmental advantage over China. There was no internal European dynamic to explain why it was the first continent to achieve sustained economic growth in the industrial form. On the Pomeranz view, what happened was that Europe, meaning firstly England, had a stroke of sheer luck in discovering coal and being brutal enough to seize the resources of the Americas.

The Pomeranz thesis depicts the English and north-western European economies as the unworthy recipients of a resources windfall. Yet mining coal and discovering distant lands cannot and do not occur unaided. They require human agency. If their stimulus is not to fade away, they need to take place in commercially active economies. The treasure of the Indies had not galvanised Spain or Portugal. That England and north-western Europe avoided resting on their laurels indicates how energetically their business people organised the mining of coal and created and responded to the flow of overseas resources.

We should not let ourselves be imprisoned by what Fernand Braudel called the 'factual record', as if only the observed line of development were conceivable. What actually occurred in history may not have been inevitable. Counterfactual alternatives to what is observed make it plain what the choices were. In the present context the proper counterfactual is whether alternatives to the import of American resources were feasible at affordable prices. As Richardson said, 'there is hardly any commodity for which human ingenuity will not find a substitute.'[14]

In reality Western Europe did acquire trans-Atlantic resources. The implications of adding Walter Prescott Webb's trans-Atlantic 'Great Frontier' to its land surface were impressive.[15] The 'ghost acreage' expanded enormously and while the total population of this vast conjoined zone was rising between 1500 and 1800, its density was falling to one-third of the initial level. What is at issue is whether England and Europe had reached a resource impasse just before they began to tap the Americas. The answer is that Adam Smith's dictum continued to apply and the Discoveries arose through 'no necessity'.

The Americas were not the sole overseas source of raw materials. Grain was available from southern Russia, cotton from Egypt and wool — which the Americas did not offer — from Saxony and Spain. English light-soil districts had switched from raising grass-fed sheep in favour of the additional cereal production obtainable within mixed-farming rotations. Feeding sheep on the rich fodder crops of the new rotations coarsened their wool and reduced its quality. Vigorous efforts to compensate by introducing fine-woolled sheep — the Merino craze — ran into the problem of coarsening. The general point was made in the *Annals of Agriculture* for 1788 by R. Valpy of Reading, who said that, 'areas which once produced good clothing wool now produce only wool fit for carpets'.[16] Yorkshire demand for wool was such that wool staplers nevertheless scoured the southern counties for supplies.[17] They resorted especially to Cirencester, Gloucestershire, where 30 or 40 waggons arrived each market day from as far afield as Pembrokeshire, Shropshire, Sussex and Kent. This meant that the Cirencester factors held on to their trade rather than that their local Cotswold wool retained its eminence in production.[18]

Agricultural change on light land such as the Cotswolds was not sympto-matic of a general deficiency in farm management but was a side effect of innovation that offered a wider range of products. The new product mix may have seemed an adaptation to scarcity but is more simply explained as a response to the changing preferences of consumers, invoking new methods of farming, extended sources of supply, and a resulting alteration of relative prices. Given that supplies of fine quality wool were available from Saxony and the Spanish Mesta, and later from Australia, the coarsening of native wool might be seen as a small price to pay for the integrated production of more meat and more (admittedly inferior) wool.

Technological changes meant that economies could be made in the use of many resources. The means was unspectacular and is often sparsely recorded, yet was cumulatively significant. One instance was the way in which wood was saved by developing finer saw blades. Although England was slower than continental Europe to start using sawmills, worker resistance in the 17th century having been violent, eventually they were introduced. A further breakthrough was the development at Southampton of the circular saw.[19] This was first patented by a sail maker in 1777 and converted into a working tool in 1781 by Walter Taylor at Wood Mills on the River Itchen.

As for communications, improvements in road building are well known, as are the ways in which rivers were canalised and artificial canals dug. Transport improved, meaning that raw materials could be profitably carried to distant industrial plants. We have only to reflect on the means whereby

Dorset clay was conveyed all the way to the Potteries. If Wedgwood could use the clay, in principle a Dorset entrepreneur could have done the same. There is little reason to think that a lack of raw materials lay behind the decline of industry in southern England.

Pomeranz denies that Western Europe had any 'ecological "advantages of backwardness," which left unexploited resources to provide ecological breathing space in the 19th century'.[20] In his view, the resource base was stretched to the limit by 1800 and all sources of energy, short of exploiting coal, and all supplies of raw materials, short of seizing them from the Americas, were used up. He nominates in this respect fibre and wood. This is not acceptable. On the contrary, Paul Warde, in an article significantly entitled 'Fear of wood shortage and the reality of Woodland in Europe, *c.* 1450–1850', concludes that, 'Europe, for all its late 18th-century problems, remained distant from any ecological frontier'. [21]

Aneurin Bevan, whose matchless Welsh oratory I once heard, described Britain as a lump of coal surrounded by fish and said it would take a genius to engineer a shortage of either. This was the view from the vantage point of industrial Britain, where coal-miners ate fish-and-chips. The environmental historian, Richard Hoffman, has suggested that the possession of rich fisheries in inshore waters meant the country could 'afford' to turn its rivers into playgrounds for rich anglers.[22] Historically, marine fish were plentiful, so much so that from the 16th or 17th century, the rivers could indeed be given over to elite fly-fishing. In the diet of the bulk of consumers, salt water fish were substituted, if they could afford them.

English rivers were thus privatised for anglers and modified ecologically for their use.[23] Maximum freshwater productivity was never aimed at; sporting fish, notably trout, were molly-coddled instead. Poor residents were excluded from the rivers and deprived of their long-standing access to freshwater protein. The monopolising of the rivers argues class injustice but does not argue a physical scarcity of resources. Since marine fish are superior as human food to England's freshwater species (except eels), shifting to them was not in principle a loss. But in practice it was, because sea fish had to be paid for in cash, locally caught fish were almost always fresher in the days before rail transport and refrigeration, and the poor were deprived of the fun of catching fish for themselves.

England accordingly held some resources out of the market. While this was sub-optimal — because it slowed growth and raised prices — it could in

Hoffman's sense be afforded. The country retained a breathing space which it never used. The prosperous men who bought landed estates were under no compulsion to leave the rivers in the public domain, to fell their timber or till every acre. They seldom needed the money; their estates were meant to fulfil dreams of politics, high society and rural amenity. What happened, or rather did not happen, on their estates was significant, since so much of the country was occupied by them. Estates already took up a large share of the land surface in 1800. A survey in 1872–1873 showed estates of more than 10,000 acres to occupy an average of 24 per cent of the counties of England and ones between 1,000 and 10,000 acres to occupy a further 29 per cent.[24]

Great resources of timber were held on these properties. Standing timber may have been managed well on a day-by-day basis but was largely a reserve which was sold irregularly. Asset strippers sometimes tried to move in, but estates were viewed as dynastic trusts and did not often come onto the market. When owners felled their woods themselves, it was likely they were cashing them in, like drawing on bank deposits to pay off abnormal debts. The Earl of Carnarvon, whose seat was at Highclere, Hampshire, described woods as an excrescence sent by God for the payment of debts, while Lord Lyttelton thought that, 'the rattling of a dice box at White's may … shake down all our fine oaks.'[25]

The topic of timber does not make for easy generalisations because the history of timber production is little studied, there are many species of trees, many differing ecological regions and almost infinitely varied items were made from wood. Craftsmen understood in the most intimate ways which wood was suited to each purpose. F. T. Evans refers to the 'iron and steel propaganda of the Industrial Revolution' and shows in detail that wood did not fall out of favour at that period.[26] It was a renewable raw material, since timber is a crop. Products made of wood continued to be of the first importance long after the industrial revolution. Following the Napoleonic wars, landowners energetically planted up heathland to grow hop-poles and wood for other purposes: rake-, broom-, hoop- and hurdle-makers used wood to compete successfully with metal throughout the 19th century. The number of makers of wooden tools like these was still climbing as late as 1908.

The timber shortage that exercised writers in the 17th and 18th centuries was localised. To the extent that it was real it was due more to poor transport and communications than physical shortages of woodland, intensively used though wood had to be. Transport costs limited how far naval and construction timber and wood fuel could profitably be carried. The potential for shortage related most to heating fuel, especially for London, but coal brought by sea from the north-east was accepted as a substitute. The fact that wood is a joint product becomes evident: it had infinite manufacturing uses as well as being a source of heat energy for domestic and industrial purposes.

Sources of Heat and Power

Wrigley has been the foremost exponent of the idea that what made industrialisation possible was inorganic energy. He urges that coal, not resources from the Americas, was the true means of lifting the limits imposed by relying on organic products. It is highly significant that he now finds the organic constraint, though ultimately unavoidable, not yet binding at the start of the 19th century.

The interpretations of the importance of coal by Wrigley and in part by Pomeranz have been criticised by Greg Clark and David Jacks.[27] They argue that the supply of coal was quite elastic, increasing during the 18th century because demand was increasing and not as a result of mining innovations. To the extent that output was held in check, the reasons were external to the mining industry and lay in high taxes and in transport costs that fell only gradually.

Clark and Jacks construct estimates to fill gaps where aggregate numbers were never collected, as Wrigley does to obtain the figures he uses. Quantification requires innumerable assumptions to create statistics on the output of agricultural land, woodland and coalmines, as well as on trade. The assumptions are brittle and impart an air of scientific certainty where none can exist. Sometimes they do not appear to accord fully with the realities of production: Wrigley seems to class all fallow land as arable, and Clark and Jacks seem to think that English coppice wood and Baltic conifers were significant sources of fuel. Yet coppice under 10 years old will not make charcoal and Baltic conifer is too hazardous to put on the fire.

Misunderstandings such as these can be corrected and the conclusion which Clark and Jacks reach, that waterpower, wind power and firewood would have been able to supply the energy needs of at least the early decades of industrial revolution, though audacious, is not unreasonable. Generations of historians have made coal central to the story but for some years now specialists have been hinting that coal was not vital for industrialisation. On the contrary, as Warde tells us, urban price data suggest that, 'energy was *always* cheap in southern England by European standards, long before the age of coal'.[28] He glosses this by stating that either an enormous energy revolution preceded the classic industrial revolution, as Wrigley's account of agriculture's non-food contribution may imply, or the traditional energy economy was remarkably efficient from the outset.

The popular view is different: it is that industry, especially ironworks, gobbled up timber, an impression reinforced by contemporary alarmist literature. In reality, industrialists went out of their way to ensure that woodland regenerated, because timber and wood were important renewable inputs. Oliver Rackham points out that, far from industry and forestry being incompatible, most of the well-wooded parts of England and Wales have an industrial history.[29] Because trees could be replanted, industrial works that moved into fresh areas were not being driven from their original sites because they had improvidently used up all the wood. They were seeking to expand production. As we shall see in Chapter 5, the rise of coal-fired furnaces in Newcastle out-competed the wood-fired glass industry of the Weald but this was not because Wealden wood had become scarce.

Nor did demand for ships' timbers for the Royal Navy and merchant shipping denude the country. Rackham points out that the innumerable complaints of a scarcity of ships' timber should have been directed at poor management and deficiencies of transport. Ship-building was not a large source of demand even though as late as 1850 less than 10 per cent of shipping tonnage was made of iron. Until after 1830, the price of oak had not risen far above the price of underwood (used for baking, for which coal was not a suitable substitute). On Rackham's figures, half of the rise in the real price of felled oak trees (150 per cent between 1690 and 1828) was due to increased demand for bark to use in tanning leather, 10 per cent to the larger size of trees, and only 4 per cent to greater demand for timber.

The expected profitability of tree-planting was hard to calculate because trees took so long to mature and tiny differences in the discount rate give widely different answers. 'The medievals did not know the method [of discounting] and — lacking our uncritical respect for figures', says Rackham, 'would not have believed it if they had'.[30] They chose a steady income from underwood rather than the apparently greater capital accumulation from planting timber. Post-medieval estate owners tended to have a longer planning horizon and retained their standing timber when they could, but even they sold the underwood.

Underwood should not be confused with coppice. Coppicing is the process of harvesting poles on 7- or 14-year rotations; the poles are for hop poles or making sheep hurdles. Coppicing was also the source of a regular supply of wood for making charcoal. Landowners planted coppice to sell charcoal to the ironmasters.[31] This was done in the West Midlands, but in the Weald too, and was no reason in itself for ironmasters to leave the Weald. Any regional competition came further down the supply chain, since the smiths who made nails and horse-shoes preferred coal and clustered on the Midlands coal seams. Ironmasters found it convenient to site their forges close to the smiths. But demand in the Midlands does not account for the additional migration of Wealden ironmasters to South Wales. Insofar as charcoal became scarce in southern England through demand for hop poles, it indicates a switch to greater agricultural production rather than industrial disability.

In contrast with coppice, underwood is not grown on a regular rotation. It is cut and gathered and used for all sorts of purposes, primarily for household heating. Since wood fuel was often expensive, the easy conclusion would be that underwood was in short supply. As a 17th-century author crowed, Londoners had to pay cash for their firing whereas in the countryside, 'we get a furze, a ferne, a green bush, or a dried cowsharn, to keep ourselves close by the fire in a cold season ...' These substitutes for wood were laborious to collect, however, and depended on the low opportunity cost of female and child labour. Moreover using some of them reduced soil fertility. The writer quoted complained about, 'the noisome burning of the Dung of Cattel, now scratcht from these Wastes for this purpose (which would more properly be left to improve and strengthen the land) ...'[32]

Burning dung on the fire superficially suggests a dearth of wood. That may have been the case in the great open field parishes of the Midlands, where woodland had been scarce for a 1000 years. Gathering dung was raised to the level of an industry there.[33] Cow-pats were collected in heaps, beaten into a mass with water, pressed with the feet into moulds like bricks, and stacked like peat by specialist workers called clatters (clodders). A dry March was desirable for what was called the 'clat-harvest', since the briquettes needed sun to dry them. They gave a steady, dull heat, without flame, suitable for the dairies and back-kitchens of farms. But this practice, which

English people associate with poverty in India rather than their own history, was declining in the 1820s and expected to die out. One place where collecting cow-dung for fuel did persist was the Isle of Portland. Fully half the land there, including the open-field strips called 'lawns' that may still be seen, had to be fallowed every year because the source of fertility was being burned instead of returned to the soil.[34]

There is nothing more chilling than damp English cold and the poor certainly suffered. They went oodn' [wooding], which is to say, scraping together sticks and twigs for the fire. A storm would bring out the village women for the sake of branches blown down. The American naturalist, John Burroughs, writing in 1882, observed that in Gilbert White's time, 'the poor people used to pick up the sticks the crows dropped in building their nests, and they probably do so yet'.[35]

Rather than a universal absence of resources, this scarcity of domestic fuel reflected high costs of transport, the sequestering of ever more land in private ownership, and low purchasing power among the poor. The problem comes out starkly in an account of the Chilterns in 1748 by the Swedish traveller, Peter Kalm.[36] He learned that anything combustible was collected, guarded jealously and sold to the day labourers. This included the chips left from felling trees, their stumps and roots, faggots and twigs from hedge-laying (the latter cut into six-inch lengths and made into bundles for sale), sawdust, dried leaves and the regularly cropped shoots of pollards.

The ecological effects were temporary and cannot easily be discerned in the modern countryside, where surviving common land has been allowed to become overgrown. Gorse, for instance, which has grown back into bushes today, was cropped for fuel and when Kalm saw it was barely four inches high. Gorse, bracken and old grass were bound into bundles for sale. Great patches of countryside were raked bare in the search for fuel. The 16th-century Weald of Kent is nicely described by Adam Nicolson as 'a shorn country'.[37] Nevertheless the scarcity of domestic fuel tells us little about any supposed lack of wood for industrial uses. It was a function of low entitlements and high transport costs. The odds and ends to which the poor had to resort were never substitutes for industrial fuel.

The bulk of the population was prepared to pay for better types of fuel, as were manufacturers in certain trades. Local entrepreneurs scrabbled to find seams of coal that could be dug in their own backyards, tending to choose common land for the diggings. This did not interfere with the growing of crops or the interests of powerful landowners, while commoners may have hoped to benefit through being paid for digging and the chance of finding fuel on the spot to heat their cottages. It was the actual enclosure of the commons they disliked.[38] Retaining sources of fuel was an important motive for deprecating enclosure which is seldom given due weight.

The endless searching for coal, sometimes repeatedly at the same spot, was probably as much an attempt to solve or cash in on the shortage of domestic fuel as to locate fuel for manufacturing. There is no one source where references to the searches are gathered together, not even the Victoria County Histories; notes appear fleetingly in antiquarian and topographical works and are seldom precisely dated. A selection follows.

A fortune was spent boring for coal at Radley, Berkshire, while efforts were made at Alderley Common, Wiltshire, and as early as 1635 to 1645 at Urchfont in the same county.[39] In 1652 and 1653 a group of Southampton merchants tried to obtain a 30-year grant of a 'mine or seame of Cole' in the New Forest, which they claimed to have been working at great expense.[40] Bristol entrepreneurs promoted borings at Shaftesbury, Dorset, and near Bruton and on Chard Common, Somerset. Coal mines were repeatedly sought among the Culm Measures (carboniferous limestone) around Exeter and in the mid-18th century workable seams were eventually found at Dunsford and Holcombe Burnell a few miles south-west of the city, but they did not pay.[41]

Anthony Wood's *Parochial Collections* of 1781 commented that at Eynsham, Oxfordshire, 'several fruitless attempts have been made at great expense to find coal tho' they dug 80 feet deep', and coal pits on Eynsham heath are shown on a map of 1769.[42] There are no outcrops of the Coal Measures here, although in modern boreholes around nearby Witney thin seams have been found only a few hundred metres down.[43] During the third quarter of the 18th century, a shaft was sunk in Malmesbury Common, Wiltshire, and legend has it that colliers from the Somerset field bribed a workman to collapse the pit.[44] At Shaftesbury, Dorset, bores were sunk for coal in 1791 and earlier; they are implausibly said to have reached over 400 feet but in any case found only Kimmeridge shale.[45]

Coal was supposedly found at Siddington, Gloucestershire, or at least welldiggers reached water too black to drink, but although they informed Mr. Bathurst, lord of the manor, he did not commission a proper inspection.[46] Nor was a small seam, uncovered only nine feet down at nearby

Barnsley, examined further. Not everyone was interested in the quest: the Bathursts had plenty of land and money already and showed no signs of wanting mines near their country seat. On the other hand, Sir John Webb of Hatherop, a few miles away, did have several places searched hard about 1773 but was unlucky despite his enthusiasm.[47]

The searches were almost all inspired by casual empiricism rather than geological theory. Geological understanding was not up to the task before the late 18th-century revelation of stratigraphy by William Smith of Churchill, Oxfordshire. The writings of Rev. William Sharpe (1724–1783) illustrate an early exception in the sense that he did rely on geological knowledge, such as it was. Sharpe had been born on the Durham coalfield and arrived as vicar of Long Burton and Holnest, near Sherborne, Dorset, in 1743.[48] In 1769 he published *Treatise upon Coal Mines*, followed the next year by *An Appendix to a Treatise on Coal Mines, containing an historical account of the several attempts formerly made to find coal in the environs of Sherborne, interspersed with remarks upon the imperfection and inefficiency of those attempts.*

Attempts had been made to sink mineshafts even before Sharpe's descent on the district — in 1690, 1705, 1717, 1720 and 1740. A site that had been dug in 1705 produced fossil wood which was just about combustible. At another site a deposit of Forest Marble was capped with blue clay almost indistinguishable from that found in true mining districts. There was a dig in 1765 at a third place where the Oxford clay looked like Forest Marble. At a fourth outcrop, material was found that would burn; it was taken to Sherborne and set alight on domestic hearths but stank beyond endurance. The same had already been learned of 'Kimmeridge coal', a readily ignitable shale used in a short-lived glass works at Kimmeridge in the 1730s. That, too, was barely tolerable on the hearth.[49] False appearances misled all these projectors but the occasional discoveries of faintly burnable material kept their hopes alive. There is coal beneath southern England but it was far too deep for the mining technology of the 18th century, when the best efforts reached down only about 25 metres (80 feet).

While it may be thought the poor would not have been able to buy enough coal to make mining worthwhile, their propensity of spend on fuel was high and there were large numbers of them. John Burnett, who relies partly on the Berkshire vicar, Rev. David Davies, *The Case of the Labourers in Husbandry* (1795), claims that home baking and brewing almost disappeared during the late 18th and early 19th centuries.[50] By about 1800 many labourers were unable to buy firing even for ordinary heating and cooking, and the cost of coal was prohibitive in many areas. The 'clat-harvest' may suggest as much, though part of what the poor had long scrabbled together was kindling and may not always have entirely represented fuel shortages. The direst or most widespread poverty did not appear until the end of the 18th century and the market may have looked reasonably promising during the previous 100 years.

Colin Clark and Margaret Haswell used data from Eden's *State of the Poor* to calculate the income elasticity of demand for food, clothing and fuel in 1795, and reported values of 0.92, 1.84 and 1.35, respectively.[51] These were higher values than for Vietnam, India and Japan in the 20th century, reflecting the severe poverty evident in other late 18th-century English sources and making understandable the epidemic of hedge-breaking to obtain firing. Mavor makes the casual assertion for Berkshire that coal was too dear for most of the poor, who burned any sort of rubbish in their grates, including stubble.[52]

Could coal have been brought within reach of the poor? If it could be mined close at hand, that may have seemed possible, especially given the large element of transport costs in the final price. But what did close at hand mean? Contemporary literature cites so many discrepant distances over which transporting coal overland might pay that little is to be gained by reporting them. Ten or fifteen miles are mentioned as great distances, for instance in 1808 the Radstock colliery was supplying Wiltshire as far as Warminster, fifteen miles away. No doubt the length of paying journeys varied with local road conditions, which did improve over time.

Fuel for industry was a different matter. The industrial heart of pre-industrial England was the Stroud valley in Gloucestershire. This is scarcely a paradoxical remark. The valley bottom was crowded with water-powered woollen mills, workers' cottages teetered close together along the sides, and the cloth called Stroud Reds, dried in racks on the lower slopes, was carried 20 miles or so by stage waggon to the head of Thames navigation at Lechlade. The original basis of all this industry was water power.

Anthony Collett wrote that Gloucestershire was saved from squalor because no coal was ever found at Stroud.[53] Perhaps so, aesthetically speaking. Romantics such as Collett would never have approved of the grime, but given local coal the cloth-workers of Stroud need not have fallen into a destitution so severe that many were driven off to Australia about 1830. Their valley need not have become a backwater where poverty produced squalor as dispiriting as the fumes of steam manufacturing.

For all this, it was not fundamentally a lack of coal that brought about the de-industrialisation of southern England. A few contemporaries agreed, citing the offsetting cheapness of labour. In 1809 Arthur Young singled out the Witney blanket industry as able to compete with the north despite the 'want of vicinity to coals' because of cheap labour — at the expense of the work people, as it was candidly put.[54] Only by the 1840s did the price of coal rise so high at Witney that steam power would not have paid, and even so the industry survived until the start of the 21st century. Elsewhere industry's need for coal, excluding the generation of steam, was met at affordable prices. The woollen industry at Exeter increasingly used coal in dye-pans and hot-pressing furnaces after 1660 and coast-wise coal imports rose 10-fold by 1700, mostly for industry.[55]

As to water power, for every stream where the mill sites were fully occupied there was another nearby where they were unoccupied.[56] Whenever they could, manufacturers tried to protect themselves against competing demands for river water from farmers, fishermen and the millers of grain. The silk miller at Gillingham Dorset, who in 1769 took a 99-year lease of the town mill which that very year was being built next to an existing mill, stipulated that if there was not enough to drive both, 'the whole stream of water should be wholly appropriated for driving the Water Wheel of the Silk Mills only'.[57] Water power continued in active use in the south and of the 100 paper mills in the country in 1700 many, including five of the largest, existed in clusters there.[58] They had often taken over former fulling mills, which meant not that manufacturing had ceased but that its type had changed.

In the south of England, industrial water power survived surprisingly late. A lack of water may have meant blowing out Wealden iron furnaces in the summer, the wheels having to be turned by hand instead, but the Weald was not the whole south, nor was iron-making the only industry. In textiles, if the head of water was insufficient or too irregular to drive fulling mills competitively, types of cloth that did not require fulling were substituted, thus extending the region's industrial life: Witney thus made blankets, Wilton carpets, Taunton worsteds, Salisbury flannels and linsey-woolseys (Salisbury's trade in fine, dyed cloth having moved elsewhere in Wiltshire).[59] A colony of Witney blanket makers even settled in Newbury early in the 19th century.

Newbury had prided itself on its fulling mills. They had all closed or been converted to other uses but, then, blanket cloth did not need to be fulled.[60]

Contemporaries commented that coal could be obtained at woollen mills in West Wiltshire and Gloucestershire at prices competitive with outlying works in the West Riding. In 1818 the price of coal in the West Riding was sometimes 9 to 18 per cent higher than Somerset coal delivered at the Trowbridge, Wiltshire, woollen mills.[61] More often coal was dearer in Gloucestershire and Wiltshire than in Yorkshire, but not so dear as to prevent the adoption of steam power, though it may have come in more slowly in the Stroud region than in Wiltshire and Somerset, let alone Yorkshire.[62] In 1850 70 per cent of the horse-power in the Wiltshire cloth industry was steam — very close to the 76 per cent in Yorkshire.[63]

According to ingenious calculations by Urdank, the crux of the problem in Gloucestershire lay in the over-capacity, and hence over-capitalisation, of the woollen mills.[64] The mill owners behaved rationally but were trapped by the costs of the steam engines they felt they must install to offset the irregular flow of the rivers. Buying expensive engines to keep their plant running when water was scarce imposed a high cost. This was additional to the capital they had already sunk in water mills. The owners of small mills found that they were using half their steam power to recycle water power instead of being able to apply it directly to production; they too had invested excessively in plant.

Arguments in terms of the indispensability of coal are too dogmatic. The assertion that the southern iron industry could not expand without coal is doubtful. The claim rests on the notion that the alternative of charcoal is too friable to carry far, something apparently supported by complaints that Wealden roads were rough and uneven through being cut to pieces by wagons full of iron goods. In truth, large loads of charcoal logs could have been carried on men's backs.[65] If this still seems likely to have restricted the distance charcoal could have been conveyed to the forge, consider that London was supplied with chairs from the Chilterns brought by pedlars or on their makers' backs. The option of portering was costly, no doubt, but threatens the argument that inaccessible charcoal stymied the growth of Wealden iron.

Industries in the Weald did compete for fuel but once again the main problem seems to have been as much transport constraints, and perhaps monopoly ownership of local woodlands, as an actual lack of wood. In 1594 the clothiers of Cranbrook and neighbouring parishes, who used quantities of fuel every year to dye a million pounds weight of wool in their great vats, plotted to breach the dam of the nearby ironworks at Sissinghurst. They wanted the wood for themselves and aimed 'to break [upp] Mr Bakers Hammer Pond'. [66] There is a hint in the sources that this may also have happened long before but the particular crisis had petered out, as it did again in 1594. Baker, who owned 16 separate woods, half of which he had bought from his neighbours, may have found it politic to sell some fuel to the clothiers. Iron and textiles continued alongside one another, which argues against any fatal shortage of wood.

Moreover, the decay of southern industry encompassed trades that did not use significant sources of heat or power, including most consumer goods industries such as buttony, boot- and shoe-making, gloving, furniture making, and leather-making The literature of economic history concentrates on wool, cotton and iron and devotes relatively little attention to consumer goods, because they did not initiate major technological changes. The situation in Bath shows how important producing consumer goods really could be.[67] The range of trades there was wide and, while most of the firms were small, there were several factories. Although in 1827 and 1828 an iron foundry and a cut-glass factory did install steam-driven machinery, it was exceptional. Yet arguments in terms of coal and steam still tend to dominate. The most important consequence is that they distract attention from the economic factors to which we turn in the next two chapters.

Endnotes

1. I am indebted for information about this and much else concerning wood to Mr. Alan Albery.
2. A. Yarranton, *England's Improvement by Sea and Land* (London, 1677), p. 43.
3. B. Trinder, *The Making of the Industrial Landscape* (Gloucester: Alan Sutton, 1987), p. 27.
4. M. B. Weinstock, *Old Dorset* (Newton Abbot: David & Charles, 1967), p. 74.
5. C. Vancouver, *General View of the Agriculture of Hampshire* (London: Sherwood, Neely, and Jones, 1813), p. 42.
6. R. Szostak, *The Role of Transportation in the Industrial Revolution* (Montreal & Kingston: McGill-Queen's University Press, 1991), p. 8.
7. L. F. W. White, *The Story of Gosport*: Southsea: Barrell [*c.* 1960], p. 85.
8. Ibid., p. 41.

9. J. B. Britton (ed.), *Aubrey's Natural History of Wiltshire* (Newton Abbot: David & Charles, 1969 edition).

10. B. C. Worssam, Iron ore working in the Weald Clay of the Western Weald, *Proc. Geol. Assoc.* **75**: 529–546, 1964.

11. E. A. Wrigley, The transition to an advanced organic economy: half a millennium of English agriculture, *Econ. Hist. Rev.* **LIX**(3): 435–480, 2006.

12. C. McEvedy and R. Jones, *Atlas of World Population History* (Harmondsworth, Middlesex, 1978), p. 43.

13. K. Pomeranz, *The Great Divergence: China, Europe, and the Making of the Modern World Economy* (Princeton, N.J.: Princeton University Press, 2000).

14. H. G. Richardson, Some remarks on British forest history, *Trans. R. Scott. Arboricultural Soc.* 35 Part I, 175, 1921.

15. E. L. Jones, *The European Miracle: Environments, Economies and Geopolitics in the History of Europe and Asia* (Cambridge: Cambridge University Press, third edition 2003), p. 83.

16. R. Valpy, On wool and the woollen manufacture, *Ann. Agric.* **IX**: 526–527, 1788.

17. H. Heaton, *The Yorkshire Woollen and Worsted Industries: From the Earliest Times up to the Industrial Revolution* (Oxford, 1920), p. 279.

18. J. H. Morris, The west of England woollen industry, 1750–1840, *Bull. Inst. Hist. Res.* **XII**: 107, 1935.

19. P. d'A. Jones and E. N. Simons, *Story of the Saw* (Manchester: Newman Neane, 1961), pp. 23, 42.

20. *Ibid.* p. 283.

21. P. Warde, Fear of wood shortage and the reality of woodland in Europe, *c.* 1450–1850, *Hist. Workshop J.* **62**: 52, 2006. Compare the equally negative conclusion of R. C. Allen, Was there a timber crisis in early modern Europe? *Insituto Internazionale di Storia Economia* 470–482, 2003.

22. R. C. Hoffman, *Fishers' Craft and Lettered Art: Tracts on Fishing from the End of the Middle Ages* (Toronto: University of Toronto Press, 1997), p. 351.

23. E. L. Jones, The environmental effects of blood sports in Lowland England since 1750, *Rural Hist.* **20**(1): 58–59, 2009.

24. J. H. Bettey, *Wessex from A.D. 1000* (London: Longmans, 1986), p. 281, t. 30.

25. K. Thomas, *Man and the Natural World: Changing Attitudes in England, 1500–1800* (London: Allen Lane, 1983), p. 200; F. Wilson, *The Courtesan's Revenge* (London: Faber & Faber, 2003), p. 60.

26. F. T. Evans, Wood since the industrial revolution: a strategic retreat? *Hist. Technol.* **VII**: 37–56, 1982.

27. G. Clark and D. Jacks, Coal and the Industrial Revolution, 1700–1869 (UC Davis Working Paper #06-16, 10 April 2006).

28. P. Warde, Woodland fuel, demand and supply, in J. Langton and G. Jones (ed.), *Forests and Chases of England & Wales, c1500–c1850* (Oxford: Oxbow Books, n.d.), p. 82.

29. See in particular O. Rackham, *Ancient Woodland: Its History, Vegetation and Uses in England* (London: Edward Arnold, 1980).

30. *Ibid.*, p. 169.

31. T. S. Ashton, *Iron and Steel in the Industrial Revolution* (Manchester, 1963), p. 15.

32. Quoted in H. G. Richardson, Some remarks on British forest history, Part II, *Transactions of the Royal Scottish Arboricultural Society* 36 (1922), Part I, p. 188.

33. Anon. [J. L. Knapp], *Journal of a Naturalist* (London: John Murray, 1829), pp. 49–50.

34. R. Whitlock, *Dorset Farming* (Wimborne: The Dovecote Press, 1982), p. 49.

35. J. Burroughs, *Fresh Fields* (Boston: Houghton Mifflin, 1885), p. 45. The meaning is rooks not crows.

36. V. Bell, *To Meet Mr. Ellis: Little Gaddesden in the Eighteenth Century* (London: Faber & Faber, 1956), pp. 56–58.

37. A. Nicolson, *Sissinghurst: An Unfinished History* (London: HarperCollins Publishers, 2008), p. 199.

38. H. G. Richardson, 'Some Remarks', 36, Part II, p. 188.

39. P. H. Ditchfield, 'Industries', *Victoria County History, Berkshire*, I (1906), p. 372; Britton, *Aubrey's Natural History*, p. 41.

40. J. U. Nef, *The Rise of the British Coal Industry* (London: 1932), II, p. 73.

41. W. G. Hoskins, *Industry, Trade and People in Exeter 1688–1800, with special reference to the Serge Industry* (Manchester: Manchester University Press, 1935), p. 49.

42. Anon., Notes on the History of Eynsham (Typescript, n.d., Oxford County Library).

43. Oxford Geology Trust, *Oxfordshire Geology for Visitors* (n.d.), p. 4.

44. Mr. Fraser, Malmesbury: the evolution of the common, *Wiltshire Archaeological and Natural History Magazine* **XLII**: 399, 1923.

45. L. Sydenham, *Shaftesbury and Its Abbey* (Lingfield, Surrey: privately printed, 1959), p. 106

46. S. Rudder, *A New History of Gloucestershire* (Gloucester, Alan Sutton: 1986 [first published 1779]), p. 23. The Bathursts did however acquire coal-mining interests far away in Derbyshire.

47. *Ibid.*, p. 480.

48. For Sharpe see Rodney Legg, *Literary Dorset* (Wincanton: Dorset Publishing Co., 1990), p. 109.

49. *Victoria County History, Dorset*, II, p. 330.

50. J. Burnett, *Plenty and Want* (London, 1966), pp. 3–5.
51. C. Clark and M. Haswell, *The Economics of Subsistence Agriculture* (London: Macmillan, 1964), pp. 146, 152.
52. W. Mavor, *General View of the Agriculture of Berkshire* (London, 1809), p. 420.
53. A. Collett, *The Changing Face of England* (London: Nisbet, 1926), p. 228.
54. A. Plummer, *The Witney Blanket Industry* (London: George Routledge & Sons, 1934), p. 85.
55. Hoskins, *Industry, Trade and People*, p. 104.
56. P. Laxton, Wind and water power, in J. Langton and R. J. Morris (eds.), *Atlas of Industrializing Britain* (London: Methuen, 1986).
57. E. E. Shaw, *A History of the Town of Gillingham, Dorset* (Gillingham: privately printed, 1973), p. 19.
58. Trinder, *Industrial Landscape*, p. 21.
59. J. H. Morris, West of England, *Bulletin of the Institute of Hist. Res.* **XIII**: 106, 1935.
60. Ditchfield, 'Industries', p. 394.
61. R. P. Beckinsale, *The Trowbridge Woollen Industry* (Devizes: Wiltshire Archaeological Society Record Branch, 1951), VI, p. xxvi.
62. S. Mills, Coal and steam — the arrival of steam power in Stroud's Woollen Mills, *Gloucestershire Society for Industrial Archaeology J.* 42–52, 2004.
63. J. Tann, Some problems of water power — a study of mill siting in Gloucestershire, BAGS **LXXXIV**: 76, 1965.
64. A. M. Urdank, Economic decline in the English industrial revolution: the Gloucester wool trade, 1800–1840, *J. Econ. Hist.* **XLV**(2): 427–433, 1985.
65. See the illustration following p. 80 in S. Bergman, *In Korean Wilds and Villages* (London: Travel Book Club, 1938).
66. Nicolson, *Sissinghurst*, p. 200.
67. R. S. Neale, The industries of the City of Bath in the first half of the nineteenth century, *Proceedings of the Somerset Archaeological and Natural History Society* **108** 132–144, 1964.

CHAPTER 4

POSSIBLE EXPLANATIONS

We know only in very general terms how the national economy was altered by realignments of local and regional economies during the eighteenth and nineteenth centuries.

Julian Hoppit, 1990

Industrialisation and de-industrialisation are diffuse processes, touching everything normally investigated by social science. Economic growth is broader still. Straightforward explanations of all these processes are indispensable for expository and teaching purposes, but the price of clarity is *a priori* judgement about what matters most. Some aspects are always sidelined. It is not to be expected that the complexity of the industrial revolution can be comprehended by simple models: that is not the purpose of models, which are tests of the power of logically combining a few selected variables. The objections that can be made to the selections underlying any explanation mean that none provides a final story of growth or decline.

The prism of the industrial revolution distorts its own origins and the setting in which it took place. Keeping regional shifts in mind makes it easier to appreciate the forces at work than does focusing on the advent of factory industry and powered machines over a fairly brief space of time. In the case of southern industry what requires explanation is the die-back of both punctiform and cottage industry. The extensive literature of rural domestic industry may be responsible for exaggerated attention to the fate of so-called proto-industrialisation. The topic is interesting but cannot cover production concentrated in mills, 'manufactories' where workers were gathered under one shed roof, or other premises outside the home.

This chapter scrutinises arguments about the causes of southern de-industrialisation other than those previously discussed, which cite inadequate supplies of raw materials and sources of energy. Contemporary topographers

91

were decidedly of the opinion that physical deficiencies were the ones that mattered most. Mudie, writing about Hampshire in 1839, could not let the point alone.[1] As we noted, Shore, describing 'Decayed Hampshire Manufactures' in 1890, was more hesitant, speculating that inertia and old ways may have impeded adaptations that might have saved some industries.[2] Inertia is a black box, or perhaps an empty box, which would need to be opened.

As we shall see, conventional economic arguments take us further than ones about resources towards understanding change, but even they seldom quite measure up, either singly or together. Few can be totally eliminated but most can be relegated to the also-ran category, leaving more central influences to be discussed. Those considered here probably imposed cost disadvantages on the south without being powerful enough to extinguish its enterprise.

Besides natural resources arguments, contemporaries, industry specialists, local historians and general historians attribute decline to a long list of causes. Many of their suggestions apply only to one trade in one place at some particular period. An historian of Worcestershire claimed — to cite a single authority — that although Worcester was well situated it may have missed out on becoming a great trading centre because the tenure of land around the city hindered building and drove enterprising men away.[3] Perhaps this was crucial in Worcester but a similar straitjacket did not stifle industrial growth in Nottingham — builders simply put up taller buildings and merrily cramped the living space of the poor. Even in Worcester it is more likely there were other reasons for the relatively weak commercial impulse. It would be exhausting to attempt to eliminate every miscellaneous suggestion, and since so many have limited application, doing so might not advance us far towards a general explanation. Frequently mentioned possibilities include a quite sufficient array of eight topics. The first three will be discussed here and the remaining five in the following chapter.

1. Adjustment to factor proportions,
2. Lack of technological invention or resistance to it,
3. Possible drag of guild and borough governance,
4. Weak networks of producers and ancillary trades,
5. Reliance on high-quality products with restricted and vulnerable markets,

6. Inadequate supply of capital,
7. Poor quality of labour and
8. Non-market competition from outside the region.

Adjustment to Factor Proportions

Among types of explanation, the factor-proportions explanation of the industrial revolution by Robert Allen is as broad as they come. It is notably coherent and seems to cover the case by stating that industrialisation took place in England because it was tailored to circumstances unique to the country.[4] The English peculiarity was a combination of high wages and cheap energy generated by economic expansion between 1500 and 1750. (This is attributed to England's success in the global economy; something that also needs to be accounted for.)

The argument is presented at the national level. For the de-industrialising south to have been an exception, wage labour would have had to be cheap and energy dear, unlike the industrialising north and more like the continent. This may seem to fit. Once coal had come to dominate, energy did become dear in the south, relatively speaking. Southern wages did fall below those of the north and, although a lower cost of living partly offset this, destitution overtook many rural workers. Yet these differences became conspicuous only in the context of the 19th-century technologies and labour conditions and were results of economic change as much as its initiators. They were not prevalent when de-industrialisation began and can scarcely explain its inception or long early phases. During the preliminary stages of industrialisation, the cost of energy did not strikingly favour the north. In any case, for many decades and in many trades, the price of coal was hardly relevant.

Beneath their doubtful fit with the complete range of evidence, problems with factor proportions models run deep. It would be surprising if they were not broadly correct, other things being equal. Why should people not wish to economise on labour when it is dear or use energy freely when it is cheap? The argument is reminiscent of Douglass North's thesis about the relations of labour and land in the Middle Ages.[5] According to that proposal, in which the Black Death was the motor of change, when the population fell, labour became scarce relative to land; thereupon workers 'should' have secured higher wages. But the most decisive observation contrary to North's hypothesis is that in eastern Europe scarce labour, far from obtaining higher wages, was harried back into serfdom. Less mechanistic factors, such as law and political structures, matter too. Models become interesting when their expectations are violated.

Factor-proportions models are hard to historicise; they do not specify lag times. Economies do eventually adjust to changes in relative prices — again, other things being equal. If they did not, price theory would have to be pulled up by its roots. But they do not respond instantaneously and their tolerances are unclear. We do not know how far or for how long the ratio between changes in wages and energy prices may have been able to alter without stifling the industrial revolution. Alterations in the levels supposedly sparked off the array of technological changes which, because they forced down the real price of manufactures, were at the heart of industrialisation. Models of this type are inducement mechanisms. What they take for granted is the response whereby people in a given region in one economy actually did create and adopt an unprecedented set of inventions.

The defects of factor-proportions arguments have long been understood. As Donald Coleman wrote in 1973, the temptation arises 'to abandon hampering history and to launch instead an argument based upon relative factor prices and rates of return'.[6] The scope for contradictory hypotheses is alarmingly wide. In short, factor proportions arguments over-extend the economic calculus. They ought to lead us instead to dig into history to learn what is actually being assumed. Nor do factor proportions arguments do a full job of explaining industrialisation when they fail to take the southern exception into account. The way to industrialisation was opened by things beyond, beneath, or at any rate in addition to, changing factor prices. Other things were simply not equal and more nuanced approaches are needed.

Lack of New Technology

The thesis that the technological inventions of the industrial revolution economised on scarce inputs and favoured using abundant ones should occasion no surprise. But if so, why did the inventions not arise earlier, say on the north-east coalfield, where similar conditions had long been fulfilled? Why were labour-using trades not maintained in the south, where workers were in plentiful supply? And if British engineers so improved steam engines after 1850 that it became profitable to use them even where coal was dear, why did this not save the Gloucestershire woollen industry, revive other industries in the south, or cause new firms to spring up? Other circumstances were generally favourable there, more so than in much of Europe. Yet the continent industrialised despite being further from the centres of powered industry in the north of England and distant from English urban markets, besides facing markets of its own which were fractured by high tolls. We have to conclude there is more to invention than adjustment to factor supplies, especially as producers ought to have been indifferent to the bias of savings attributable to a given invention. If costs came down, did it matter much where the economies lay?

An assumption that little technology was devised in the south during late pre-industrial and early industrial times would be incorrect and rather irrelevant. The emergence of new technology can be demonstrated and it was not all trivial. Aside from showing that southern industrial society was far from inert, this does not however advance us far. The idea that home-grown technological ideas are what matter to an economy is a fallacy, though it is kept alive today in the form of American fears about scientific competition from China and India.[7] Technology is geographically mobile and what matters is whether it is installed in the production system.

Northern and southern England were not separate zones. They lay in a national market in which up-to-date technology could be, and sometimes was, transferred from one to the other. The south had probably adopted the spinning wheel sometime after the mid-16th century, prior to which the sparse documentary references to them suggest that spinners were using the spindle and distaff.[8] Spinning wheels may have been taken up late, but taken up they were; the region was not incapable of change. Practical difficulties were associated with bringing in new machinery but in a vigorous investment climate these could have been overcome. The problem was that manufacturing *investment* so often shunned the south: innovativeness was weaker than inventiveness.

Dear coal, a lack of steam-powered looms and inadequate capital are discounted by K. G. Ponting as crippling deficiencies in the cloth industries of Wiltshire and Gloucestershire. In these respects, the areas were not far behind Yorkshire, adopting Australian wool as quickly, and pioneering machines for finishing the cloth.[9] Furthermore, Ponting points out, the Yorkshire industry expanded *before* the introduction of the power loom, and he decides tentatively (as the fragility of the evidence requires) that rash expenditure by Wiltshire and Gloucestershire businesspeople was the problem.

This suggestion of wholesale incompetence scarcely draws a firm line under the issue.

Allen's insistence that no-one would invent where the results would not be used is excessively *a priori*. It ignores the nation-wide market for ideas and also the human capital context, which is to say that in the south as well as in the north there were clever people interested in devising and developing technologies. Inventors in rural neighbourhoods might eventually miss the stimulus of larger groups working on technology but people maintained contact during the 18th century by prodigious feats of letter writing. Regular contact was kept with places as distant as the American colonies. Science and invention did not entirely depend on local industrial surroundings but arose from diverse places, or rather people, who had the income, education and avocational interest to engage in them.

Contrary to expectations that rural society was a scientific and engineering vacuum, there were individuals and little groups of friends who discussed and experimented with new methods. It is easy to pick a garland of these people to ornament the point without the slightest hope that the list will be complete. John Aubrey commented on a number of them in 17th-century Wiltshire, for instance the Seend blacksmith, 'an ingeniose man' turned clockmaker and fiddle-maker, who smelted in his forge lumps of iron picked up in the street.[10] A vicar of Amesbury devised hydraulic engines and pumps, and in 1716 applied for a patent for a water-raising device which was later discussed by a French philosopher.[11] Technologies even spread out from the south of England: the burial is recorded at Breage, West Cornwall, of a Somersetshire man, 'that brought that rare invention of shooting the rocks [blasting] which came heare in June, 1689 ...'[12]

At Chipping Camden, Gloucestershire, in the early 18th century, Jonathan Hulls invented a steam boat.[13] Hulls' background reveals the conjoining of science and commerce possible in rural districts. He went to Camden Grammar School and his occupation was farming and clock repairing, though in documents of 1764 he is described as a joiner. He was a self-taught mechanic who had two mathematically minded friends, one a maltster, the other a schoolmaster. The trio published *The Maltmakers Guide, for the Use of Maltsters, and Excisemen in Gauging Malt* in 1750, and a little later *The Trader's Guide*. In 1754 there followed a patent for a slide rule and in 1763 one for an instrument to detect fraud by counterfeit gold. The most striking notion seems to have been Hulls' alone: he filed an immensely thorough patent for a steam paddle boat. The boat failed when tried on the Warwickshire Avon but was nevertheless emblematic of the ferment of ideas possible in small places.

The list continues and need not be comprehensive to make the point. Valentine Strong (1609–1662), Oxfordshire mason, whose sons were Wren's master masons for St Paul's Cathedral, built something more useful when he made the first malt kiln of stone to resist fire; his model was three times more economical on fuel than the previous type.[14] An Oxford cutler created 'an engine' (as almost any mechanism was called) for cutting knife handles. John Kay was a resident of Colchester, Essex, when he invented the fly-shuttle in 1738. At Henley-on-Thames, Oxfordshire, Rev. Humphrey Gainsborough, brother of the painter, was a renowned projector who actually died (in 1776) while talking about the locks he had constructed, having in his pocket at the time £70 of the capital for such schemes.

To continue, William Plenty arrived at Newbury from Southampton in 1779 and established himself as a wheelwright. Newbury was almost an inland port where boats were built; Plenty developed the precursor of the lifeboat there in 1816 and subsequently manufactured lifeboats alongside his business of making farm implements and lock-gates. A Portsmouth man, Dr. Lind, associated with chemical works and the salterns at Lymington, Hampshire, introduced a purifying distillation process. In 1786 John Bull of Worcester invented a machine for embossing and crimping leather which was adopted in the glove industry, while in the same decade a method of varnishing leather was devised and used in coach-building. About 1825 Mr. Lewis of Brimscombe, Gloucestershire, invented a cross-cutter to sheer the nap off cloth which was not entirely superseded as late as the 20th century. In 1837 Isaac Pitman, son of a hand-loom weaver from Trowbridge, Wiltshire, and himself a schoolmaster at Wotton-under-Edge, Gloucestershire, devised a system of shorthand which became the most widely used in the world.

In 1820 Thomas Hancock, from Marlborough, Wiltshire, patented India rubber springs. Although Hancock was by then living in London, the fact that one of his brothers produced the first reliable passenger steam buses and another was responsible for the submarine telegraph cable, further testifies to the vitality of scientific and technological life possible among the natives of small towns. Ideas could be imported and extended in out-of-the-way places, since information networks existed over vast distances.

The supreme achievements of southern England were in puddling (refining) and rolling iron. They were inspired by demand from the Royal Naval dockyard at Portsmouth, which during the 18th century was the leading industrial complex in the world. Portsmouth was a centre for ship-building and ship-fitting, where many of the great 19th-century engineers were trained. Foreign potentates were brought there to be awed by British naval might.

The breakthroughs in iron were owed to Henry Cort, whose patents of 1783 and 1784 revolutionised iron production and constituted a signal advance in world industrialisation.[15] He had secured a contract from the Navy Board to supply Portsmouth dockyard with mooring chains and similar iron equipment and moved to an old forge at Fontley, near Fareham, not far from Portsmouth, which had a water-powered hammer and used charcoal from the woods around.[16] He switched to using coal, which had to come round the coast from north-east England. Others had tried to use coal in making iron but his were the first successes. Despite approaching Boulton in 1779 about acquiring a Boulton & Watt engine, he never managed to employ steam power in the mill.

The machinery to make ships' blocks, invented by Walter Taylor and his son at Wood Mills on the River Itchen, also at first supplied the Royal Navy. It ended up in the Portsmouth yard, subsumed in Marc Isambard Brunel's works and often attributed to him.[17] This was part of a world-class advance in interchangeable parts manufacture and, under Brunel, in assembly-line production. The Taylors had begun by developing a machine to drive bolts true and then built improved ships' pumps.[18] In 1781 they installed the first steam saw mill in the country at Wood Mills, although it was not a success. Walter Taylor is also credited with inventing the circular saw.

The Taylors secured contracts between 1758 and 1805 to supply the yard with pulley-blocks. The blocks were needed in large numbers by sailing vessels and, when made by hand, were inconveniently uneven and subject to splitting of the wood. The uniformity of the Taylors' blocks meant they could be stored in British colonial harbours along sea routes and, being uniform and interchangeable, slotted in to replace broken or defective ones. The blocks were half the size of previous ones, which was an obvious economy. Prices at the Taylors' firm nevertheless rose 20 per cent during the 1790s and Brunel soon took over. His machinery was in reality an assemblage of about 45 special purpose machines of 22 types, able to be adjusted to make the parts for over 200 sorts and sizes of pulley-blocks.

The French arsenals had already moved towards assembly lines and making interchangeable parts. The American system of manufacture was shortly to be based on the concepts. In England their use for producing civilian goods was slower to develop than in the United States. Military contracts had guaranteed sufficient demand to set the system afoot but when contracts fell off after the Napoleonic wars, the baton had already passed across the Atlantic. Some of the ideas had anyhow originated in the States, where Brunel — father of the protagonist of the Great Western Railway — had lived, while Samuel Bentham, re-organiser of work routines in Portsmouth dockyard, had worked in Russia.

Their machines were so well made that with them 10 unskilled workers could produce as much as 110 skilled men previously, and the capital cost was recovered in three years. Brunel's machines were turning out 130,000 blocks per annum from 1808, more than enough for the navy. Three of the machines were still in use in 1965! An impressive parallel was Bentham's rationalisation of the workflow, which included putting up a circular Panopticon from which supervisors could observe the men; this economised on supervisors, who were far scarcer than labourers.

What Brunel and Bentham established, together with their metals man, Maudsley, was a benchmark in both mechanical and industrial engineering. The insistent question is why did their methods not spread mass production to other industries in England? Learning about their practices was straightforward since the Portsmouth yard was perfectly well known; it was a favourite tourist destination. Possible explanations include the high price of wood in England compared with the United States or Germany, and the less equal distribution of income, which restricted English demand for manufactures and led English labour to resist mechanisation. England remained, or rather became, the land of the Rolls-Royce rather than the Model-T Ford.

It has to be conceded that southerners were sometimes indebted to midland, northern or metropolitan enterprise, as the following examples show. When Ralph Allen built a railway in 1731 to carry stone from his great quarries to build Bath, the railway was modelled on one in Shropshire. Jonathan Hulls employed a Birmingham artisan to mill the parts for his steam boat. Humphrey Gainsborough was a friend of James Watt. The Leominster cotton spinning experiment capitalised on the Bristol-to-Manchester trade in cotton that passed through the town, as well as using cotton spindles made in the midlands or north. The plush industry at

Banbury gained from midland energy. And although the Hancocks came from Marlborough, they worked mainly in London.

Were workers in the south able to slow the introduction of machinery? It is almost conventional to contrast southern resistance with northern willingness to adopt machines. This may have something in it. Strikes and protests against the flying shuttle and gigs did occur in the second half of the 18th century, more in Wiltshire than Gloucestershire. Moir does not think that innovation was genuinely held up in Gloucestershire.[19] She reports that the Stroud clothier who first used flying shuttles, finding the weavers anxious about them, actually sold them to the men for their own use. On the other hand, Somerset clothiers who wanted their cloth dressed by gig mill were obliged to send it long distances; one sent his cloth 90 miles from Frome.[20]

Protests against technological change may have been aimed at drawing attention to grievances during trade depressions. Each depression left fewer weavers in Wiltshire. At Banbury during the second quarter of the 19th century there was a 'diminished trade-club' in the plush industry; it seems to have prohibited women from working, enforced seven-year apprenticeships for boys, and permitted each man to have only a single apprentice.[21] Restrictions like these — though in this instance new technologies were not specifically targeted — were a throw-back to a less competitive age and did not persist for long. Workers' resistance to change did not apply to all trades and seems have been a minor impediment.

The Achilles' heel of southern industry lay in deficient innovation rather than workers' resistance or inventive feebleness. Although there were instances of innovativeness in the early years, like the use of cotton-spinning machinery at Leominster 'many years' before it was taken up in Manchester, this was far from the general rule.[22] Bull's machine for embossing and crimping leather would have been useful to the shoe-makers, but they did not adopt it.[23] The method of varnishing leather, devised by the coach-builders in the 1780s, did not spread to other products until the early 1830s. Opportunities to invest in manufacturing were either not enticing, which pushes the problem of explaining conditions in the south one step back, or they were not seized, which does raise questions about the responsiveness of producers and investors. Alternatively non-industrial opportunities were drawing investment away. We will return to the issue of investment in later chapters. There was another problem, requiring us first to consider the collective behaviour of manufacturers.

The Drag of Borough and Guild Governance

The guilds were sidelined in economic history for many years when institutionalism was out of fashion. In the *Economic History Review* of 50 years ago, Kellett lamented that the loss of control by the London guilds over crafts and retail trades during the late 17th and 18th centuries was passed off as an inevitable process rather than being investigated.[24] Until recent years little notice was taken of his complaint. What underlay the virtual dismissal of this matter — once thought to have been central to economic change — was a form of neo-classical economics in which the drive to maximise returns was assumed to override all else. In short, whatever the institutional arrangements, the assumption was that the economy would hunt out (and find) the optimal allocation of resources and as a result maximise profit. Institutions were irrelevant by assumption.

Issues concerning the guilds have returned with a vengeance during the past 10 or 15 years, vengeance being *le mot juste* given the vitriolic disputes that have arisen. Dispute is not entirely new; the topic was contentious as long ago as the 1890s. The point at issue today is whether guilds were rent-seeking institutions, dedicated to securing exclusive privileges for their members and resistant to technological change, or socially useful instruments which enforced minimum standards of product quality.

For present purposes, we need to ask whether collective modes of governance harmed the prospects of southern industry. A categorical answer might be artificial, because the experience of too many industries in too many towns over several centuries would have to be captured in a single summary. Added to this, the sources for early modern times have not survived well. They are better for the late 18th and early 19th centuries but by then guilds and corporations were relinquishing active roles as super-managers and retreating to their social, ceremonial and charitable purposes. The records do not always illuminate their industrial functions.

In theory, corporations or guilds possessed the power to adjudicate on four functions: entry to a trade, quality control, setting prices and determining the quantity produced. In the guilds and towns of southern England, entry and quality were the considerations most mentioned. Entry was controlled by limiting the number of apprentices a man might take or limiting the number of individuals permitted to acquire the freedom of practising a given craft in a given place. If these stipulations had been enforced, and not just reiterated formally in the documents, they would clearly have held back competition. This would confirm the charge of rent-seeking. The concern with quality control seems to have been designed to maintain a town or guild's reputation, and hence the prices its producers might hope to charge, while incidentally protecting consumers from shoddy wares.

Insofar as a pattern is discernible, it is that phases of industrial expansion led to lax enforcement of regulations. During good times, manufacturers were eager for hands and merchants clamoured for product; non-freemen were let in readily and other regulations were overlooked. Undoubtedly the rules were costly to enforce when trade was busy, especially in the bigger places where employees might play off one employer or one putting-out merchant against the next. By the late 18th century, the guild of shoe-makers at Banbury concluded that any benefit from their charter, bestowed by King John, forbidding non-members from carrying on the trade in the town, 'was neutralized by the trouble and odium of enforcing it'.[25] They had a feast and finished by literally consigning the charter to the fire! On the other hand, whenever trades turned down, a chorus of complaints arose about the flouting of regulations. Meanwhile the decay of the guilds separated masters and men. To protect their interests in the absence of guild control, workmen began to combine to press for higher wages, and even to form the half-substitutes of trades unions.[26]

Regulations accordingly adapted to circumstances, but with a lag. In downturns it sometimes proved possible to re-impose the rules that still lay on the books. Mostly, however, this was no longer possible. Broadly speaking the guild system weakened as if on a ratchet which could not easily be reversed. By 1792 the Weavers' Company in Newbury was actually reduced to begging 'strangers' to enter its clothing trade, promising no interference.[27] It was too late and there was an exodus of distressed weavers. Under Basket-makers Company rules, apprenticeships were for seven years. Yet a boy could learn the trade in three years, which left the master with four years of cheap labour to compensate him for teaching the apprentice and for any materials he had spoiled.[28] When more attractive jobs became available in other trades, the seven-year apprenticeship was waived and was down to four years by 1900.

We should not expect to account for the withering away of collective control over southern industry purely via industrial logic. The joker in the pack was the national shift in elite opinion, which the courts partly shared.

The judges often declined to support the restrictiveness that the guilds sought to impose or re-impose. Small towns could rarely afford to bring every case to court and soon gave up trying. As early as the start of the 17th century, towns had been losing cases they took to court with the aim of compelling new arrivals to join their craft guilds. A key case concerned Newbury and Ipswich in 1616. The ruling in this instance became a common law precedent, to the effect that 'foreigners', men from outside a borough, could not be compelled to enrol as freemen.[29] The confiscation of goods during raids by guilds had been declared illegal even earlier, in 1599.

The decline of the guilds was an irregular process, often voluntary, and slower in some cases than others.[30] In the 18th-century Dorset silk trade, the Throwsters Company ceased to enforce an edict of 1662 which restricted the occupation to those who had served a seven-year apprenticeship. There is little evidence that the Company of Weavers, Fullers and Shearmen at Exeter prosecuted its members for experimenting or economising on materials during the 18th century. But only at the end of the century do we find a note that the regulations of the Company of Blanket Weavers in Witney were no longer enforced.

Guilds, then, showed a tendency to relinquish their powers in good times. In bad times they tried to pull back to the old regulated ways but mostly failed in the attempt. Did their efforts have any general effect on the decline of southern industry? The difficulty is to separate cause and effect. No-one to keep more than two apprentices at any one time, trumpeted the Weavers' Company in Newbury, a town which had possessed large enterprises in the 16th century. But as Dell recognised, this edict 'either helped to bring about the era of the small man or reflected the state of affairs already existing'.[31] 'The latter seems more probable ...' he concluded, '[because] the big clothier had gone of his own volition'.

Even so, the guilds almost certainly made some minor contribution to decline. Their response was uncertain, impeding responses to commercial challenges and new methods in some towns and hence giving others (and ultimately northern ones) an advantage. There were individual employers who seem to have kept to the regulations merely because of the threats of legal action and the social ostracism that might accompany it in small communities. W. G. Hoskins thought there was a world of difference between the Exeter Weavers Company in the 18th century, when a merchant-cum-banker (one of the Barings) had to teach it to keep accounts, and the experimental, market-seeking, men of Halifax, with whom they were contrasted at the time.[32] He thought that throughout the century the Company was inbred and conservative, letting in little fresh blood after about 1700.

The Exeter Company had continued to insist on seven- or even eight-year apprenticeship, which inculcated sound but increasingly out-dated and inflexible methods.[33] There were instances when it prevented non-freemen from manufacturing woollens at all and brought many prosecutions for cutting prices or reducing quality. The company was also opposed to the employment of women, but then Exeter was notoriously conservative. It had not shared in the usual medieval flowering of guilds and, apart from the Company of Weavers, Fullers and Shearmen (Charter of 1621), was ruled by the Mayor and Chamber of Twenty-Four. 'As to the Chamber of Exeter', an antiquary wrote to the historian, Lysons, in 1820, 'you will find them jealous and illiberal in all their measures'.[34] This was not quite the only southern town where competitive shocks produced defensive responses, hampering adjustment to the lower costs and prices achieved elsewhere.

Endnotes

1. R. Mudie, *Hampshire: Its Past and Present Condition, and Future Prospects* (Winchester, n.d. [1839]), Vols. I and II.
2. T. W. Shore, Decayed Hampshire manufactures [1890], in *Hampshire Papers* (Southampton: Hampshire Field Club, 1908-1911), p. 102.
3. T. C. Turberville, *Worcestershire in the Nineteenth Century* (London, 1852), p. 18.
4. R. Allen, *Nuffield College Annual Report: Academic Report 2007–2008*, pp. 53–55.
5. E. L. Jones, Institutional determinism and the rise of the Western World, *Econo. Inquiry* **XII**: 114–124, 1974.
6. D. C. Coleman, Textile growth, in N. B. Harte and K. G. Ponting (eds.), *Textile History and Economic History* (Manchester: Manchester University Press, 1973), p. 4.
7. The fallacy is condemned by Amar Bhide, *The Venturesome Economy* (Princeton: Princeton University Press, 2008).
8. D. Peacock, *Jack of Newbury* (Reading Ph. D. thesis, 2003), p. 47.
9. K. G. Ponting, *A History of the West of England Cloth Industry* (London: Macdonald, 1957), pp. 145–146.

10. J. Britton (ed.), *The Natural History of Wiltshire by John Aubrey* (London, 1847), p. 21. Walloon weavers who came to Wiltshire in Henry VII's reign built the handsome houses at Seend but found the iron in the water bad for fulling and washing cloth, and so moved on. (A. Powell, *John Aubrey and His Friends* (London: The Hogarth Press, 1988), p. 117.) But they did not need to quit the south, where there were plenty of other places they could have settled.

11. J. Chandler and P. Goodhugh, *Amesbury* (Amesbury: The Abbey Society, 1989), p. 43; P. Goodhugh, *The Rev. Thomas Holland* (South Wiltshire Industrial Archaeology Society: www.southwiltshire.com).

12. F. E. Halliday, *A History of Cornwall* (London: Duckworth, second edition, 1975), p. 253.

13. C. Whitfield, *A History of Chipping Campden* (Windsor: Shakespeare Head Press, 1958), pp. 164–166.

14. R. Plot, *The Natural History of Oxfordshire* (Oxford, second edition, 1705), p. 257.

15. H. W. Dickinson, Henry Cort's bicentenary, *Trans. Newcomen Soc.* **XXI**: 32, 45, 1940–1941.

16. Fontley was excavated in 1964 by the initiative of Stephen Weeks, then a 16-year old schoolboy. See S. B. Weeks, *Fontley Iron Mills: A South Hampshire Trust Excavation* (January 1965). See also N. Pevsner and D. Lloyd, *The Buildings of England: Hampshire and the Isle of Wight* (Harmondsworth, Middlesex, 1967), p. 238. I visited the excavation in 1964 and also photographed Cort's building in Gosport, which the Hampshire authorities have since permitted to be destroyed.

17. K. R. Gilbert, *The Portsmouth Blockmaking Machinery* (London: HMSO, 1965); C. C. Cooper, The production line at Portsmouth block mill, *Industr. Archaeol. Rev.* **VI**(1): 28–44, 1981–1982; C. C. Cooper, The Portsmouth system of manufacture, *Technol. Cult.* **25**(2): 182–225, 1984.

18. B. B. Woodward *et al.*, *A General History of Hampshire* (London n.d. [1862]), I, pp. 126–127.

19. E. A. L. Moir, The gentlemen clothiers: a study of the organization of the Gloucestershire cloth industry, 1750–1835, in H. P. R. Finberg (ed.), *Gloucestershire Studies* (Leicester University Press, 1957), p. 260.

20. *Victoria County History, Somerset*, **II**: p. 417, 1911.

21. R. P. Beckinsale, The plush industry of Oxfordshire, *Oxoniensia* **XXVIII**: 60, 1963.

22. R. Jenkins, Industries of Herefordshire in Bygone Times, Hereford City Library: LC Large pamphlet 17262, p. 176.

23. G. Riello, Nature, production and regulation in eighteenth-century Britain and France: the case of the leather industry, *Hist. Res.* **81**(211): 86, 2008.

24. J. R. Kellett, The breakdown of gild and corporation control over the handicraft and retail trade in London, *Econ. Hist. Rev.* **10**(3): 381, 1958.

25. A. W. Excell and N. M. Marshall (eds.), *Autobiography of Richard Boswell Belcher* (Blockley: Blockley Antiquarian Society, 1976), p. 8.

26. W. R. Amphlett, History of Worcester glove trade, Worcester Public Library M5.252 (1954), p. 13; Bichard, *Baskets*, pp. 19, 59.

27. Walter Money, The guild of fellowship of the cloth-workers of Newbury, *J. Br. Archaeol. Assoc.* 265–266, 1896.

28. M. Bichard, *Baskets in Europe* (Fyfield Wick, Abingdon: Fyfield Wick Editions, 2008), p. 59.

29. Kellett, 'Breakdown', p. 384, where the general breakdown of the legal powers of guilds is also described.

30. A. Plummer, *The Witney Blanket Industry* (London: George Routledge & Sons, 1934), p. 110; Symonds, silk industry, p. 82; J. Youings, *Tuckers Hall Exeter: The History of a Provincial City Company Through Five Centuries* (Exeter: University of Exeter and the Incorporation of Weavers, Fullers and Shearmen, 1968), p. 169.

31. Dell, The decline, p. 63.

32. W. G. Hoskins, *Industry, Trade and People in Exeter 1688–1800, with special reference to the Serge Industry* (Manchester: Manchester University Press, 1935), p. 53.

33. Youings, *Tuckers Hall*, p. 177. For criticism of the conservatism of apprenticeship, see R. Eberts and C. Eberts, *The Myths of Japanese Quality* (Upper Saddle River, New Jersey: Prentice Hall PTR, 1995).

34. W. G. Hoskins, *Old Devon* (Newton Abbot: David & Charles, 1966), p. 13.

CHAPTER 5

FURTHER POSSIBILITIES

'Minor practical changes in ways of doing and making, unrecorded because unsensational, are so often the true origin of cumulative gains in productivity that it would be arbitrary to contend that none occurred ... (between the Middle Ages and the Industrial Revolution)'.

D. C. Coleman, 1973

This chapter discusses the remaining five of the eight types of explanation listed near the start of the previous chapter. They are:

1. weak networks of producers and ancillary trades,
2. reliance on producing high-quality goods with restricted and vulnerable markets,
3. inadequate supply of capital,
4. poor quality of labour and
5. non-market competition from outside the region.

The division between the two chapters is for ease of reading and does not imply that the issues fall into two distinct groups.

Weak Networks of Producers

The point is sometimes made that southern firms or towns where manufacturing took place did not possess large local networks of suppliers or ancillary workers. Given the state of overland communications, isolation from neighbouring towns of any size was greater than linear distances might now suggest. Towns had to produce much of what they consumed. The presence of only a handful of specialists and limited overall support were competitive disadvantages.

Weak networks may therefore have been as or more important than some other impediments. It is, for instance, usual to attribute the retreat of fulling from mills in the older woollen towns of east Gloucestershire to locally inadequate water power. Better heads of water could be found in the steep valleys of the Cotswold escarpment, to which firms gravitated.[1] The eastern mills turned over to grinding grain or sometimes making paper. Yet the benefit of a denser network of firms further west in the Stroud area may have been a more significant reason why the cloth industry congregated there than the attraction of water power. The retreat of fulling from inadequate water power may be a false positive 'energy' explanation.

Framework knitting illustrates how isolation from networks of skill was a matter of moment. When Lee's invention of the stocking frame was taken to Venice, Rouen and Amsterdam in the 17th century, the industry withered there for lack of skill at repair work.[2] This may seem surprising, especially for Amsterdam in the industrially busy Netherlands, but the frame was complex for the period. It was comprised of over 2,000 separate pieces of steel and lead and required a great deal of maintenance. A sense of what was missing in Europe, and later in outlying areas of the trade in England, may be gained by listing the remarkable variety of ancillary workers in the vigorous framework knitting areas of Nottinghamshire in 1739: there were frame-smiths, setters-up, sinker makers, stocking-needle makers, joiners and turners, altogether perhaps as many hands as actual stockingers. Despite lacking anything comparable, the hosiers of small, isolated Tewkesbury did make headway during the 18th century, but about the year 1800 a spate of inventions in Lancashire finally reduced their advantage. Tewkesbury began to suffer from its remoteness from East Midlands' developments in production and design.[3]

Consider, too, the experience of the Quaker cloth manufacturer, Thomas Fox of Wellington, Somerset.[4] In 1790 he ordered horse-powered machinery for spinning and weaving wool from Joseph Taylor, Machine Maker of Manchester, but at that date the demand for machinery was so high that it was supplied late, had been roughly handled on the canals, and was poorly made in the first place. On two occasions the machines arrived broken in pieces because they had been badly packed. Taylor supplied a mechanic who walked almost 200 miles from Manchester but proved useless when he arrived. Another Manchester mechanic who had come to install the machinery proved a better workman, but was obliged to return to Manchester to rebuild the machine himself. By September 1791, horse-driven spindles were finally in use at Wellington, but this was too late to compete with the big new factories in Yorkshire. In 1801 Fox was corresponding about machinery with firms in Leeds, Birmingham, Stroud, and Staverton in Wiltshire, because he thought the local machine makers were 'a troublesome sett whose estimates were much overstrained'.

Richard Roberts, spinner and weaver of linen at Burton Bradstock, Dorset, provides another illustration.[5] In 1803 he established the first swingling machine capable of separating flax fibres in south-west England. By 1814 he had brought two mechanics down from Leeds to construct and erect the latest style of machinery. Roberts sent one of his own employees to the little textile town of Castle Cary, Somerset, to learn how to set up machinery, but this man found his way back into Roberts's mill and made drawings of the machinery which he sold to competitors, for whom he also made parts.

The costs of being remote from established centres are clear. Whereas the West Yorkshire worsted industry was in close contact with the inventors of Lancashire, the worsted weavers in Norfolk relied on yarn from Suffolk and from Yorkshire itself.[6] Therefore they had no interest in improving the spinning process, which languished in Norfolk. It was difficult for an industry to catch up once it fell behind. More generally, successful districts may have gained competitive advantage through the built-in insurance of possessing several trades. They could offset a downswing in any one of their number.

This does not explain how the concentrations actually began in the north. There may have been some almost chance factor, perhaps the energy of small groups of entrepreneurs — co-religionists such as Quakers or Baptists — the benefits of which accumulated. The Quakers educated their children at their own schools, married within their own community, and passed capital around among their own kind. To repeat, although networks conferred growing advantages, the fact of their existence does not explain how they emerged in the first place. It was not an initial advantage for men setting up textile factories in the Pennine valleys that within a few years a range of specialist craftsmen was to become available locally. Only when cadres of support personnel had become established could they reinforce the north's superiority over the more scattered firms of the south.

Valuable though networks could be they were not all-powerful. Businesses could sometimes prosper well away from others. The Northampton boot-and-shoe industry is an example and framework knitting in Leicester and hat-making in Luton are others. The production of whiting at Kintbury in

Berkshire (which lasted until 1930) and blanket making by the Early family at Witney, Oxfordshire (from 1669 until their last mill closed in 2002) were isolated survivors. Locating near markets and sources of raw materials protected southern wheelwright firms from competition until after the First World War, when army surplus lorries arrived, followed by vehicles mass produced in city works, usually in the Midlands. A presence close to customers and attention to local ecological conditions prompted the founding of agricultural implement firms across the south in the 19th century, and several of them lasted until recent decades.

Reliance on High-Quality Goods

English attention to fashion was, comparatively speaking, limited; trying out new materials to tempt consumers was left to the Parisians, especially in the lace industry.[7] Yet when the mass market began to be captured by lower-cost and later by more mechanised producers, some southern manufacturers did begin specialising in fashion items. The West Country clothiers, finding by the 18th century that Yorkshire was under-cutting them at the cheaper end of the trade, shifted to producing superfine cloth.[8] They cashed in on rising prosperity across northern Europe as far as Russia, while in 1766 a Bradford-on-Avon clothier invented 'cassimeres', a superior type of cloth that became popular across the Atlantic.

Shifting to high-quality goods was risky, because the fashion trades are unstable: demand listeth like the wind, and reputations for style are easier to lose than gain. Wartime interruptions of trade sometimes forced firms with narrow ranges of products out of business. They were less likely to be re-established in the south than the north. These difficulties do not explain general southern decline, however, because they applied only to a minority of trades, notably textiles in the valleys of the Cotswold escarpment.[9] The problem was probably not so much the lack of prudence in concentrating on the fashion market as it was the higher costs facing southern producers.

The alternative response to competitive pressure was to move the opposite way, downmarket, into producing cheaper types of cloth that could still be made on the hand-loom — shalloons for instance. The small firms of some southern towns may have gained as much as a generation's extra life by switching to cheaper products. The catch was that there was a floor to wages below which the operatives would starve and once competitors embraced machinery they were able to undercut even the cheapest hand-loom weavers.

After decisions had been made to concentrate on high- or low-quality goods, producers were criticised for becoming wedded to their choice. In the late 17th-century Wiltshire woollen industry, says G. D. Ramsey, inventive and technical skill were not lacking but the clothiers of Salisbury and Wilton 'inevitably' declined.[10] They produced white broadcloths and 'were too conservative to change their methods' even though demand had shifted to medley and other new fabrics. A similar charge of conservatism was levelled at Worcester in that period. And in the late 18th century the clothiers of Gloucestershire stuck to traditional woollens and let Yorkshire get ahead with the manufacture of worsted.[11] Since the production of worsted is simpler and lends itself to cheaper workmanship, Gloucestershire fell back in the struggle to cut prices. Only in the 1840s did the clothiers display any marked initiative when they worked the newly opened China market.[12]

A charge of conservatism, though descriptively plausible, does not penetrate far; there must have been tangible reasons why producers were reluctant to alter their product mix again. Maybe textile industries were profitable only for limited spells and could not accumulate enough capital to re-tool. Fashion goods were seldom made in bulk and the economies of scale available to producers of run-of-the-mill broadcloth were hard to achieve. 'Conservatism' may have had some force when applied to manufacturers trapped in their old ways by promises of contracts dangled by government purchasing agents. Sole customers could jilt a business overnight. The Wealden iron industry — not of course a fashion trade — is said to have lasted as long as it did only because it had the Office of Ordnance as its customer. But the government constituted such a minor share of the market for all goods that this provides no general explanation for southern decline.

Inadequate Supplies of Capital

The largest holders of capital were landowners, who were reluctant to invest in industry, especially on their doorsteps. Admittedly some Midlands and northern landowners did become involved with the early stages of mining or manufacturing but agricultural improvement and fixation on rural amenities characterised those who acquired estates further south. Some southern industrialists gentrified, siphoning capital from their businesses in order to buy land: in Gloucestershire they became known as the 'gentlemen clothiers'.[13] Social climbing on the part of rich clothiers is well attested and they continued to build country houses right into the Cotswold industry's death-throes. The last was erected by a Gloucestershire clothier as late as 1888. Ironically, that was 30 years after northerners with money from the clothing industry had begun to move down and build or buy country houses in the county.

At Newbury in the early 16th century, John Winchcombe and Thomas Dolman had spent fortunes outside business. The descendants of Thomas Stumpe, who had turned Malmesbury Abbey, Wiltshire, into a manufactory, climbed into the peerage. There were significant purchases of land elsewhere in Wiltshire, and sometimes marriage into the country gentry, by clothiers who profited from the expansion of trade after the Restoration.[14] Successful commercial families thus penetrated the landed classes. As if to balance this, the younger sons of great families were apprenticed to skinners or maltsters, as the sons of large farmers long continued to be. Serious prejudice against trade set in only after the 17th century.

The supposedly deleterious consequence of gentrification for industry is a version of the Buddenbrooks hypothesis (named after Thomas Mann's novel) which has become familiar to economists: successive generations of successful business families bring about their commercial decline by diverting the firm's resources to unproductive pastimes.

This has little general force. While it is reported that taking capital out of the woollen industry to buy land, 'not infrequently led to the failure of a clothier whose assets were not sufficiently liquid in times of trade depression', there is no reason we should be concerned when one family fell if another rose in its stead.[15] For the removal of capital to cause industry-wide decline, fresh entrants would have had to be blocked. The only mechanism even hinted at that might have had this effect was when manufacturers took water-mill sites out of commission and declined to sell them to new entrants. A few owners do seem to have switched their mills to corn-milling (which may imply higher returns in agricultural processing than manufacturing) but there was little sign of mills being withdrawn entirely from commercial uses. Nor is it clear that alternative water-power sites would not have been available. Furthermore the explanation cannot be generalised across all types of manufacture.

The small scale of early manufacturing meant that it did not place heavy demands on the impersonal capital market. Northern industrialists relied first on their own and family resources, expanding their premises by reinvesting their profits. In the south, capital was in principle forthcoming from the merchants and attorneys of the market towns. They were capable of mobilising any sums likely to be needed, as is shown by their role in costly transport projects.[16] Lack of incentive rather than lack of means seems to have been the constraint on local investment in manufacturing.

Southern manufacturers mostly worked on a small scale, the main exceptions being textile production along the Cotswold valleys, Portsmouth dockyard and the tannery at Wantage, which at the start of the 19th century was the largest in the country. Entry to many trades was relatively cheap, requiring little more than make-shift premises, a shed or two, maybe one's dwelling house (or in the case of putting-out merchants, the workers' own cottages) and a line of credit. Small Gloucestershire clothiers often enough failed in trade depressions, when they could no longer obtain credit from the Blackwell Hall factors. They did not have deep pockets themselves. Complaints are recurrent about the power of the Blackwell Hall factors, who disposed of the cloth in London.[17] They did not settle their debts promptly and stand accused of keeping the country clothiers short of credit.

Spells of weak profitability risked sudden death play-offs. The disturbed conditions of the Napoleonic wars forced closure on small firms in the pin-making industry, which was two-thirds concentrated in Bristol and Gloucester.[18] In other industries, many firms carried on but may have been 'living dead', their enfeebled condition exposed only when a mill dam burst or a workshop burned down. The plants were then abandoned rather than repaired or rebuilt, which suggests they had been barely hanging on. While they were covering their variable costs, the operators were able to continue operations from day to day. But if they were not making enough to cover their fixed costs, they could not accumulate the funds to replace lost capital stock. Watching their fathers live from hand to mouth, the sons of the operators shied away from following them. Outsiders were rarely willing to assume the risk. Writing in the 1860s, Jevons implies a similar principle by pointing out that when accidents destroyed water corn mills they were not replaced and their work was transferred to steam mills.[19]

Daniel Bourn bought some of Paul and Wyatt's spindles for cotton spinning in his mill at Leominster and in 1748 obtained his own patent for a machine to card wool and cotton, but in 1754 the factory was destroyed by fire and the project abandoned.[20] The mill was later rebuilt as a corn mill.

The *Manchester Mercury* heard that Bourn lost over £1600, while his partners also lost money. The website of the Herefordshire Council Sites and Monuments Record states that Richard Arkwright, who lived on the nearby Hampton Court estate, was a rival of Bourn and later used elements of Bourn's, and Paul and Wyatt's, machinery in his own successful machine.[21] (Sir) Richard Arkwright was supposedly implicated in the fire — but the Arkwrights can be exculpated. Hampton Court was not bought until 1809, and the purchaser was not the original Richard Arkwright but his son, Richard Arkwright Jr., and even he did not settle there. It was Sir Richard's grandson, John Arkwright, who took up residence, and then not until 1819. More likely Bourn had not rebuilt the mill because he had lost too much money. The slack in cotton spinning was taken up in Lancashire before anyone thought it worth trying again in Herefordshire.

A similar fate awaited many more routine enterprises, once more implying that they had been covering their variable costs but not making enough to cover prime costs. The three plush factories at Banbury in 1838 all wove on looms that were very old — they had not been updated — and in the middle of the century, an explosion in a new-built factory there bankrupted the firm.[22] Declining trades suffer a continual attrition of their stock of workplaces. The fact that this was so slow in the south merely helps to disguise the low profitability of industry there.

When whole streets of tenements in the poorest clothing towns burned down, they were repeatedly replaced by dwellings made of equally hazardous materials, in particular thatched roofs. East Devon was notable for this.[23] Elsewhere in the south, towns that burned down in the frequent fires of the period from 1650 to 1850 were quickly rebuilt and increasingly upgraded to non-flammable materials, brick and tile or brick and slate. Much of the rebuilding predated effective fire insurance and argues for the ready availability of capital and credit. Had there been a strong incentive to expand manufacturing, funds could have been tapped for that as well.

A lack of incentive is certainly indicated by the experience of Herefordshire, always a marginal county from the manufacturing viewpoint, where Lord Scudamore's bequest languished uselessly at interest.[24] No-one applied for the £400 available to any responsible person who would establish a woollen manufacture at Hereford, and thus employ the poor, from 1668 to 1772! Although the terms of the trust were widened in 1764 from woollens to any type of business, only trivial enterprises drew on the fund. Despite the notorious difficulties of entering the county by road, cloth could be brought in at lower prices than Herefordshire men thought they could match.

Poor Quality of Labour

A negative opinion of the quality of labour in rural areas is expressed by Allen, who speaks of it as being deskilled by the collapse of proto-industry and by the enclosure movement.[25] These processes supposedly left the population only menial farm work to do. Allen claims that enclosure narrowed the mental life of the rural population, farm workers becoming mere ploughmen. Were that so, it would have left the quality of labour unimpaired in parishes that had never housed rural domestic industry or were not enclosed.

The dog that did not bark in this story was society's failure to supply adequate education, or in many parishes any education at all. The decline of small independent farms and proto-industry would have caused less suffering had people been reasonably well taught. Lindert has shown that under-investment in primary education is the biggest single impediment to economic development and that elite rule typically fails to invest enough in it.[26] Contrary to its mythology, England began to slip back relative to other countries during the 19th century and spent less on primary schooling than some countries with lower average incomes. Even the National Education Act of 1870 provided only a few short years of elementary schooling, featuring the four 'Rs' of reading, writing, 'rithmetic and religion. The diaries kept by village schoolteachers show children continually taken out of school for potato picking and similar tasks.[27] The interests of farmers, over-represented among school governors, were paramount.

Had passable education been offered it is reasonable to suppose that outcomes would have been different, probably taking the form of much more domestic and overseas migration, with the eventual result of higher real wages for those who remained. Once the pedagogic defects were partially remedied by the Education Act of 1944, the suppressed talent in the countryside was released. This shows there is no case for stigmatising the rural population as inherently lacking in ability.

Gladwell takes the negative line further with a blanket dismissal of European 'peasants'.[28] He asserts there is a permanent difference between the skilled background of Asian labour and the unskilled heritage of agricultural workers in Europe. European 'peasants' allegedly worked only 1,000 hours per year, and drank and hibernated the remainder of the time. They developed a taste for long holidays and did not learn to make complex calculations. This placed them in a weak position *vis a vis* the descendants of Asian rice farmers, who worked 3,000 hours, and mastered tasks such as draining the land and selecting among many varieties of rice, operations necessitating mathematical calculation. Supposedly this means that modern Asian labour is superior to Western labour today. In Gladwell's account the difference is a given; there is no motor in his explanation, unless one wants to refer right back to the origins of wet-rice cultivation in Asia versus rain-fed farming in Europe.

Over-generalised interpretations such as these smack of the hypothetical history written by 18th-century scholars. There are at least six objections.

1. While they may apply to the tedious routines of gang labour in arable areas during the 19th century, the characterisations do not apply to earlier periods when there were vastly more independent small farmers. Moreover they exaggerate the simplicity of farm work as a whole. As a close observer wrote in 1860, agricultural employment was a harder-learnt all-round task than was supposed.[29]

2. The characterisations cannot apply to workers who engaged in specialist tasks such as dealing with livestock or floating water-meadows.

3. They do not apply to workers in the numerous other trades that persisted in the countryside, some of them highly skilled, such as wheelwrighting. Similarly, advanced female skill was apparent in the lace industry, an occupation that could be and was taught. Adding in millwrights and men who had lost industrial jobs, the potential number of artisans would have remained high enough to keep a manufacturing sector in operation — had the low quality of labour really been the limiting factor.

The range of skills needed was wide but it could have been supplied. Some tasks required practical training or personal dexterity; others were fairly easily learned or could be self-taught. New entrants with little training were soon able to weave worsteds; half the weavers around Taunton, Somerset, at the start of the 18th century had never been apprenticed.[30] The deeper functions of apprenticeship included providing employers with some years of cheap labour and protecting employees from competition until young entrants had been socialised in current practices.[31] Both sides colluded to insist on the value of the time spent as an apprentice. In the Gloucestershire woollen industry the enforcement of apprenticeship nevertheless dwindled during the 18th century, but when there was an influx of workers after the Napoleonic wars men began to protest against the relaxation of the rules, though clothiers rejoined that apprenticeship was actually unnecessary because it did not take long to learn to weave by machine.[32]

The argument that there was no-one to teach proto-industrial skills is contradicted in two ways, on the one hand by the existence of a reservoir of skills able to cope with complex operations and on the other by the limited skills needed to undertake other jobs.[33] Asserting that workers could not acquire skills because they had no teachers is a cultural fixity thesis, implying that change was out of the question.[34] This line of reasoning actually underplays the economic calculus, which stresses substitutions. Ordinarily economists anticipate response to incentives.

The movement of firms into the south and the establishment of new ones, small though both trends were, imply that manufacturers did not regard local labour as uniformly hopeless. The usual example is the arrival of Heathcoat at Tiverton, but he brought lace workers with him. A better example may be the Clarks, who established shoe-making at Street, Somerset, in 1825. There was also a marked expansion of industry in 19th-century Kent.

4. Denigrating the quality of southern labour wrongly homogenises opportunities for employment between arable and woodland districts or open and closed parishes. Up to a point, the region shared a common history but it never became a uniform desert populated by the unskilled. Admittedly, in closed parishes (squires' villages) tasks might be restricted to domestic service, gardening and estate and farm work, but there were plenty of open villages — all liberty and swearing, as Richard Jefferies said of them — where opportunities of other kinds might be taken by small tradesmen and dealers.

5. The arguments are condescending employer-class stereotypes that do not allow for the intelligence of many 19th-century manual workers. They lacked resources, education and refinement but did not lack wit.[35] A reasonable assumption is that there was a normal distribution of intelligence among them.

6. To reinforce a point made above, the interpretation represents a cultural fixity thesis which implies that culture cannot be unlearned. In reality innumerable descendants of Victorian farm workers work in skilled occupations today, many in the highest ranks of the professions.

To sum up, far from being 'supine peasants', the ranks of southern labourers contained many individuals of considerable energy. Despite poor circumstances, they displayed remarkable fund-raising ability and independence of mind. Evidence of this is their building of chapels in the middle of the villages, right under the noses of the clerical establishment. The willingness of others to emigrate suggests that the problem of labour was not a low intrinsic level of ability, or the extent of deskilling, but restricted opportunities for a reasonable life. Much enterprise went into emigrating, which tended to siphon off the most forceful, as may be seen by contrasting the verve (or brashness) of the populations of North America or Australasia with that in England.[36]

Non-Market Competition

None of the explanations so far discussed is forceful enough on its own to account for southern decline. Many apply only to one trade, or one place, or one period or one phase of the trade cycle. Nor do they offer a knock-out blow when combined. They were often correlates of manufacturing decline rather than its origin and amounted to defensive responses that may have made recovery more difficult but did not start the slide. Business history has little to say about differences in the behaviour of southern employers and employees between good times and bad.

A final possibility is that southern industries were driven out of business, not by market forces at all, but by non-market competition. This is a live possibility. Sometimes there was direct cheating, as when a Birmingham tradesman pirated Jonathan Hulls' instrument to detect counterfeit gold. Beyond commercial piracy, the urge to suppress competition was perennial. The Whitechapel Bell-foundry's purchase of numerous small foundries in the early 19th century, only to close them down, was mentioned in a previous chapter.

As to entire industries, 'by 1700 the deindustrialisation process [in the Sussex Weald] ... was almost complete, well before the generally acknowledged establishment of coal-fire manufacture elsewhere'.[37] Glass-making declined early and fast — the last furnace closed in 1618 — supposedly being out-competed by the rise of coal-fired furnaces in Newcastle. But this is a false positive instance of the resource advantage of the coal regions. Far from competition, a Royal Proclamation of 1615 had forbidden the use of wood fuel in glass-making, ostensibly to protect sources of timber for merchant shipping.

Admiral Sir Robert Mansell in Newcastle, a favourite of James I and corrupt Treasurer of the Navy, obtained the monopoly of glass-making, and vigorously prosecuted wood-burning transgressors. He opened his works on the Tyne in 1619. The next year he made sure that two importers of glass were imprisoned. Mansell's monopoly even evaded the 1624 Statute of Monopolies, which declared other monopolies null and void. Faced with a typically egregious Stuart monopolist, it is small wonder that the descendants of the French glass-makers brought to the Weald in the mid-16th century moved on north or west, while local part-time producers reverted to full-time farming.

Ironically, the Mansell family already owned a glass works at Newnham, Gloucestershire, and others were distributed here and there across the south, at Buckholt, Hampshire, for instance. The making of glass with coal is the subject of priority disputes of the type that occur commonly in the history of technological change (and which indicate the level of inventive activity and many-layered nature of technology). But there is no doubt that Sir Robert Mansell was the industrial victor. His monopoly meant that England's scatter of glass furnaces dating from the mid-16th century was wiped out, and the production of cheap small glass went with them, whereas luxury glass boomed.

A later instance of non-market competition was the Regulatory Act (known as the Tewkesbury Act) of 1765.[38] East Midland hosiers, normally opposed to regulation and ashamed to ask the Company of Framework Knitters to impose it, secretly petitioned Parliament to have the cotton hosiery produced in Tewkesbury outlawed or at least marked as more flimsily constructed than usual. They were alarmed because stockings so made could be sold 25 per cent cheaper than their own, as a result of extra skill developed by spinners in the Tewkesbury district. Consumers eagerly bought cheap Tewkesbury stockings and disregarded the accusation that they did not last. The Act was copied into the standard legal work, Burns' *Justice*, but no-one was ever convicted under it. Henson, a Nottingham stockinger himself, said it was badly worded and those he called the 'Tewkesbury frauds' slipped around its provisions.

We may mention, lastly, the ring of London ironmasters who did not resort to the law but simply combined to raise the price of iron. By running Henry Cort into a £10,000 loss, they almost forced him out of business.[39] Once again, protectionism did not succeed, and the conclusion about attempts to employ methods other than price competition must be that they were usually ineffective. In the larger scheme of things, protectionist measures were ad hoc and directed at a scatter of trades at diverse dates. Even had they been successful they would not have swept southern industry by the board.

Endnotes

1. E. A. L. Moir, The gentlemen clothiers: a study of the organization of the Gloucestershire cloth industry, 1750–1835, in H. P. R. Finberg (ed.), *Gloucestershire Studies* (Leicester University Press, 1957), p. 226.
2. J. D. Chambers, *Nottinghamshire in the Eighteenth Century* (London: P. S. King & Son, 1932), pp. 95, 101.
3. T. Rath, The Tewkesbury hosiery industry, *Textile Hist.* 7: 140–153, 1976.
4. H. Fox, *Quaker Homespun: The Life of Thomas Fox of Wellington, Serge Maker and Banker 1747–1821* (London: George Allen & Unwin, 1958), pp. 50–55, 93–94.
5. M. B. Weinstock, *Old Dorset* (Newton Abbot: David & Charles, 1967), pp. 97–99.
6. W. Smith, *An Economic Geography of Great Britain* (London: Methuen, second edition, 1953), p. 104.
7. R. A. Church and S. D. Chapman, Gravener Henson and the making of the English working class, in E. L. Jones and G. E. Mingay (eds.), *Land, Labour and Population in the Industrial Revolution* (London: Edward Arnold, 1967), p. 151.
8. L. Haycock, *John Anstie of Devizes 1743–1830: An Eighteenth-Century Wiltshire Clothier* (Stroud: Alan Sutton and Wiltshire Archaeological and Natural History Society, 1991), pp. 11–12.
9. J. de L. Mann, Textile industries since 1550, in *Victoria County History, Wiltshire*, IV (1959), p. 176.
10. G. D. Ramsey, *The Wiltshire Woollen Industry in the Sixteenth and Seventeenth Centuries* (Oxford University Press, 1943), p. 116.

11. *Victoria County History, Gloucestershire*, II (1907), p. 195.

12. A. Urdank, Economic decline in the English industrial revolution: the Gloucester wool trade, 1800–1840, *J. Econ. Hist.* **XLV**(2): 428, 1985.

13. Moir, 'Gentlemen Clothiers', pp. 242–243; Powell, *John Aubrey*, p. 116.

14. Ramsey, *Wiltshire Woollen Industry*, p. 127.

15. R. Perry, The Gloucestershire woollen industry, 1100–1690, *Trans. Bristol Glo. Archaeol. Soc.* **68**: 114, 1945.

16. A rare study of the financial situation in a market town and its district is Audrey M. Taylor, *Gilletts, Bankers at Banbury and Oxford: A Study in Local Economic History* (Oxford: Clarendon Press, 1964). Gillett had retreated into banking from less profitable plush manufacturing.

17. Ramsey, *Wiltshire Woollen Industry*, pp. 135–137.

18. H. I. Dutton and S. R. H. Jones, Invention and innovation in the British pin industry, 1790–1850, *Bus. Hist. Rev.* **LVII**(2): 175, 1983.

19. Quoted by N. Rosenberg, *Perspectives on Technology* (Cambridge: Cambridge University Press, 1976), p. 204.

20. Jenkins, Herefordshire, p. 186.

21. Sites and Monuments Record, Herefordshire, Pinsley Mill SMR 726, SO 5010/5906. Compare E. L. Jones, Industrial capital and landed investment: the Arkwrights in Herefordshire, 1809–1843, in E. L. Jones and G. E. Mingay (eds.), *Land, Labour and Population in the Industrial Revolution* (London: Edward Arnold, 1967), pp. 48–71. The website is in process of being corrected.

22. Beckinsale, Plush Industry, pp. 59, 63.

23. E. L. Jones, Fire disasters: the special case of East Devon, *Devon Hist.* **20**: 11–17, 1980.

24. W. J. Rees, *The Hereford Guide* (Hereford, 1806), pp. 47–48.

25. R. C. Allen, *Enclosure and the Yeoman* (Oxford: Clarendon Press, 1992), pp. 288–289.

26. P. H. Lindert, Voice and growth: was Churchill right? *J. Econ. Hist.* **63**(2): 317, 330.

27. E. L. Jones, The land that Richard Jefferies inherited, *Rural Hist.* **16**(1): 89, 2005.

28. M. Gladwell, interview on BBC4, 24/11/08, based on his book *Outliers: The Secret of Success* (London: Allen Lane, 2008), which was reviewed favourably in *The Economist*, 13 Dec. 2008.

29. J. Wilkinson, History of Broughton Gifford, *Wiltshire Archaeol. Mag.* **VI**: 38, 1860.

30. S. Ogilvie, Can we rehabilitate the guilds? A sceptical reappraisal, CWPE 0745 (September 2007) [on Google Scholar], p. 27.

31. M. Bichard, *Baskets in Europe* (Abingdon: Fyfield Wick Editions, 2008), p. 59.
32. W. E. Minchinton, The beginnings of trade unionism in the Gloucestershire woollen industry, *Trans. Bristol Glo. Archaeol. Soc.* **XXX**: 137–138, 1951.
33. Allen, *Enclosure and the Yeoman*, pp. 261, 289.
34. For objections to cultural fixity, see E. L. Jones, *Cultures Merging: A Historical and Economic Critique of Culture* (Princeton: Princeton University Press, 2006).
35. K. Amis makes a telling observation in his *Memoirs* (London: Penguin, 1992), p. 96.
36. It may be apposite to draw attention to B. Frey, D. Savage and B. Torgler, 'Who survived the Titanic and why?' on Tyler Cowen's website, *Marginal Revolution* (2009).
37. B. Short, The de-industrialisation process: a case study of the Weald, 1600–1850, in Pat Hudson (ed.), *Regions and Industries: A perspective on the Industrial Revolution in Britain* (Cambridge: Cambridge University Press, 1989), p. 169; G. H. Kenyon, *The Glass Industry of the Weald* (Leicester: Leicester University Press, 1967); *Isle of Purbeck website.*
38. G. Henson, *History of the Framework Knitters* (Newton Abbot: David & Charles Reprint, 1970), pp. 359–363; Rath, 'Tewkesbury', p. 140.
39. H. W. Dickinson, Henry Cort's bicentenary, *Trans. Newcomen Soc.* **XXI**: 32, 1940–1941.

CHAPTER 6

PROSPERITY, POVERTY AND BOURGEOIS VALUES

One of the most pathetic stories of the 16th century is that, I think, of the efforts of Lord Burleigh ... to prove his descent from a Welsh princeling who probably never existed, and who, if he did exist, was probably hardly distinguishable from the sheep of his native hills.

F. J. Fisher, 1957

An immense stir was provoked in 2007 by the thesis about the origins of economic growth in Greg Clark's stimulating book, *A Farewell to Alms.*[1] The argument combines demography and culture. Clark urges that well-to-do late medieval and early modern families in England had more surviving children than the poor — more than the available opportunities. Many were therefore obliged to move down the occupational scale. While this was unfortunate for the individuals concerned, society gained because descendants of the prosperous carried with them the values of hard work, ingenuity, innovativeness and reverence for education. These values were supposedly characteristic of the successful households in which they had grown up. They spread their bourgeois values through society, presumably civilising a proportion of the feckless poor in the process. Supposedly, this was enough to account for England's growth and industrialisation.

The thesis is so bold that it bears repeating. Deirdre McCloskey conveniently excerpts a summary of Clark's case:

> For England ... 1250–1800 ... the richest men had twice as many surviving children as the poorest ... The superabundant children of the rich had to ... move ['cascade'] down ... Craftsmen's sons became laborers, merchants' sons petty traders, large landholders' sons smallholders... Patience, hard work, ingenuity, innovativeness, education ... were thus spread biologically

123

throughout the population … England's advantage lay in the rapid cultural, and potentially also genetic, diffusion of the values of the economically successful through society.[2] (D. McCloskey, 2008)

What depends on this thesis? In principle the entire industrial revolution does, since despite earlier episodes of economic growth elsewhere, the industrial primacy of Britain is incontrovertible.[3]

The issues raised may be expanded to include:

- When and why did better-off families adopt bourgeois values?
- Did they rear more children than the poor?
- When did the status-fertility crossover occur and the poor start raising more children than all but the extremely rich?
- Did the rich really imbue their children with bourgeois values?
- Were these transmitted to descendants who tumbled down the occupational scale for lack of attractive positions or enough land?
- Were the values genetically encoded?
- Was it these values that brought about industrialisation?
- Why did industrialisation not arise evenly across England and bourgeois values not protect old-established industry in the south?

Several reviewers quickly took Clark to task. Three of the sternest points of rebuttal were that the numerical effect cannot have been large enough to produce the result claimed, the behaviour of the offspring would quickly regress to the mean, and the values espoused by the most successful in the medieval period were anyhow not those of regular, creative effort: they were redolent of violence, disdain for labour, perpetual hunting and killing of animals, and an easy facility for securing favours from the powerful.

We may take our cue from one of the reviewers, Robert Solow, who wrote that:

one would really like to see some direct evidence that the trait of responsiveness to pecuniary incentives had spread more widely in English society than it had earlier or elsewhere by the end of the eighteenth century. Even if it had, only the most minute micro-research could hope to demonstrate that this was the result of the mechanism proposed by Clark.[4] (R. Solow, 2007)

Family History

What follows takes it cue from Solow. It considers Clark's thesis in the light of the long-term experience of a small number of families in a block of southern counties, Gloucestershire, Wiltshire, Berkshire and Hampshire. The data refer to a dozen families. The arena is even smaller than implied, comprising a thin slice of what has been rather awkwardly termed 'East Wessex', stretching from Southampton Water to the Cotswolds, and often relating to parishes on county boundaries, which the 18th century called frontier parishes. This reflects the localism of life at the time and the significance of county identity; it has made tracing the history of these families slower than it might have been because of the need to locate sources for several of them in at least two counties. Frontier parishes were often thinly populated and being, so to speak, on the edge have not always generated as many records as more central ones.

It is relatively unusual for economic history to deal with individuals.[5] The parent disciplines discourage this approach, economics as an article of faith, history if a historian's own ancestors are involved. When economists turn to long-run growth their analyses are depersonalised. Likewise democratic historians, in Tocqueville's view, attribute nothing to the individual and employ a structuralism which Himmelfarb criticises for trivialising even Hitler.[6] But a micro-study ought to assess how an individual's *habitus* or personal disposition interacted with the structure and culture of societies and economies.[7] This means integrating biography and economic history, a difficult task when dealing with people who left traces of themselves in official documents but almost no literary remains of their own.

Is it academically useful to study family history?[8] Over the past generation the genealogies of innumerable ordinary families have been teased out by their descendants. Despite the presence of some 250,000 hobbyists in England alone, the pursuit is frowned on by the history profession, as may be judged from the dismissive reaction of the Oxford history faculty to Simon Schama's proposal for a course on the subject.[9] Long before the invasion by amateurs, scholarly standards in genealogical history admittedly left much to be desired, contaminated as they were by extremes of wishful thinking. The index to Horace Round's *Studies in Peerage and Family History* is scathing, not to say hilarious, about this, listing such gems as: ancestors, fictitious; records, imaginary, cited; Heralds' College alters its 'recorded' pedigrees; its defective record of grants; fabulous pedigrees constructed by members and more of the same.[10] Small wonder that Round's aim was to rescue family history, 'from the hands of those pedigree-mongers who made of it a byword and a reproach'.[11]

More to the present point, may the scholar cite his own family? This is not merely unfashionable, it is deeply unpopular. I toyed with disguising the fact that my sample consists primarily of my own ancestors and set Jack Fisher's remark as the epigraph of this chapter in warning to myself against retrospective hubris. Yet to refer to family A, family B, and so forth would make for unreadable writing and obscure the fact that it applies to real people whose other descendants I have met and who lived in places, sometimes in houses, that may still be visited today.

A merit of working with family history data for anyone accustomed to the aggregated and manufactured statistics of economic history is to be confronted with how fragile and full of gaps the historical record is. Too often documents are illegible, incomplete or just plain missing. A safe containing the records of one of the parishes included in the present study (Combe, Berkshire, formerly Hampshire) was tossed into a pond in the woods in the course of some forgotten dispute. It was rescued but black patches obliterate whole pages. Three miles away at Ashmansworth there are no registers before 1810, the earlier ones having been destroyed when the parish clerk's cottage burned down. Nevertheless, where documents do survive, the approach offers immediacy. Furthermore, it is a spur to labours few scholars would undertake professionally; acts as a focussing device which reduces the scatter of examples without wholly eliminating their diversity and humanises the writing.

A personal approach brings one close to what really may be authenticated, besides demonstrating that economic history is not only a set of abstractions but concerns the verifiable actions of individuals.[12] It would seem illogical to be able refer to other peoples' ancestors but not one's own, as some historians demand. The alternative pretends to an implausibly 'scientific' detachment and would debar people whose forebears were prominent from writing history.

Next, are small samples to be rejected because they may be unrepresentative? Clark's own work has an extremely narrow evidential base, despite the mountain of hypotheses piled on it. Reviewing *A Farewell to Alms*, Jan de Vries quipped, 'had this book been written by an historian its subtitle might have been: Some Findings from Suffolk Testators, 1620–1638'.[13] There seems no *a priori* reason to think that the sample here, though equally small, behaved very differently from any other demographic, genetic or cultural sample. The assumption may be that society was fractal, with the world contained in a grain of sand.

Insofar as there were differences within the sample they may have derived from ecological variety: the Cooks, for example, who farmed low fields by the upper Thames at Latton, Wiltshire, were only a dozen miles as the crow flies from the Abells and Havilands, high up on the bare Cotswolds at Winstone, Gloucestershire. This may seem inconsequential to anyone unfamiliar with the ground, yet as farmers they faced strikingly different challenges and opportunities. The dates of their harvests would have differed, as they do today, and though hay was sparse on the hills it was abundant by the Thames. The sample was thus more inclusive of agricultural patterns across southern England than its small size may suggest. Yet demographic and socio-economic behaviour do not seem to have differed drastically at the level of analysis attempted here.

The families in my sample were my ancestors and my wife's, with one or two relating to close friends. They lived in two fair-sized groups of villages and small towns between the New Forest and the Cotswolds. The main examples (Abells and Havilands on the one hand and Joneses on the other) did not live in the same county until 1865 and were not related until my parents married in 1922. Nor is the sample quite as small as appears: over the centuries the number of individuals and satellite families is in the hundreds.

Long family trees are hard to come by. As Anthony Camp says, 'the great wealth of Lord Nuffield and all the genealogical expertise that he could muster could not take the ancestry of his yeoman family beyond about 1580 with certainty'.[14] I have been luckier and can muster unbroken lineages back to Norman times for two families (Jones and Haviland), two others less consecutively back to the Middle Ages (Noyes and Goater), three (Abell, Cook and Mansbridge) to the 16th century, and have shorter trees for the remaining four or five, consecutive only since the 18th century. There is some occupational and a little biographical material, although the latter is far from complete.

Most of the trees have been assembled by the families' own historians, especially Penny McKay in her prize-winning study of the Havilands; the Utah Mormon, Eldon A. Jones and other assiduous distant relatives, occasionally as many as four working independently per tree.[15] I have cross-checked and fleshed out the material, more with respect to historical experiences than the 'who-begat-whom' dimension on which the whole nevertheless rests.

I hope to show that the opinion of the historian Peter Spufford is unimaginative, when, rather like Edward Gibbon, he claims that, 'a long descent can only be of interest to the historian when it is accompanied by continuous possession of property, office or title and a continuous participation in the active life of the nation'.[16] Gibbon, a Hampshire man until he retreated to Lausanne, thought a family tree was a positional good, its value stemming from the fact that others are excluded from sharing it. He wrote that, 'the knowledge of our own family from a remote period will be always esteemed as an abstract pre-eminence since it can never be promiscuously enjoyed but the longest series of peasants and mechanics would not afford much gratification to the pride of their descendant'.[17] Given that his claims about his own descent were wrong, Gibbon was not in a strong position to assert this. My own set of families started well enough but did not hold what they once had, and it is precisely the long tumbledown which brings their history to bear on Clark's thesis.

Of the three chief families whose experiences will be reported, the Joneses arrived in Wiltshire from South Wales in the early 16th century. They were a father, son and the son's wife, a junior branch of a family originating from Llanarth, a country house in Monmouthshire.[18] In Wiltshire they rented a farm and rabbit warren from the Hungerfords, who had been the greatest sheep-masters in the county during the 15th century and were still very extensive landowners. The Havilands, who had been merchants in Guernsey and mayors of Poole, arrived in the Gloucestershire Cotswolds in 1573 in the person of John Haviland, Rector of Winstone. Fifty years later one of his sons had become a well-known London printer (i.e. publisher) and in the mid-17th century another son and a grandson took their degrees at Christchurch, Oxford.[19] The Abells moved to Winstone from further south in Gloucestershire about 1600 and were yeomen and husbandman. For several generations Abells married into the Havilands, who had lost their ecclesiastical and London connections and remained in the village as farmers. The other families in the sample were all at one time landowners or farmers, though by the late 19th century most had become minor tradesmen or labourers.

The Joneses became poor but stayed honest. Things went more drastically wrong for the Havilands and Abells. In 1806 a Haviland and an Abell were transported to New South Wales for jointly stealing a horse. The vast majority in all of the families stayed in England, however, most of them becoming poorer as time passed: this implied marrying among the poor and less educated, which trapped them in a similar condition of low achievements and expectations. A fringe example was Mary Brin, who seems to have been a member of one family into which the Abells later married. Examined for bastardry in 1715, this unfortunate young woman could date the relevant event only by admitting that, 'Robert Hawkins of Shellingford, wooll comber, has several times had carnal knowledge of her body, first time in Eastfield, Newbery about a fortnight before the last great Eclipse and also about a fortnight after the same eclipse in Mr Merriman's meadow in Newbery, and at several times since'.[20]

Does the Demographic Record Support the Clark Thesis?

Clark was not the first to emphasise the fecundity of successful people. Anthea Jones cites Sir John Blaket of Icomb Place, Gloucestershire, who was killed at Agincourt.[21] His granddaughter was the wife of Simon Milbourn, 'who had by her eleven daughters, from whom are descended (I think) a thousand knights, gentlemen and others … They speak loud of their great blood, and there is no smoke without a fire …'

Not quite everyone accepts that the rich were or remained biologically more successful. Razzell and Spence argue that in the 18th and 19th centuries the death rates of the wealthy were as high as those of the poor. This they attribute to self-indulgence, but theirs is a distinctly minority viewpoint.[22]

What does my sample show? Demographic data relating to the Haviland, Abell and Jones families may be compared for two equal periods divided at 1750, when downward social mobility became evident.[23] This enables us to contrast the period 1600–1749 with 1750–1899. From one period to the other the median age of marriage for men fell from 30 to 27 years and for women from 27 to 24 years. Life spans rose from 51 years to 60 years for men and from 53.5 years to 57 for women.

Thus, contrary to what may be expected from Clark, both sexes tended to live longer in the latter period, despite markedly lower social standing. Six or seven now lived into their eighties or nineties. My three-greats grand-mother, Mary Abell (nee Haviland), was left £30 per annum for life by a brother and went on collecting this until she died at 95 in 1830. Admittedly my four-greats grandfather, Edward Jones, was on parish relief when he was buried at 85 in 1813 by the vicar of Aldbourne, Edward Jenner's disgruntled friend, Rev. Thomas Preen. Preen specially noted this great age in the register. Edward Jones had probably out-lived his savings, although another four-greats grandfather, Henry Johnson, did not do so: he was living in Ashbury on independent means at the age of 90 in 1841, despite having worked as an agricultural labourer.

On the other hand, as Clark would expect, more children were raised to marriage age in the former period, 93 children as against 54 in the latter. Scholars knew before Clark that the status-fertility relation reversed at some stage but it does not seem to have happened in these families, at least before 1899.[24] Apart from two or three particularly large Victorian families, the poorer families tended to be smaller in the later period.

Does the Social Decline Fit Clark's Pattern?

The answer is 'yes' for most families. Certainly the Abells, Havilands and Joneses were of higher status in the earlier period than they later became. The Havilands and Joneses had been of still higher status in the Middle Ages and 16th century. The situation for both was almost that of Y. Euny Hong, descendant of Korean feudal monarchs, who writes, 'my family's heyday, in fact, had ceased by the time the last Plantagenet breathed his last'.[25]

Enough information survives for nine families in the sample to demonstrate downward mobility during the 18th and 19th centuries. In particular, from 1600 to 1749 the main lines of the Abells, Havilands and Joneses were landowners, yeomen and husbandmen, but during the period 1750 to 1899 they became horse-dealers, tailors, gamekeepers, iron moulders or domestic servants. Five patterns of events brought about the change.[26] Half-a-dozen lines were afflicted by what might be called the 'surplus sons' phenomenon, whereby the sons of farmers tumbled down to become wheelwrights, wheelwrights' sons became carpenters and carpenters' sons became labourers. There were three bankruptcies, all significantly in 1817: a farmer-dealer, a wheelwright and an innkeeper. There were three cases of business mismanagement or deaths of parents leaving young orphans. Two cases of crime resulted in transportation. And in two cases male lines failed, followed by ruinous marriages on the part of daughters.

Some flesh may be put on these dry bones by describing the life courses of the main families: the Joneses did buy some land of their own but during the 16th and well into the 17th century were primarily tenants on a Hungerford family farm at Mildenhall, near Marlborough. The farm included a commercial rabbit warren and they paid 400 couples of rabbits annually as rent for the manor house.[27] The eldest sons in three generations made socially advantageous marriages. William Jones, head of the family at the end of the 16th and start of the 17th century, was a land speculator who acquired several manors in different parts of Wiltshire. He appears to have been taking very long leases, tantamount to freehold, of manors that had formerly been owned by the Hungerfords. One parish where he obtained land in 1584 was Stratton St. Margaret, now swallowed up in Swindon. There he tried to carve out a new manor called, without false modesty, Stratton Jones.[28]

William Jones was trading on the connection with his Hungerford land-lords but overreached himself. He died in 1611, his eldest son having predeceased him by a few months. They had become involved in an obscure conflict which was recorded on a plaque, now missing, but seen in Mildenhall church in 1660 by the great topographer, John Aubrey, and briefly resurfacing during church restoration in 1981.[29] The plaque referred to the Jones's enemies; strangely, it had not been erected until 1642 although father and son had died 30 years earlier. It was probably written for purposes of his own by the incumbent, a prominent Royalist who under Charles II became bishop of Worcester and then bishop of Winchester.

A descendant of William Jones sold 'Stratton Jones' in 1625, while the last of his properties was disposed of by later descendants about 1670. This may have coincided with the collapse of the Hungerford holdings; the senior member of that family, aptly known as 'the Spendthrift', spent his time at the Restoration court gambling away manor after manor. The place name 'Stratton late Jones' continued to appear in legal documents until the mid-18th century, one century and a quarter after it had been sold. This attests to the need for establishing pedigrees of ownership as firmly as possible in the absence of anything approximating to a land registry.

My cadet branch of the family became tradesmen in Marlborough, owning in the 18th century only a few small properties, then in the 19th century the direct line became gamekeepers, owning nothing. Like some of the families into which they married, they fell to the level of the 'second

poor', that is to say able to keep themselves off poor relief but only just —
and in the case of the aged Edward Jones at Aldbourne at the very start of the
19th century, not even that.

In a society where the law of primogeniture obtained, descent from a
succession of younger sons was disastrous. A farmer could seldom provide
well for more than his eldest son, to whom he left the farm or to whom he
might reasonably expect the landlord would grant the tenancy. Younger sons
tended to be pushed out of farming. To cite only one among my other
constituent families, the Goaters were yeomen farmers at Ashley, Hampshire.
In the 16th century the lord of the manor tried to enserf them, or as he
conceived or pretended to conceive it, to re-enserf them. He claimed that the
family and all their possessions belonged to him. This was an attempt to
oblige them to pay a fine in order to keep the wealth they had created. It
failed but, regardless of that, the logic of demography worked to extrude
some Goater sons from farming. By the late 18th century my direct Goater
ancestors were coppice dealers in the neighbouring parish of Sparsholt, where
as an auxiliary occupation they served as parish clerks in an unbroken line for
well over a century. A similar trajectory was followed by several of the families in the sample, though the dates differed. For example the Mansbridges,
who married into the Goaters, were farmers in a small way at Sparsholt as late
as the 1850s, but afterwards retreated into carpentery. Like the Goaters, they
descended from a long line of yeomen farmers, but I suspect they were
under-capitalised and found themselves caught up in the general evaporation
of the small farmer class.[30]

Coincidentally, the Havilands had depended, like the Joneses, on the
patronage of the Hungerfords — to whom they were actually related. John
Haviland, who was literate and Latinate but not a graduate, became Rector
of Winstone through the offices of a Hungerford relative who lived in the
manor house and was patron of the living. The Hungerfords later sold out
and moved away, however, and the Havilands lost their support.

More is known about the Havilands than any of the other families,
thanks to Penny McKay's work. The Rector farmed the glebe while one of his
sons and a grandson took Oxford M.A.s, and a daughter married the M.A.
who succeeded her father as rector, thus keeping property in the family.
Another son and a full six of the Rector's grandsons became Stationers or
members of other London companies. The son, also called John Haviland,
was the printer. He died in 1638 and left a fortune of £6000 to his Winstone

kin, though in the event they received a smaller sum. Nevertheless they erected to his name a fulsome plaque which is still in the church.

The disturbances of the Civil Wars broke the London connection for the Havilands. Future generations stayed at home, farming on the Cotswolds. The high premiums charged for entering London companies after the wars prevented them from returning to take up apprenticeships. Some family members crossed the Atlantic: one slightly distant relative was a plantation owner in Barbadoes at the same time (1664) as an illegitimate grandson of the Rector was transported there. It is worth noting how much the fortunes of members of the family had begun to diverge.

Otherwise the Havilands continued to farm in Winstone, like the Abells. Five Haviland yeomen lived there in the mid-1740s and the family's peak influence was reached in the 1770s, when Susanna Haviland and Thomas and Comfort Abell were co-grandparents of nearly 30 children. Only in 1770 did a Haviland, who was a maltster and shopkeeper, break the agricultural connection completely by apprenticing his son to a Cirencester surgeon.

Winstone was enclosed in 1782, which reduced the number of small farms, although the decline in family status between 1781 and 1790 was not solely for that reason. A lack of male heirs in certain branches seems to have been more immediately responsible. There were nevertheless still too many sons for the available land and some of the Havilands turned to inn-keeping, possibly through the influence of an in-law, Thomas Abell, innkeeper at Duntisbourne Abbots. Two of the innkeepers subsequently became Freemen of Gloucester. Penny McKay's Haviland line were tailors whose descendants spent some generations as domestic servants. Others became soldiers and eventually army officers, London distillers, King's Messengers (which seems remarkable), and one became a watchmaker. A distiller's son, Thomas Heath Haviland (1795–1867), was a colonial administrator in Prince Edward Island, Canada, and his son, also Thomas Heath Haviland (1822–1895) lieutenant-governor of the province.

For the Abells the 19th century was particularly rocky and my own line became innkeepers and none-too-scrupulous horse-dealers. My great-great grandfather, a horse-dealer, acquired a farm (perhaps only a 'dealer's farm' for keeping the horses in which he traded, and probably through marriage) but went bankrupt in 1817. His son and a grandson returned to horse-dealing, the Victorian equivalent of being second-hand car salesmen.

As we have seen, the reasons for economic and social decline varied. Mismanagement and bad luck figured prominently, but there are two features of wider interest: first, the system of inheritance and sequence of occupations among farmers and tradesmen, and second, a descent into criminality, which from its timing may have been a response to a sudden increase in commercial distress about the time of the Napoleonic wars. We have already noted the three bankruptcies in 1817.

Lucky tradesmen might prosper more than their farmer-brothers, as was the case in two families in the sample. One younger son was apprenticed to a London draper and made a considerable fortune. After his death outright adventurers courted his two daughters, leading to suspicious deaths and ruinously expensive court cases.[31] Rural tradesmen more often found themselves on the slippery slope of downward mobility. When primogeniture prevailed and the eldest son inherited the farm, the starting point was always too many sons and only the one farm. This becomes clear if we return to Winstone,

The widow of the first Winstone Haviland, John the Rector, was a grandmother at least 35 times over. Not all of her grandsons could be provided with land and after the Civil Wars the former option of London apprenticeships was too dear. Most farmland in the parish was let on three lives and opportunities to rent or buy more acres were few. A landowner promised and then reneged on selling to the Havilands. As a result, in the early 18th century grandsons and great-grandsons found themselves obliged to spread out across Gloucestershire and Wiltshire. They began by working away on other men's farms, none married before the age of 30, and all married women from parishes some distance from their home village. Occasionally they inherited land from their wife's family. By such devices most Abells and Havilands managed to stay on the land into the second half of the 18th century.

In Wiltshire and Hampshire, two families into which the male line of the Joneses married tumbled down from farming to become wheelwrights in other villages. For this capital was essential, because timber had to be bought and kept for years until it was seasoned, and farm wagons were long in the making. Eighteenth-century insurance policies for one of these men include substantial premiums to cover the value of timber in the yard. We can only guess where the capital came from: likely sources were subventions or loans from their fathers, through marrying an employer's daughter, or borrowing locally on the strength of perceived craftsmanship, probity and business sense.

The whole tumbledown cycle started again when a wheelwright had too many sons for them all to be employed in his business. Some had to become carpenters, which was a sort of tributary trade. The wheelwright could do anything the carpenter could do, but the carpenter supposedly did not possess all the wheelwright's skills, the difference being the ability to construct wheels. This was not very likely for the sons of wheelwrights, growing up as they did in homes next to their fathers' yards, where they could watch the great wagons being built, like ships of the line. It is more likely there was insufficient capital and too few openings.

In earlier centuries carpentry had been a fairly advanced craft but the skills had become generalised, and probably simplified, tools were made cheaper, and the returns fell. Not every son could work for his carpenter father — one of the families branched out successfully into building and other trades but the prospects were not infinite in a village and it was not possible to commute far to a job every day. The carpenters had to go to work for wages, which is never a way to accumulate capital. It is easy to guess what happened next: the carpenters had too many sons, some of whom declined into labouring.

The downward ladder was not always neatly farmer-wheelwright-carpenter-labourer. One or two generations might intervene, some individuals were more fortunate or skilful than their brethren, and some managed to enter other occupations. As mentioned, inn-keeping was a favourite resort of Abells and Havilands. For those among them who moved off Cotswold down into the city of Gloucester this was sometimes a success. But by late in Victoria's reign some of the great-grandsons or great-great grandsons of the farmers of the early 18th century had been reduced to wage labour.

Not every family line moved the same way at the same time but many of those who descended through younger sons married women from impecunious households, which meant limited education, few contacts and reduced expectations. It meant converging near the bottom of the socio-economic heap. This accords with Clark's thesis: the descendants of successful men were progressively driven down the social scale by demography acting in agricultural societies with little spare land and no very rapid economic growth. The period when this took place was later than Clark envisages but the principle is similar.

Contrary to the usual claim that the poorer you are, the closer home you will marry, the percentage of spouses originating in the same parish was lower during the second period. The percentage fell from 39 per cent to 14 per cent, and the average distance between the parishes from which spouses came rose from nine miles to thirteen miles. The extrusion of people in the sample from agriculture meant more people had to work away from home. They met partners from further afield.

Were Bourgeois Values Retained and Transmitted during Downward Mobility?

Maybe: the wooden grave marker at St. Mary Bourne, Hampshire, of my wife's four greats-uncle, William Bower (1774–1851), read, 'for forty years the faithful servant of Mr. Robert Longman, of this parish. He maintained himself by his own honest earnings during life'.[32] His immediate forebears had been tradesmen and some of his relatives farmed a little land and prospered considerably as maltsters. Despite having become a farm worker in the rock-bottom period for labourers in the south of England, he left £90 in the Andover Savings Bank. As with Henry Johnson of Ashbury, and as a pure guess in both cases, the savings may have come from the sale of a cottage or some other small property. Medical expenses prompted sales like that and meant downward steps in individual fortunes.

The difficulty is that documentation is thin for the successful periods in the history of the families because personal records for medieval and early modern times are scarce, and it is thin for the unsuccessful periods because by then the people concerned were too obscure to attract much attention. The sources provide demographic and occupational data of the type used here to trace and compare family size and downward mobility but do not provide direct evidence about values professed, held or transmitted. It would be extraordinary if they did.

Nothing appears about child-rearing practices and, other than the works printed by John Haviland in the early 17th century, only the tiniest asides touch on literacy or education. Most of the families remained true to the established church but public professions of religious belief are no guarantee of honest behaviour. The church plaques for William and John Jones and John Haviland may be discounted; everyone's geese are swans in public testimonials.

The only literary item is a poem by Matthew Haviland, published in the English Poetry Full-text database. This is addressed 'To my Posterity' and entitled 'A monument of Gods most gracious preservation of England from Spanish Invasion, Aug. 2 1588 and Popish Treason, Novem. 5 1605'. But this Matthew was from a branch of the Havilands that had split off before John Haviland, the Rector, came to Winstone. Matthew was Mayor of Bristol in 1608 and three times Master of the Merchant Venturers' Company.[33] He was apparently one of a group who obtained Royal leave in 1610 to found a plantation in Newfoundland. Everything one needs to know about the poem is contained in its title. Matthew was clearly an extreme Protestant nationalist. There is no reason to suppose his Winstone relatives, bound up as they were with Anglicanism, would have thought differently.

According to Lawrence Stone, the ruling elite was, 'the only group whose lives and thoughts and passions are recorded in sufficient detail to make possible investigation in full social and psychological depth'.[34] The rest of us are left with the economist's tool: revealed preference. Here are some points referring to revealed behaviour:

- Leaving aside the remote case of Mary Brin, there were illegitimate births in several of the families. John Haviland, the Rector, was himself guilty, but there was only one other illegitimate Haviland birth between 1600 and 1750, although at least five between 1750 and 1800.
- John Haviland the printer and his partner engaged in sharp practice, publishing in Edinburgh to evade censorship in London. How venal the evasion of censorship is I leave to the reader's judgement. At least Haviland and his partner were not alone: one study reports that 30 per cent of members of the London Stationers' Company broke its ordinances in the early 17th century.[35]
- There were a few 18th-century disputes that reached the civil or ecclesiastical courts. The case of Abell vs. Haviland over responsibility for tithes took place at a date when the families were inextricably intermarried and living cheek by jowl in little Winstone. There was also a contested Haviland will in 1758. And the marvellously named Comfort Abell at Winstone, and Elizabeth Goddard, a Hampshire ancestor, both brought defamation cases. Testimony in the latter instance suggests a pointlessly bitter affair but ecclesiastical court records consist of accusation, testimony

or verdict, never any two of these, let alone all three. It is impossible to tell whether the women involved were contentious or wronged.

- There was a sudden onset of criminality in some families, the fact that the first six entries for Abell in the Gloucestershire Record Office catalogue are wills and the next six gaol sentences being especially piquant. During the Napoleonic Wars the Abells, even yeomen members of the family, were fined several times for poaching, besides for the nebulous offence of possessing deer skins without adequate explanation. As previously mentioned, William Abell and Richard Haviland were actually transported to New South Wales in 1806 for stealing a horse. By 1818 Abell had been secondarily transported to Van Dieman's Land, whereas Haviland prospered enough to become Castrator of Government Stock in New South Wales and to be allotted a convict servant.

A Wiltshire family called Tarrant was first involved with the Joneses as long ago as 1818. By complete chance, one of their descendants, Michael Tarrant, became a close friend of mine in Melbourne, long before we knew of the connection. In England the Tarrants were classic tumbledown people, that is to say farmers who fell on bad times. They were framed for an affray in the 1780s by the Marlborough banker who was the Earl of Ailesbury's agent, subsequently undertook a campaign of poaching, and saw five sons (including an army deserter) and a cousin transported together for stealing and poaching in Berkshire in 1818.[36] One of the convicts subsequently acquired by marriage a New South Wales farm and ended his life as 'a well-known fruiterer' of Mudgee. Abell and Tarrant brothers who had not been involved in the crimes were (entirely independently) gaoled for attacking the officers of the law who came to make the arrests. Members of both families continued to poach.

Finally, there was a possible arson and insurance fraud by a relative of the thrifty William Bower, previously mentioned. Almost all such incidents took place in the worsened, even desperate, circumstances during and immediately after the Napoleonic wars. They had little or no precedent in the earlier history of any of the families, nor were they representative of the behaviour of a majority of their members, then or later.

At this point we may raise the question of how criminality should be defined. Australians remain abnormally sensitive about the 'convict stain' and even now are concerned to assert what is obvious: that a proportion of convicts in the population has not poisoned the gene pool and prevented the emergence of a law-abiding and effective society.[37] Richard Haviland did well enough in Australia and the descendants of the Tarrants have been in business or the public service for generations.[38]

Does this imply that genetically coded entrepreneurial tendencies lay buried deep beneath their crimes, to spring up again as entrepreneurship did in China after the reforms of Deng Xiao-ping? Should criminality be redefined as entrepreneurship? It is nothing if not enterprising. Crime does not however create a bourgeois economy, which requires contractual certainty. In any case, if genes were involved, is it not more likely that the traits of enterprise and effort were so diffused that almost anyone might respond to fresh opportunities or be driven to crime?

Consequences

Anthony Wagner, who presaged part of Clark's thesis, says endogamy in the ruling class spreads genetic characteristics within it more evenly and reinforces its class character.[39] It seems unlikely that comparable homogeneity could have been achieved within the yeomanry, described by Wagner as 'an estate of people almost peculiar to England living in the temperate zone between greatness and want'. Like the rank of gentleman which, it is said, attached to anyone who could 'bear the port of a gentleman', the title of yeoman was assumed by anyone who could persuade his neighbours to accept it. Yeomen had an interest in keeping their children around them for the traditional reasons of old age insurance, cheap labour, and continuity of the farm business. They were covetous of land and the dictum of Tennyson's Northern Farmer's applies: property, property. They liked their sons to marry local farmers' daughters, which may have happened anyway in tiny local marriage pools. But yeomen did not invariably succeed in keeping marriage within strict class bounds.

The essence of success, then and later, was as much a matter of non-market competition as of competition in the commercial marketplace. The practice of lettings on three lives kept farms off the market for long periods, restricting agricultural opportunity. Land did not automatically fall into the hands of people who may have intended to make more productive use of it. The Havilands and Joneses will have taught their children how to manage farms but more profitable lessons would have been how to marry advantageously and curry favour from social superiors. Jane Austen gets closer to the heart of English life than many a history book.

If values were formative, why did the families in the sample make a poor job of transferring them to effect? The families were immensely more prosperous in early periods than they were later to become. They conveyed neither the facility of securing patronage nor (despite retaining the work ethic) of maintaining prosperity. All of them entered spells lasting two or more centuries when their occupations became pedestrian, finally falling to the humblest levels. The early exceptions were mainly people who emigrated to the United States.

Despite Clark's emphasis on the transfer of talent between the generations and his view that the dispersion of economic abilities was reduced over time, neither genes nor inherited culture conferred much advantage during the economic expansion of the 19th century.[40] We might concentrate more usefully on the demand side (the openings available to talent) than on the supply. Family fortunes did not recover until the 20th century. Early efforts at betterment fell foul of a sequence of occupations that looked promising but one after the other became over-staffed and subject to declining real incomes — carpentery, iron-moulding, the assembling and repairing of cars.

During the 20th century the most notable ascents in single lifetimes were those of a William Jones and Albert Mansbridge. William Jones's father had been apprenticed as a carpenter before founding a small building firm.[41] William left school at 14 but married a schoolteacher who persuaded him to go to night school, where (astonishingly) he learned critical path theory and the turnpike theorem. These he put to use in quantity surveying and gave the firm a competitive advantage. He crowned his career by becoming President of the National Federation of Building Trades Employers. Albert Mansbridge, descendant of a long line of farmers but likewise the son of a carpenter, founded the WEA (Workers' Educational Association). He wrote several books, received an honorary M.A. from Oxford, and was father of the painter, John Mansbridge, some of whose works hang in the National Portrait Gallery.[42]

Widening the focus to other families, the best explanation of their 'recovery' was the opportunity afforded by the 1944 Education Act. Depending on how widely among the descendants the net is cast (I do not have information about all of them), there are or recently have been academics, schoolteachers, authors, doctors, dentists, civil servants, computer programmers and a mayor of Southampton. Is the revival explicable by latent genes, inherited culture or both — characteristics that mysteriously hung fire during the downhill generations?

The variety of temperament and attainments among descendants of the families was and is considerable. The great-grandfather of the lawyer and Tory landowner who became lieutenant governor of Prince Edward Island (Thomas Heath Haviland, 1822–1895) was brother of the horse thief transported to Australia. No-one who belongs to a family will be surprised by the discrepancy nor by big discrepancies within single generations. No common culture, unless vacuously defined, and no common genes seem likely to explain the dispersion of personal outcomes.

Wagner asked whether circumstances bring particular types of men to the top.[43] They may. Temperaments not only vary, they change. They were notoriously volatile during the Middle Ages and calmed down later. 'Pressure towards foresight and self-constraint' is explained in the theory of Norbert Elias as stemming from market relationships, to which may be added the effects of political pacification and the rise of secular law.[44] These influences were external to the individual and suggest that personality and behaviour were moulded and expressed within particular sets of circumstances.

Circumstances were not propitious for the majority of family members who stayed in rural southern England. As Richard Rumbold declared on the scaffold in 1686, 'the mass of mankind has not been born with saddles on their backs nor a favoured few booted and spurred, ready to ride them'.[45] But the time had past for egalitarian sentiments. In southern England the landowners maintained a society of nepotism and patronage. Investment in public education was woefully inadequate. Established society was efficiently replicated generation after generation.

Without greater market expansion than was forthcoming, most people would be held by a sort of reverse Peter Principle in situations beneath their capacity, where any ingenuity they possessed made small difference. Joseph Ferrie found from census data that whereas over 80 per cent of unskilled males in the United States moved to higher-paying occupations between 1850 and 1920, in Britain fewer than 51 per cent did so.[46] Only fresh opportunities would reveal England's buried talent and enable other than the most exceptional individuals to improve their lot.[47] Occasional very bright children from these families won some of the vanishingly small number of grammar school scholarships before the war, but the 1944 Act was the first time the net was spread widely enough to make a real difference.

An apparent defect of Clark's thesis is that it is couched at the national level and cannot cope with divergent regional experiences. The potent values supposedly spread by the downwardly mobile were not enough to preserve, let alone renew, industry in the south. Yet Clark's hypothesis may perhaps be saved by arguing that enterprise was not snuffed out there but was switched from manufacturing to farming, agricultural processing, the communications sector and the service occupations required for their smooth operation.

In the sample examined here, outcomes relative to income (or wealth) class and downward occupational mobility partially conform to Clark's thesis. Whether these features diffused bourgeois values through society and whether those values explain economic results are different matters. The dispersion of personal fortunes suggests that no tight complex of values was transmitted or that, if it was, social circumstances cramped its expression. As McCloskey observes, the 'virtue' of the Middle Ages was less bourgeois values than skill at acquiring patronage. The Havilands and Joneses lived by that until their luck ran out. Genetics and culture were sidelines compared with economic opportunity.

Endnotes

1. G. Clark, *A Farewell to Alms* (Princeton: Princeton University Press, 2007).
2. D. McCloskey, 'You know, Ernest, the rich are different from you and me': a comment on Clark's A Farewell to Alms, *Eur. Rev. Econ. Hist.* **12**: 138–148, 2008.
3. E. L. Jones, *Growth Recurring: Economic Change in World History* (Ann Arbor: University of Michigan Press, 2000, second edition).
4. R. Solow, Review of Clark, *A Farewell to Alms*, in *The New York Review*, Nov. 2007.
5. But see J. R. T. Hughes, *The Vital Few: The Entrepreneur & American Economic Progress* (New York: OUP, 1986, enlarged edition).
6. Gertrude Himmelfarb, *On Looking into the Abyss: Untimely Thoughts on Culture and Society* (New York: Alfred A. Knopf, 1994), pp. 42–44.
7. See S. Mennell, *The American Civilizing Process* (Cambridge: Polity, 2007), p. ix.
8. E. L. Jones, 'Tumbledown People: What Use is Family History?' *NIAS Newslett.* **35**: (Fall), 9–11, 2005.

9. *Observer Magazine*, 16 Oct 2005.
10. J. H. Round, *Studies in Peerage and Family History* (New York: Longman Green, 1901, vol. 2).
11. J. H. Round, *Peerage and Pedigree Studies* (London: James Nisbet, 1910), p. xii.
12. Inappropriate levels of abstraction are criticised in K. Basu, E. Jones and E. Schlicht, The growth and decay of custom: the role of the new institutional economics in economic history, *Explor. Econ. Hist.* **24**: 17–18, 1987. E. L. Jones, Economic adaptability in the long term, in Tony Killick (ed.), *The Flexible Economy* (London: Routledge, 1995), p. 98.
13. J. de Vries, Review of Clark, A Farewell to Alms, in *J. Econ. Hist.* pp. 1180–1181, 2008.
14. A. Camp, *Everyone Has Roots* (London: W H Allen, 1978), p. 83.
15. I have also received valuable research assistance concerning Berkshire and Hampshire from Stephanie Albery.
16. Quoted by Camp, *Everyone Has Roots*, p. 147.
17. E. Gibbon, *Memoirs of My Life* (Harmondsworth, Middlesex: Penguin, 1984), p. 41.
18. The originating family stayed in Wales, eventually changing its name to Herbert. The last male heir was an M.P. and First World War general but the line became extinct when his daughter died without issue.
19. P. McKay, The book of the clerk, *J. Inst. Geneal. Heraldic Studies* 20(167) (April 2001) to 21(173) (October 2002).
20. Berkshire Record Office: D/P109/15/2.
21. A. Jones, *The Cotswolds* (Chichester: Phillimore, 1994), pp. 107–108. In genealogical terms the daughters were by Simon Milbourn out of his wife.
22. P. Razzell and C. Spence, The hazards of wealth: adult mortality in pre-twentieth century England, *Soc. Hist. Med.* **19**(3): 381–405, 2006. See also their letter in *Int. J. Epidemiol.*, 3 March 2005, and the reply by Simon Szreter.
23. The sizes of the families may be undercounted for lack of full data in the parish registers. Birth dates were seldom cited for women, whose first appearance was when they 'married in'.
24. Vegard Skirbekk *et al.*, 'From rich, large families to childless success. Why and to which extent the status-fertility relation reversed', Research Training Network Meeting, Vienna, 2005 (Extended abstract on Google Scholar).
25. Y. E. Hong, Ancestor worship, *Finan. Times Mag.* 27 May 2006.
26. The families were Abell, Batt, Bower, Cook, Goater, Habgood, Haviland, Jones, Mansbridge, Noyes and Tarrant. The sources are so numerous and fragmentary that it would serve no good purpose to reference them all; the Victoria County Histories and county archives are the best places to start. Some family trees are available on the Internet.

27. The lease of Mildenhall Warren in 1586 is printed by J. Bettey (ed.), *Wiltshire Farming in the Seventeenth Century* (Trowbridge: Wiltshire Record Society, Vol. 57, 2005), p. 296.

28. E. C. Elwell, Account of the Manor of Stratton St. Margaret (MS., n.d., Wiltshire Studies Library).

29. J. E. Jackson (ed.), *Wiltshire: The Topographical Collections of John Aubrey* (Devizes: Wiltshire Archaeological Society, 1862), p. 339. In the 1590s, William Jones owned the manor of Milton Lilbourne and it is possible that the conflict was related to the fact that he sued his neighbour at Fyfield Manor for a large, unpaid debt. There was a subsequent enquiry into the deceased Jones property to determine what feudal rights might be said to belong to the Crown. G. S. Fry and E. A. Fry (eds.), *Abstracts of Wiltshire Inquisitiones Post Mortem ... Charles the First* (London: Wiltshire Archaeological Society, 1901), pp. 120–124.

30. The steps whereby the yeomen swallowed up their small neighbours, only to be bought out in turn by men with outside capital, is well described for a next-door village by N. S. B. Gras and E. C. Gras, *The Economic and Social History of an English Village (Crawley, Hampshire) A.D. 909–1928* (Cambridge, Mass.: Harvard University Press, 1930).

31. J. Habgood-Everett, *Habgood Versus Habgood in Chancery* (Orpington: Latton Publications, 1995).

32. J. Stevens, *A Parochial History of St Mary Bourne, Hants* (London: Whiting and Co., 1888), p. 210.

33. P. Wardley (ed.), *Bristol Historical Resource CD* (2000).

34. L. Stone, A Life of Learning, The Charles Homer Haskins Lecture of the ACLS, 1985, p. 13.

35. Cited by S. Ogilvie, Can we rehabilitate the guilds? A sceptical reappraisal, *CWPE* **0745**: 15, September 2007.

36. By an astonishing coincidence, one of the gamekeepers was my three-greats grandfather and one of the poachers was Michael Tarrant's three-greats grandfather. This was the Tarrant who acquired the farm in Australia.

37. *The Age*, 26 Jan 2009.

38. One of the Tarrants re-offended in Australia and was sent to the punishment camp of Norfolk Island. Curiously, when Haviland became Castrator of Government Stock his manager was Thomas Arkell, who, having been born at Cutsdean, Gloucestershire, may have known, or known of, Richard Haviland. Cutsdean was 15 miles from Winstone as the crow flies. Perhaps there was patronage in the colonies too.

39. A. Wagner, *Pedigree and Progress: Essays in the Genealogical Interpretation of History* (London: Phillimore, 1975), p. 25.

40. G. Clark, In defense of the Malthusian interpretation of history, *Eur. Rev. Econ. Hist.* **12**: 187, 2008.
41. Anon, *Built by Jones: J. M. Jones and Sons, Maidenhead 1918–1968* (London: Newman Neame, 1968).
42. Some are reproduced in *Encyclopaedia Britannica.*
43. Wagner, *Pedigree and Progress*, p. 116. As the legal owners of real estate and as the dominant sex, the word men is correct here.
44. Mennell, *American Civilizing Process*, p. 110.
45. Quoted by G. Holmes in J. Cannon (ed.), *The Whig Ascendancy* (London: Edward Arnold, 1981), p. 9.
46. Quoted in *The Economist*, 11 June 2005.
47. On suppressed talent in the working classes, see K. Amis, cited in E. L. Jones, *Cultures Merging: A Historical and Economic Critique of Culture* (Princeton University Press, 2006), p. 239.

CHAPTER 7

DE-INDUSTRIALISATION AND THE LANDED SYSTEM

The causes which lie behind this long 'dying fall' of the [Berkshire clothing] industry must therefore be sought mainly in the 17th century. The developments of the Industrial Revolution after 1780, with new sources of power developed mainly near the coalfields of the north, are much too late to be considered in this connection.

R. F. Dell, 1954

Southern de-industrialisation involved hundreds or thousands of closures of small manufacturing businesses, most barely documented, their individual histories scarcely recoverable. References to them read like paragraphs in yellowing newspapers, of passing interest, and then only to local residents. Alternatively they are summarised at a high level of abstraction, ready to be dismissed as collateral damage in the onrush of the industrial revolution. The other side of the coin has been ignored to an even greater extent: the establishment of new businesses in the agricultural sector. These firms have left equally little documentary trace but we may at least consider the circumstances in which they arose.

Sectoral Adjustment

The south, meaning lowland England, had a *site advantage* in the form of gentler slopes, better soils and lower rainfall than the north, that is, the highland zone west of the Tees-Exe line. The north's agricultural environment, at least where concentrations of industrial mills first developed, was relatively unattractive. It was not accidental that the Lancashire mills were so often built by local yeomen who spied opportunities for entering industry whereas southern farmers stuck to their last. The Liverpool economic geographer, Wilfred Smith, wrote of the West Yorkshire clothing districts, 'the agricultural poverty of the district was evident'.[1] These districts were bleaker and less fruitful than East Anglia, the West Country or the Vale of York (which despite its northern location also lay within the English Plain rather than in the Highland Zone). Not every northern district was agriculturally disadvantaged; some were destined to achieve the highest per acre crop yields in the country, but that tended to await the growth of demand from the large northern industrial cities.

Until the northern cities expanded, the great food market remained London, for which the south had the *locational advantage* too. Improved communications across the region were increasingly aimed at making it easier to convey agricultural produce to London. Associated with this flow was the processing of food and brewing of drink. Granaries and maltings were placed by rivers and canals to reduce the bulk to be carried. Growing, gathering, processing, shipping and carrying agricultural goods created business opportunities not only for farmers but also for professionals such as lawyers and auctioneers. A few of their businesses have survived, sometimes under different names: auctioneering firms such as Dreweatt Neate of Newbury and Moore & Sons of Tewkesbury were founded as long ago as the 1750s. Most such firms lack early documentation, though solicitors in Berkshire still hold the early 18th-century deeds of Jethro Tull's Prosperous Farm at Shalbourne.

Since the agricultural sector demanded and rewarded service personnel, their elegant Georgian houses in market towns and many villages, together with the growing civic amenities and mannered society of the era, are perfectly explicable. Food processing and transportation drew increasing amounts of capital and promised returns to local investors that seemed preferable to industry. Lowerson notes that the opportunities for substantial investment in Sussex were limited and capital tended to go into the canalisation of rivers or turnpiking with the aim of moving farm produce, rather than into industry.[2] As to Kent, 'there are but few *manufactures* in this country', said Hasted's *History and Topographical Survey* in 1797, 'as well owing to the great attention paid to agriculture and grazing, as to the great number of easy and lucrative employments in the disposal of government ...'[3] Either way, Kentish funds did not pour into industry. In Essex, Thomas Griggs (1701–1760) moved from producing textiles to speculating in real estate, fattening livestock and malting barley.[4] Likewise in Hampshire, where James Wyatt had profitably built ships in the 1740s, his descendants went in for farming.[5]

The eventual extent of the adjustment to expanding food markets is undoubted but its pace may possibly be exaggerated, as Everitt pointed out for the 17th century and Pawson for the 18th century.[6] Piecing their remarks together, a picture emerges in which before 1660 only 'islands' of southern development were in contact with the London market, whereas during the first half of the 18th century only undeveloped 'islands' remained isolated from it. Occasional pockets of awkward land resisted taming even later. One was the surprisingly lawless area a few miles south of Newbury, despite the fact that this was a town well connected to London. From 1830 into the 1840s the pocket of recalcitrant land was turned into residential estates by Rev. John Harvey Ashworth, a clergyman-cum-land speculator.

The Diversions of Landownership

Capital obtained from political favours, court offices, government sinecures, the law and trade entered the southern countryside, as successful men sought to fix their position by buying estates. Most gentrified or made sure their sons did, not that their social arrival necessarily debarred continued searches for offices of profit. A piquant example was the Rushouts of Blockley. This originally Huguenot family introduced silk throwing to Blockley and continued to own the mills while residing nearby at Northwick Park. From this land-locked, semi-industrial, semi-rural position an 18th-century member of the family, St. John Rushout, contrived to become treasurer of the Navy.[7] More commonly, the purchasers of estates became rentiers and concentrated on rural affairs.

The sources of capital for purchasing estates were innumerable, comprising almost every post, profession or business capable of making substantial sums of money.[8] In an ample number of cases this represented the return of a younger son of a landed family, now able to flaunt his metropolitan achievement to the people among whom he had grown up and whose good opinion he sought (or whose noses he wished to rub in the glory of his success) by buying land where the system of primogeniture had meant he inherited none.

This is not to imply that every fortune created in London or Bristol was deposited in the countryside but many were, perhaps most of the very large ones. Profits from the Bristol slave trade were poured into landed property; Donn's map of 1769 marks 'houses of note' within 12 miles of the city, many with African or West Indian associations, and there were others much further out.[9] Northern industrialists sometimes bought land in their own region with fortunes made in the dark, satanic mills but increasingly they came south. Having bought an estate, they usually wanted to shake off the concerns of business, not wishing to have to go on watching, as one of them said, 'either personally, or by deputy, the processes by which 6d. a piece is to be gained, or 2/6 to be lost, in the production of beggarly printed calicoes'.[10]

Not all fortunes were, so to speak, ruralised and a new species of urban bourgeoisie also arose in the 18th century. Some small towns developed communities of rich residents, for example the 'Dawleish circle' in Devon, whose members had colonial connections and supported Australian exploration. People such as these have been called pseudo-gentry, which seems harsh given their prior military, administrative and professional attainments.

Histories of estate purchases are bedevilled by the choice of different sets of examples from different periods, but the abiding impression is that monetary return was not the attraction. Farm rents may have been important to the lesser gentry, whose cumulative wealth determined that before the Restoration, maybe later, the bulk of English wealth still rested in provincial hands.[11] Incomers with funds from London were another species and had grander ambitions. Once the fashion for blood sports took hold among them, there seems to have been little variance about the mean of their behaviour. They have attracted more attention than the small Tory gentry, not because there were more of them but because they were usually richer and set on making a splash in the countryside. They represented dynamic exchange between the larger economy and rural England rather than any sluggish continuity.

The 'fleering' contempt of the cavaliers, and Puritans as well, for their social inferiors was noted at the time of the Civil Wars. During the late 17th century class distinctions hardened in the provinces, while in the 18th century the number of lesser gentry melted away. Many a landowner became sunk in debt as a result of excessively ornamenting his estate and pursuing the extravagant lifestyle that went with it. The purpose of ownership included gaining political influence in the shires (less exacting and cheaper than politics at Westminster), and acquiring social position, this being bolstered by participating in fox-hunting, coursing, game-bird shooting and angling. Yet absentee landlords, their estates left in the none-too-tender hands of agents, also became a recognised and much criticised category.

For the majority of purchasers who settled in the countryside, blood sports were a prime attraction. As a self-serving judge declared in 1820, 'if you do not allow men of landed estate to preserve their game' — set man-traps and spring-guns — 'you will not prevail on them to reside in the country. Their poor neighbours will thus lose their protection ...'[12] The farming routines of the tenants took second place to the owner's pastimes.[13] Landowners, among whom were the rich 'squarsons' of the Church of England, rode roughshod over their tenants and dominated the society in their districts, which is not surprising given their elevated rank in the distribution of income. A single example of this will do — and not from the higher reaches of landownership either: at East Lockinge, Berkshire, the value of the Rector's annual hogshead of red wine in the early 18th century equalled the yearly earnings of a male worker.[14]

Before we come to the economic effects of the landowning system, consider the attitudes of landed proprietors as a class. They could do much as they pleased. An example is the layout of the church at Well, Lincolnshire (east of the Tees-Exe line). This is a Palladian structure modelled on St. Paul's, Covent Garden, and was erected in 1733 as part of the redevelopment of the Well estate. In the fashion of London money buying land, Well belonged to Sir James Bateman, member of a merchant family; he or an ancestor had been Lord Mayor of London. His architect located Well church on a line-of-sight from the front of the big house, to present a temple-like appearance when viewed from the windows of the house. This meant having the entrance at the east end of the church. With extraordinary effrontery the architect (presumably at the instigation of his employer) placed the altar *at the west end*.

The example of Well is exceptional but if a landowner could so trample on established church practice, was there any meanness he might not do on a whim? Very few, it seems. When William Benson (1682–1754), son-in-law of a Bristol slaver, lost his seat in Parliament for a misdemeanour, he stood again for Shaftesbury, Dorset. He received only four votes, whereupon he immediately turned off the town's water supply.[15] When Lord Fortescue gave the medieval glass from Tattershall church, Lincolnshire, to Lord Exeter in 1757, the villagers objected strongly. But Fortescue's steward defaulted on his promise to reglaze the windows, 'as it would only please the people, who have no concern therein, as the chancel belongs entirely to my Lord'. The church was left open to the weather for 50 years.[16] At Milton Abbas, Dorset,

Joseph Damer made sure that a house belonging to someone who defied him was flooded during the creation of an artificial lake.

Stewards were even more high-handed than their employers and possessed unchecked authority when working for absentee landowners. In the abuse of power in the countryside the Church of England was similarly complicit. Richard Jefferies described it as a 'huge octopus' sucking the strength out of the land in the form of tithes.[17] At a petty but still telling level, according to the diarist Francis Kilvert, the Rector of Langley Burrell used to watch the boys playing football on Sunday afternoons and, when the ball came near him, snatch it up and plunge his knife into the bladder.

Rev. John Keble, author of the then best-selling *The Christian Year*, and his Gloucestershire neighbours, the Hicks Beach family, were among the rich people eager to suppress the common man's alehouse. Another Gloucestershire clergyman wrote to his patron in 1859, 'I succeeded at length in entirely abolishing the races, banishing the stable, suppressing the public house, closing the shops on Sunday, and putting an end to the Sunday games and sports, and wrestling, boxing, cock-fighting and cricketing which had been usual on the village green.'[18] Mary Sturge Gretton's view later in the 19th century was that in curtailing the pleasures of the poor the Sunday Observance movement had a lot to answer for. She entered into detail on the efforts that shut down Wychwood Fair.

Contrary to common opinion, new landowners were not necessarily cold-shouldered by rural society.[19] Deep pockets made origins in trade acceptable, especially if they were good for loans and the new family would play by the norms of rural sport and entertainment. A desire to insert their children into county society made that probable. The upper reaches of society were always comprised of successive layers of entrants. Here is an entry scratched in his diary by crotchety old John Biddulph, of the bankers Biddulph and Cox, an investor in Mexican mining and a landowner in Herefordshire. After dining in 1833 with 'Ricardos, Col: Drummonds Webbs; Dowdeswells &c.', he wrote, 'I could not help looking round the Table and thinking of the Private History of Each Family, all living in Luxury and opulence, all well received in the best Company which their Education & Conduct deserve, & yet more than half would have been Excluded a Century ago ... but Such is the alteration of times — Two of the Ladies Natural Children — One Gent & Wife are Uncle and neice (sic) — one the Son of a Peasant of the lowest Grade'.[20] The appropriate text for this is Goldsmith's *She Stoops to Conquer* (first produced in 1773) which, though ostensibly about the barriers of class, may be read as showing money could surmount them.

The male descendants of the newcomers were soon socialised as country gentlemen, fixated on sport, detached from the day-to-day management of wealth, and less businesslike or entrepreneurial than their forebears. They had joined Veblen's Leisure Class. Against this may be cited the involvement of midland and northern landowners in canal building, urban development and mining. Yet many of those ventures seem to have been responses to special expectations of profit, in other words adaptations to opportunities that just happened to arise on or near their properties. Newcomers to the land were more concerned to seal their arrival by remodelling their estates for the ends of conspicuous consumption. They did not wish to remain within sight of the factory chimney.

The usual illustration of landowners' desires relates to their role in enclosing the common fields, but there is a better test which has not been utilised by scholars: road capture. With enclosure the aim may have been either to appropriate a larger share of the land or to bring about a rise in productivity, or both, but privatisations of rights of way suffered from no such ambivalence. They afforded no public benefit. Gains in productivity did not enter into it. The highway was not a physical strip of land maintained for the use of traffic.[21] It was a legal concept, a 'right of passage' for every subject of the crown over another's land, solely for the purpose of passing and re-passing, but this changed in the 18th century. Public authorities thereafter shifted or straightened roads to accommodate new patterns of traffic in ways they hoped would be socially beneficial, but where roads were closed or turned by a private party at the expense of all others we are dealing with dis-improvement and the judicial theft of the subject's rights.

Diversions and closed rights of way were and are astonishingly common. The direct routes of early times have often been blocked, although the evidence is sometimes hard to find beneath later landscape features. As Kipling wrote in 'The Way through the Woods', a poem which if taken literally would refer to a closure in the 1820s:

> They shut the road through the woods
> Seventy years ago
> Weather and rain have undone it again,
> And now you would never know …

But there is a large category of examples where the evidence may be found, once one realises what to look for. The road system contains hundreds of sharp, inconvenient, unnecessary and dangerous bends where the original route has been captured by a landowner and the road diverted. The rolling English road was not made by the rolling English drunkard; Chesterton's poem was wrong about that. It was made by powerful men seizing public property. With a full quarter of England in estates of over 10,000 acres by the 1870s, landowners had infinite opportunity to usurp rights of way for their private ends.

Standard theory postulates that privatisation was vital for economic growth, on the grounds that assets in individual hands will be put to their most productive use, free from the hindrances of multiple ownership. The assumption slips in that this is what actually happens. Yet privatisation does not automatically have this effect. When individuals diverted roads or paths they were not channelling over-exploited common resources into individual productive use but the exact opposite; they were abstracting them from everyday use and redirecting them for the frivolous purpose of embellishing parks and pleasure grounds, besides fencing off *hoi polloi*. Landowners typically cared nothing for inconveniencing other users by making their journeys roundabout.

The legal requirement that two magistrates must agree to a diversion was no safeguard. Occasional personal antagonisms apart, neighbouring magistrates would sign the necessary orders on one another's behalf, since diversions seldom discommoded the well-to-do in their carriages or on their horses. Some county record offices are full of highway diversion certificates, which usually recite the formulaic claim that altering a given route was in the public interest, even when patently it was not. Lists would be tedious but there is plenty of evidence.[22] Few members of the public were likely to stand up to a landowner if he wished to make his ground more private; local people were all too likely to be dependent on his patronage or employment.

The proprietors of land were free to be overbearing. Only rarely might they meet their match, as one did in Gloucestershire in 1826.[23] There, a nephew of Col. Kingscote approached a surveyor for the Ordnance Survey and demanded, 'in a most haughty tone of voice', what he was doing along the course of a road. He abused the surveyor in foul language, threatening to knock him down and beat his brains out with the butt of his gun. The surveyor's brother complained to Col. Kingscote, threatening 'other modes of redress', perhaps a duel, if the reply were unsatisfactory: 'My Brother demanded his name, and, upon Mr Kingscotes giving it, observed, I thought so, — concluding that no one but a Man of consideration in the County would act in such a manner.' Col. Kingscote did apologise for his nephew but it is unlikely he would have apologised to someone who did not turn out — as the surveyor did — to be the son of a general.

If road capture has been overlooked by historians, the large-scale establishment of pleasure parks and sporting estates is recognised, but even here the implications have seldom been brought out. One result was that some land was taken out of productive use and on much of the remainder blood sports interfered with farming routines.[24] A reduced use of agricultural resources was thus an unintended result of London's growth, a negative feedback from the depositing of metropolitan capital in the land and a perverse drag on the very growth that the capital's food market had set in motion.

Country houses were built and rebuilt on a scale hardly imaginable from the number surviving in the modern landscape, though that is an appreciable total, despite 1,116 having been demolished in the less-than-salad years of 1875 to 1974.[25] House building was not as materially unproductive as medieval church building had been but was hardly the equivalent of investing in houses for the populace at large, let alone investing in factories. Around their mansions, landowners extended ornamental parks in which farming was reduced to the desultory grazing of cattle or sheep to keep down the tall grass. The number of parks established in the Home Counties virtually doubled between 1760 and 1820.[26]

Few places had a village Hampden to stand up against the drastic changes in land use that establishing parks involved. Modifying the landscape mostly went unchecked, although Thomas Raikes (a governor of the Bank of England who was apparently also engaged in the slave trade) did find himself taken to court, and lost the case, when he tried to drain the pond on which the village of Daglingworth, Gloucestershire, depended for water. And, not content with appropriating everything they could, landowners wished to monopolise the view itself. At Eaton Hastings (Berkshire, now Oxfordshire) Rev. Richard Rice removed an entire island in the Thames opposite his land. At Nethercote in Lewknor, Oxfordshire, a landowner demolished the village school because it obstructed his outlook.[27] As *The Buildings of Oxfordshire* remarks, 'C18 landowners who required the fashionable ideal landscape on their estate had little social conscience'.[28]

The greatest name associated with this wave of development was that of the landscape designer, 'Capability' Brown, who was no innovator but operated on a grander scale and at more locations than his predecessors. Brown worked for clients in the Home Counties, south-central England and the South Midlands, only occasionally venturing north of the Trent. On their estates, landowners subordinated all to the romantic prospect. To extend his park, says Maurice Beresford, the Earl of Nottingham gave up £600 per year in farm rents, 'as the price of his satisfied eye'.[29] Goldsmith caught the spirit of the age in 'The Deserted Village' (1770), where,

The man of wealth and pride
Takes up a space that many poor supplied.

Goldsmith stoutly defended the accuracy of his observations but there was no call for his nervousness; examples are there to be traced on the ground, or their archaeological remains are, the type specimen being Milton Abbas, Dorset.

Around the parks, walls were built. Around Fonthill, Wiltshire, William Beckford had a wall erected that was 12 feet high and seven miles long.[30] He had the Nine Miles Walk cut, planted one million trees on either side, and turned a fishpond into a lake. This was in the 1790s and was funded by the fortune his ancestors had gained from the sugar plantations. Beckford was extreme but not unique: read Pevsner's account of the Duke of Portland's building works at Welbeck Abbey.[31] The walls that surround parkland are visible on any journey through the English countryside.

Inside the parks lay stables and kennels larger and better designed than most estate cottages, the stables often matching the big house in style. In a later period, Nancy Mitford was obliged to admit that at Asthall, Oxfordshire, 'there was water & electric light in the stable but not the cottages'.[32] The scale of values was plain. The skimping of materials and workmanship is to be seen in the servants' quarters of great houses open to the public; for example Pugin's half-finished Gothic monstrosity at Woodchester Mansion, Gloucestershire, which was commissioned by a Liverpool shipowner. Many parks also contained follies or sham ruins that cost more to put up than cottages.

R. H. Tawney said that the 'bloody minded barons' had been muzzled by Henry VII and thereafter turned to hunting and capitalist farming. Thus began their abandonment of violent politics that the Civil Wars only temporarily reversed. Men who had been extruded from national politics or dropped back into county affairs after the wars, together with the incomers who rusticated themselves in the course of self-gentrification, engaged thereafter in displacement activities. They expended their energies on park landscapes, took a prying interest in genealogy and heraldry, and engaged in what has been termed cultural capture by filling their houses with Italian statuary and paintings acquired on the Grand Tour.[33] These were diversions from productive activity and sinks for money made outside the landed sector. The students of country house building, Wilson and Mackley, find that the role of landowners in industrial, agricultural and transport investment has been exaggerated.[34] Most were collectors, builders and gardeners, busily investing in houses, furnishings and picturesque landscapes.

Above all, though, country gentlemen became obsessed with blood sports, about which the most telling comment was made by Veblen, who understood that these pastimes had social bonding as their latent function. Without the addition of that function, 'it is quite beyond the reach of imagination,' he commented, 'that any adult male citizen would of his own motion go in for the elaborate futilities of British shooting …'[35]

For all their crazes for collecting foreign antiquities and prettifying houses and land, it was the pursuit and slaughter of birds, animals and fish that occupied the landed classes. Few went in for more creative activities, even few of the parsons, despite the Church's boast that it had placed an educated man in every parish. One Gilbert White of *Selborne* does not make a summer. An occasional family did turn to intellectual pursuits, such as the Knights, ironmasters who bought Downton Castle on the Teme in 1778, and produced a number of authors and antiquarians. But they were unusual and became more so as landed society around them dug itself into greater depths of rusticity. John Betjeman pointed out that collection-building in most country-house libraries stopped at the end of George IV's reign, except for adding works on husbandry, law, pedigrees of family and livestock, and sporting books.[36]

In their woods and policies, sporting landowners had their gamekeepers wage war against protein-starved poachers by setting mantraps, which was not made illegal until 1828. Gardens, hedged and walled to block the view in the mean English fashion, were ringed with spring-guns. It is unsurprising that people whose chief pleasure was the killing of wildlife were negligent towards the human inhabitants of the countryside, let alone towards the slaves on the sugar plantations from which a number of them had extracted their fortunes. Exceptions were just that, exceptions, as country people well knew. 'For one act of kindness in eighty years', asked Richard Jefferies, 'why should they feel grateful'?[37]

Relationships even with upper servants were at best like those with pet dogs. Employees were disposable cogs in the estate machine. A head keeper who asked the Duke of Marlborough for a day off because he was ill got a message straight back: 'The lower orders are *never* ill.' Munsche, historian of the game laws, quotes a young gentleman in Oxford who, when lamenting the death of the family gamekeeper in 1833, added that before another season was over he would have forgotten him, 'such is the extent of our sorrow for the loss of those so much below our station'.[38] Servants' personal names were changed to James or Mary to save their employers the trouble of remembering what they had been christened — a habit copied in the farm-house.[39] The dumb waiter was adopted for dessert courses at dinner in order to dispense with servants who might overhear upper-class gossip, the way news of landowner intentions still leaks out in the 21st-century countryside.

Old money is said to be more tolerant than new money but modern analysis does not bear this out.[40] Coupled with condescending attitudes was a resistance to educating the poor. Even the so-called reformer, Hannah More, described her plan of education for the working classes as 'such coarse work as may fit them for servants. I allow of no writing for the poor. My object is not to make fanatics, but to train up the lower classes in habits of industry and piety'.[41] It would be intolerable, some ladies thought, if their maids could read, for then they could not leave their letters lying about.

The standard rejoinder to criticisms of unjust behaviour in the past I shall call the *autres temps, autres moeurs* defence. It urges that circumstances were different — the past is another country. This will not do once we find, as we do, that a minority of opinion was all along opposed to the landed interest's overbearing manner. When some people, albeit a small minority, were willing to stand up and be counted over injustices, it cannot be argued that it is anachronistic to think that behaviour might have been different. Ethical issues are not time dependent. In the Christian theology to which the landowners formally subscribed, and the squarsons preached, evil is evil.

In sum, the south became a landscape of great houses and estates devoted to pleasure for the few and toil for the many. The arrival of a moneyed family on the estate, the placing of the younger sons of successive generations in church or army, the marriages with daughters of similar families from one or two counties away, are evident from the self-congratulatory plaques on the walls of village churches. They celebrate the London merchant, office holder, or lawyer who first made the money, and recount the titles, military honours and Oxford degrees of his descendants. Some families died out or lost their money, but others were always pushing upwards to replace them, adopting the colouration of the country gentry and acting as to the manor born.

Consequences of the Landowning System

What difference did this laundering of metropolitan money make to the economy of the south? Capital was withdrawn from commerce and applied to rustic futilities offering minimal social return. Astonishingly, writers at the start of the 19th century turned to decrying the landscape effects, even the landscape gardener, Humphrey Repton, sounding aghast at his old profession.[42] The indictment included the felling of timber, the enclosing of commons, the erecting of lofty palings not to keep the deer in but to keep the people out. Old benches for resting were removed, the stiles replaced by warnings about mantraps and spring guns, and notices posted by the enclosure commissioners to say the footpaths had been stopped up. This may sound like something by Oliver Goldsmith or John Clare and was indeed a continuation of the grasping privatisation about which they — and *sotto voce* Alexander Pope — had complained. Now Thomas Peacock and others added their voices. In 1860 Edward Fitzgerald, translator of the *Rubaiyat of Omar Khayyam*, was still complaining about 'the petty race of Squires' who have the 'Pathways stopt up'.[43] But no protestations halted the perpetual tradition of restricting access to the countryside.

This might have mattered little to the national economy if the removal of industrialists into the land had cleared space for new families to ascend the business ladder. That was surely the case; new men were inspired to climb. The effects on the regional economy were a different matter. Incoming capital was rarely applied to productive uses outside agriculture and even there the maximising of returns was held down in favour of sport. Funds were more likely to be spent acquiring extra land through enclosure or purchase. Landowners were efficient at passing on the commercial risks of farming to their tenants and, in a cascade of delegation, they in turn passed on as much of the risk as possible to a sort of reserve army of labour.[44]

What the landowner did not do was spend his capital on local industry. John Galt's *Annals of the Parish* (1821) noted that when a cotton mill had been built in 1788, 'some of the ancient families, in their turreted houses, were not pleased with this innovation'.[45] They frowned on the handsome houses erected for the weavers, which were altering expectations concerning desirable cottages and about working away from the farms or in domestic service. The example is Scottish but catches the mood.

The landowner was likely to have around him people for whom non-utilitarian changes were costless. Just as vernacular architectural historians regret that every new wife demands a remodelled kitchen, so a new lady of the manor would demand the latest style of house, furnishings, garden and park. Her children were likely to second these ambitions. Like charity, social climbing begins at home.

In the estate office were professional men pleased to curry favour by adorning the land. Here lurked the stewards, bailiffs and agents, eager to distance themselves from mere farming tenants and unlikely to be tender towards the poor. Agents may have prided themselves on being practical men but they were dedicated to technical agriculture and subject to what is known in agricultural economics as the 'prize marrow fallacy', whereby technical perfection is sought ahead of the level of profit. They blandly accepted that the return on investment in large estates would be lower than elsewhere in the economy and are suspected of encouraging the over-capitalisation of agriculture in the depression at the end of the 19th century.[46] In earlier times their profession had been active in promoting enclosures and suggesting to their employers the forming of ornamental layouts, establishing of plantations, and damming of streams to make lakes.

Landowners were prepared to block non-rural development if they felt able to forego the extra income. A whim could bring industrial plant in the countryside to a halt. The lease pertaining to the silk mills at Sherborne, Dorset, permitted Lord Digby to turn the Oborne water out of its course at intervals throughout the year. During the 1770s, the tenant, William Willmott, suffered repeatedly from this. Willmott could in no way persuade his lordship, 'to sink his pond water even 1/8 of an inch abt Thursday in every week just to gain a head to serve either me or my people & for no other reason than her Ladyship wishes to see their pond always full'.[47] Driven to despair, Willmott admitted, 'I had resource (sic) to the expedient of bribing the person who has care of the water, so that this week I hope to go on pretty briskly.' His was not a universal problem but the amenity motive for holding land was strong.

In addition to lavishing capital on less than maximally productive works, and occasionally blocking operations in the manner of Lord Digby, landowners did not favour industry. What they failed to do was as significant as what they actually did. They did nothing to foster a suitable workforce, being unwilling to invest in educating the rural working classes, who tumbled down from small farmers to hired hands. Large proprietors tended to own property in their neighbouring town and exert authority over its affairs. As Richard Jefferies wrote (perhaps of Cirencester, which elsewhere he called Fleeceborough), the 'Cornleigh' steward stopped up footpaths and enclosed odd corners, meaning that, 'the whole town was straitened, and a band as it were drawn tight about it so that it could scarce breathe'.[48] Such an overshadowing influence, symbolised in modern Cirencester by a high wall and the tallest yew hedge in Europe, was unfriendly to development. The landed interest could live alongside artisans and craftsmen with their backyard workshops, since they constituted little threat and supplied consumer goods. Larger manufacturers might constitute too independent a political force, their establishments sully the air, and their employees scout deference.

Brian Short claims that the attitudes of landowners were responsible for perpetuating the de-industrialisation of the Weald through treating their estates as cultural and political investments, alongside which grubby industry and disorderly workers would have sat badly.[49] Industrialists who laid out estates in the north of England felt the costs that manufacturing cities could impose through incessant poaching by factory hands. When poaching finally became insupportable in the 1870s, shooting estates moved away to the high moors — explicitly advertised by estate agents as thinly populated.[50] It was an attraction of the south that, contrary to common supposition, poaching was less there than around the northern towns.

Hence the amenity motive for estate-building goes some way towards explaining how the south had withered to the rural by Victoria's reign. Landed proprietorship created a milieu in which manufactures were disapproved and new industries unwelcome. The system of landownership was as if the countryside were held in a sort of Iron Maiden. Social and political motives for owning estates applied not merely in the Weald but throughout the south.

Endnotes

1. W. Smith, *An Economic Geography of Great Britain* (London: Methuen, second edition, 1953), p. 83.

2. Discussion in M. Palmer (ed.), *The Onset of Industrialisation* (Nottingham: University of Nottingham, 1976), p. 73.

3. Quoted by J. Whyman, Industrialisation by Fits and Starts: the Kentish Experience, in Palmer, *Onset*, p. 15.

4. K. H. Burley, An Essex clothier of the eighteenth century, *Econ. Hist. Rev.* 2 ser. **XI**: 291, 1958.

5. A. J. Holland, Shipbuilding, mainly for the Crown, in the Southampton area 1650 to 1820 (University of Southampton M.A. thesis, 1961), p. 199.

6. A. Everitt, *Change in the Provinces: the 17th Century* (Leicester: Leicester University Press, 1969), p. 38; E. Pawson, *Transport and Economy: The Turnpike Roads of 18th-Century Britain* (London: Academic Press, 1977), p. 313.

7. Monument in Blockley church.

8. H. J. Habakkuk, *Marriage, Debt and the Estates System: English Landownership, 1650–1950* (Oxford: Clarendon Press, 1994), p. 413.

9. P. Wardley (ed.), *Bristol Historical Resource CD* (2000).

10. Quoted in J. Cannon (ed.), *The Whig Ascendacy: Colloquies on Hanoverian England* (London: Edward Arnold, 1981), p. 159.

11. A. Everitt, *Change in the Provinces*, p. 16.

12. Quoted in *Transactions of the Bristol & Gloucestershire Archaeological Society*, **122**: 161, 2004.

13. E. L. Jones, Environmental effects of blood sports in Lowland England since 1750, *Rural Hist.* **20**(1): 51–66, 2009.

14. J. Collins, *The Reverend John Aldworth and His Parish of East Lockinge 1684–1729* (Wantage: The Black Swan Press, 1989), p. 81.

15. M. Longyear, William Benson Earle, Grateley Community Website.

16. M. Barley, *Lincolnshire and the Fens* (London: Batsford, 1952), p. 65.

17. R. Jefferies, *The Dewy Morn* (London: Wildwood House, 1982 [first published 1884]), p. 352.

18. J. R. Walton, The rise of agricultural auctioneering in eighteenth- and nineteenth-century Britain, *J. Hist. Geogr.* **10**(1): 27, 1984.

19. The Duke of Norfolk wrote at once to invite Richard Arkwright to dine and offered a few does to replenish the deer park when Arkwright bought Hampton Court, Herefordshire, in 1809. It was an exceptionally churlish local landowner who in 1833 still called Richard Arkwright a tradesman, when his son, John, had been appointed High Sheriff of the county in 1831. E. L. Jones, Industrial capital and landed investment: the Arkwrights in Herefordshire, 1809–43, in

E. L. Jones and G. E. Mingay (eds.), *Land, Labour and Population in the Industrial Revolution* (London: Edward Arnold, 1967), p. 60.

20. J. Biddulph's Diaries, 1828–1839, Hereford City Library 963.

21. Pawson, *Transport and Economy*, p. 65.

22. Partial lists may be extracted from county histories and similar sources; for example, F. Woodward, *Oxfordshire Parks* (Woodstock: Oxfordshire Museum Services, 1982).

23. The original letter of complaint is printed in H. P. R. Finberg (ed.), *Gloucestershire Studies* (Leicester: Leicester University Press, 1957), pp. 168–169. Should we be surprised that the track south-south eastwards from near Kingscote church to the lodge looks like an anciently privatised section of the road to Easton Grey?

24. Jones, Blood Sports.

25. R. Wilson and A. Mackley, *Creating Paradise: The Building of the English Country House 1660–1880* (London: Hambledon and London, 2000), p. 225.

26. H. C. Prince, *Parks in England* (Shalfleet, Isle of Wight: Pinhorns, 1967), pp. 7, 9.

27. F. Woodward, *Oxfordshire Parks*, p. 29. The maps and tables in this booklet make it a comprehensive study of the history of parks in a single county but with far wider implications.

28. J. Sherwood and N. Pevsner, *The Buildings of England: Oxfordshire* (New Haven, Ct.: Yale University Press, 2002), p. 417n.

29. M. W. Beresford, *History on the Ground* (London: Methuen, 1971), p. 228.

30. S. Thurley, *Lost Buildings of Britain* (London: Viking, 2004), pp. 46, 63.

31. N. Pevsner, *Nottinghamshire* (Harmondsworth, Middlesex: Penguin, 1951), pp. 196–198.

32. C. Mosley (ed.), *The Letters of Nancy Mitford* (London: Hodder & Stoughton, 1993), p. 450.

33. A. Nicolson, *Earls of Paradise: England and the Dream of Perfection* (London: HarperPress, 2008), pp. 104, 178; L. Gibson, Lecture on Landscape — A Very English Obsession, West Ox Arts Lecture, Bampton, 25 Sep. 2009.

34. R. G. Wilson and A. L. Mackley, How much did the English Country House cost to build, 1660–1880? *Econ. Hist. Rev.* **LII**(3): 466, 1999.

35. T. Veblen, *Imperial Germany and the Industrial Revolution* (London: Routledge/Thoemmes Press, 1995 [originally published 1915], p. 142.

36. J. Betjeman, *Guide to English Parish Churches* (London: HarperCollins, 1993), p. 44.

37. Jefferies, *Dewy Morn*, p. 235.

38. P. B. Munsche, The gamekeeper and English rural society, 1660–1830, *J. Br. Stud.* **XX**: 105, 1981.

39. Farmers' behaviour was harsh when labour was cheap. Examples are legion, but see S. Markham, *A Testimony of Her Times: Based on Penelope Hind's Diaries and Correspondence 1787–1838* (Salisbury: Michael Russell, 1990), p. 138.

40. V. Burris, The myth of old money liberalism: the politics of the *Forbes* 400 richest Americans, *Soc. Probl.* 47(3): 360–378, 2000.

41. Quoted by G. E. Evans, *Ask the Fellows Who Cut the Hay* (London: Faber & Faber, 1965 edition), p. 163.

42. R. Porter, *Enlightenment: Britain and the Creation of the Modern World* (London: Allen Lane The Penguin Press, 2000), pp. 317–318.

43. Quoted by J. Tennyson, *Suffolk Scene* (Bury St. Edmunds: Alastair Press, 1987 edition), p. 250.

44. D. R. Stead, Delegated risk in English agriculture, 1750–1850: the labour market, *Labour Hist. Rev.* 71(2): 128–144, 2006.

45. Quoted by H. Jennings, *Pandaemonium 1660–1886: The Coming of the Machine as Seen by Contemporary Observers* (London: Andre Deutsch, 1985), p. 88.

46. E. Richards, The land agent, in G. E. Mingay (ed.), *The Victorian Countryside* (London: Routledge & Kegan Paul, 1981), II, p. 455.

47. M. Weinstock, *Studies in Dorset History* (Dorchester: Longmans, 1953), pp. 92–93; H. Symonds, The silk industry in Wessex, *Proc. Dorset Nat. Hist. Antiq. Field Club* **XXXVII**: 68, 1916.

48. Jefferies, *Dewy Morn*, p. 134.

49. B. Short, The de-industrialisation process: a case study of the Weald, 1600–1850, in P. Hudson (ed.), *Regions and Industries: A perspective on the Industrial Revolution in Britain* (Cambridge: Cambridge University Press, 1989), p. 173.

50. H. Osborne and M. Winstanley, Rural and urban poaching in Victorian England, *Rural Hist.* 17(2): 187–212, 2006.

PART II

ECONOMIC CHANGE

CHAPTER 8

POLITICS AND IDEAS

Mercantilist regulation and pressure group politics has been rather "crowded out" by economic analysis, concerned to bring demand and supply, prices and costs to the foreground.

P. K. O'Brien, T. Griffiths and P. Hunt, 1991

Industrialisation sprouted within an economy which already had a fairly high level of investment. The progressive concentration of manufacturing reflected competition brought about by improvements in transport and communications and we shall concentrate here on the ideas and political developments that fostered them. Specifically, this requires us to consider the acceptance of market ideology and the Enlightenment, and the political changes brought by the Glorious Revolution. The effects of ideas and political change have been under-rated in economic history, while the impact of highly visible technology has been correspondingly easy to exaggerate. The earliest investments in communications did not rely on new technology, they replicated existing methods. The peculiar intensity of investment in the sector is what most needs to be explained.

The History of Thought and the Enlightenment

A widespread set of enquiring people became evident during the 18th century, some imbued with curiosity about science, others convinced that the proper study of mankind is man, many decidedly entrepreneurial in temper, and all convinced that human progress was possible. Those involved were almost all men, though a contribution by women is nowadays being recognised.[1] The individuals concerned constituted a better-informed, more educated and inter-connected elite than before, stretching down into the middle class. Some were investing on their own account but their main influence lay in the encouragement they gave to the investment community at large.

The expansion of that group can be traced a long way back, certainly from the late 16th century. Thereafter it edged up the levels of investment, invention and innovation. The availability of capital was not a serious limitation. Michael Postan observed that any 15th-century baron could have afforded to promote the early stages of the 18th-century cotton industry.[2] None felt inclined to do so. Nor did the rising bourgeoisie respond to the opportunity until later.

By the 18th century the situation had altered. Improved transport and postal services meant people were better able than before to meet and correspond, and thanks to cheaper printing to buy, read and annotate more books. Yet the mundane advantages of the Georgians are not the leading point. There had been individuals and groups like them in the 17th century too. It is conventional to trace the advent of scientific enquiry and practical thought to the Royal Society in the 1660s, but more interesting to ask what had previously impeded such activities. The answers come filtering upwards in the commotion of the Civil War, the censorship that was ended only 50 years afterwards, and the politico-religious strife that persisted into the late 17th century and beyond.

Even this does not touch the deepest point, since the potted biographies in John Aubrey's *Brief Lives*, for example, disclose a society of ferment and thought in the 17th century. Does the history of thought ground at that time? Not wholly: there was nothing inherently new about debate, though it had tended to collapse into religious conflict. Accordingly, the Renaissance, which ushered in man-centred enquiry, and the Reformation, which formalised the splintering of religion, may seem better points of outset. But if we range so far back any connection with industrialisation becomes obscure.

Locating a fixed origin would be attractive because it would end the regress from each upheaval to the one before. Yet it raises problems. First, if specialists in later periods are right to say that certain currents of thought were now vital to the production of novelties, what explains the technological changes of the High Middle Ages? Second, more fundamentally, should we really emphasise what intellectuals wrote? Every conceivable opinion was advanced by someone, and every novelty propounded, few being of practical import. Third, the extent to which currents of thought were related to market activity seems hard to assess.[3] Might it not be better to pass over conceptual arguments and restrict enquiry to economic outcomes?

A retrospective reading of the history of thought may well over-emphasise the role of intellectuals (it is after all written by bookish academics) and is probably distorted by its attachment to individuals and concepts that scholars have traditionally extolled. 'Often in the history of ideas', states Diana Stanciu, 'one aspect of an author's writings is picked up, used, and amplified by succeeding generations to the exclusion of many other (and perhaps more important) points'.[4] The best-known figures may be the ones who most deserve to be paraded but there are conventional and subjective elements in the way they are ranked. Even Hobbes and Locke have assumed a prominence they may not have attained among their contemporaries. The opinions of lesser figures are likely to be occluded. Not everyone pays attention to them, although Stanciu properly devotes a chapter of *Shaftesbury's 'Characteristics'* to her author's critics.

Compared with religious violence in the 16th century and political violence in the 17th century, the 18th century had it easy, its notions sped by legal, commercial and technological advances. At a deeper level, space was cleared as the poisoned tide of theology ebbed into stylised commentary. Non-conformists, although discriminated against, were eventually permitted to go their own way; many ministers made shift to continue preaching to the committed following their ejection from the church after the Restoration.

At first there was harassment and persecution, as witnessed by Edward Calamy, *The Nonconformist's Memorial; an account of the lives, sufferings, and printed works of the Two Thousand Ministers Ejected from the Church of England, chiefly by the Act of Uniformity, Aug. 24, 1662*.[5] But times changed. Arguments like that of Thomas Edwards, in his widely read *Gangraena* of 1646, denigrating religious toleration because it might lead wives and children to espouse religions different from the head of the household and hence break up the family, were spurned as eccentric.[6] Trimmers such as Henry Bennet, Earl of Arlington, who in 1665 advised Charles II to grant liberty of conscience but later was zealous in oppressing non-conformists, became fewer in number. Religious opinions became more lax and energy was diverted into secular life, some of the novel forbearance stemming from the need for alliances among different sects rather than from points of principle. David Hume placed the change in attitude between 1690 and 1740, a period during which Shaftesbury brought out the revised edition of his writings as the '*Characteristics*' (1711).[7]

None of this argues that progress was linear, for restrictions on enquiry had continually to be fought. The lower levels of society clung to magical beliefs after the gentry and upper clergy had discarded them. Even at the higher levels, as Roy Porter is careful to point out, there was no complete 'end of ideology' slumber. Opposition towards Roman Catholicism and the foreign powers that embraced it remained unyielding. A small example is that of the Jervoise family of Herriard, Hampshire.[8] In 1711 Thomas Jervoise moved to Leiden with his father, because of the latter's debts, but became mentally ill. It was difficult to prove his lunacy because he had lucid intervals, until he made the mistake of turning Papist and threatening to 'go to Rome to ye Pretender', whereupon his family were able to deem him lunatic enough to strip him of his inheritance for life.

When Shaftesbury wrote a *Letter Concerning Enthusiasm* (1707), urging that the principles of the Glorious Revolution and the Act of Toleration (1689) should be extended to 'enthusiasts' such as French Protestant refugees, it was a Broad Churchman, Edward Fowler, Bishop of Gloucester, who replied most angrily.[9] The direct divine inspiration in which the enthusiasts believed would compromise the status of Biblical prophecy, Fowler insisted, not to mention undermining the status of the church and its bishops. But *odium theologicum* was on the retreat. Whatever the likes of Fowler desired, vagaries of policy under Charles II and James II made the enforcing of spiritual jurisdiction difficult. Despite the ousting of dissenters after the Restoration, presentments to church courts fell rapidly from the late 1680s. Moreover, censorship was replaced by fines, which had the happy consequence of raising revenues while supposedly suppressing dissent. The fines may have been set so as to maximise revenue but were in reality too low to eradicate dissent.

In the world of ideas, honey was made in the entrails of the lion, to use an image contemporaries would have recognised. To select a later metaphor, there was a stilling of Brownian motion, but at the same time the centre of gravity of the whirling mass of ideas shifted. The covering term for what emerged is the Enlightenment, which did not wait for the texts of Montesquieu, Vico and Voltaire in the 1720s and 1730s but originated in the disputes of 1689 — a wrangling with refugees and warring with pamphlets in London clubs and coffee houses. Although this took place within the international republic of letters, the movement had 'a unique inflection in England', as Porter invokes it. The shift was evident in politics, too, with a waning of revolutionary heat in favour of incipient party politics.

Following George I's ascent in 1714, progressive ideas triumphed. Thence most opinions could be published, despite laws against blasphemy, obscenity and seditious libel which remained on the statute book, as indeed they still do. Throughout the first-third of the 18th century the most advanced ideas were English, spreading after 1745 to Scotland, where some think they reached their greatest glory with Hume and others.[10] Surprisingly, the new attitudes sanctioned the defence of the status quo, which intellectuals in most ages find less enticing than criticism.

A definition of the Enlightenment is hard to pin down. Although the term was used at the time, it had a self-congratulatory tinge which subsequent scholars have accepted a little uncritically. The word refers to what people tell us they thought, and since someone may be found saying everything conceivable, the problem of sampling is severe. How do we know which ideas were influential or that those disinterred by historians truly bore on economic action? The topic is as slippery as a greased pig. Max Weber thought that material and 'ideal' interests rather than ideas directly govern men's conduct. He immediately qualified this by saying that ideas nevertheless create 'world images' which determine the tracks in which 'the dynamic of interest' pushes action.[11] Faced with such sophistries of intellectual history, as well as the descriptive tangles of political history, an economist may be forgiven for thinking the approach of his profession is neater. Revealed preference: what was done, not what was said.

Ordinarily my inclination would lean this way, perhaps citing the fact that the protective duties of 1689 to 1786 were levied just when free trade views were being expressed.[12] This is a case where the lack of connection between word and deed is entirely plain. Yet there seems no doubt that rent-seeking — the seeking of gain by means other than the market — did beat something of a retreat during the 18th century. For this no adequate theory seems to exist and further discussion is needed.

Corruption

From rent-seeking a step further along the road to perdition is corruption. English society was corrupt enough. Was it becoming less so and did reducing corruption help the economy to grow? Surprisingly, the question may be put the other way round: may it not have been that growth was becoming sufficient to absorb the costs of corruption? Were bribes a form of transfer payment which, despite diverting contracts from the people who were best equipped to carry them out, proved too insubstantial to weigh a buoyant economy down?

That there was a good deal of corruption is undoubted. Government granted sinecures to favourites and paid unearned emoluments and pensions out of the public purse.[13] Undeserving individuals in what might be called the upper elite, such as the Bathursts, acquired a great deal of cash. Over a 40-year period two families alone received between them sums approximating to the cost of governing the young United States. A well-paid set of ludicrously archaic positions survived, courtesy of the taxpayer. These anomalies persisted until at least the second quarter of the 19th century, when accumulated reforms (individually none was decisive) finally curbed them.

Hence the system was at length reformed, or reformed itself. By the middle of the 19th century the Old Corruption, as Cobbett labelled it, had more or less evaporated. Possibly the elite had saved its political power from evaporating along with it by putting its house in order, pre-empting attacks from Whigs such as the banker, Robert Biddulph, and from the Evangelicals.[14] By mid-Victorian times the state was a minimalist affair and the civil service relatively purposeful, very different from the military-fiscal state of the 18th century. The point is that it was under the old arrangements that growth and industrialisation had gained a head start. This is the oddity: corruption had not been sufficient to sink industrialisation during its most vulnerable years.

Is a high level of corruption then tolerable? Economists make no bones about it: it is intolerable, distorting activity, rewarding those whose only claim to efficiency lies in manipulating the political system, imposing what is effectively a tax on consumers and other producers, and above all cutting the total level of investment.[15] The subject has attracted attention in recent years from Transparency International, which publishes an annual list of countries ranked by how clean businesspeople think they are as places for commercial transactions. The Scandinavian countries and New Zealand repeatedly top the list, while Nigeria, Indonesia and China jostle at the bottom. But China cannot be accused of a low growth rate. It remains moot how much higher still the rate might be if Chinese society were ruled by independent law.

Defenders of corruption, including MBA students from less-developed countries, repeatedly assert that bribes 'grease the wheels' of business. They see bribery as a routine cost of competition and do not reckon the macro effect. The opinion is an old one, perhaps as old as corruption itself. That shrewd observer, Cecil Torr, a former barrister who became a landowner in late 19th- and early 20th-century Devon, claimed that inefficiency in public bodies was a sign of honesty: 'when a public body is corrupt, the members take good care that everything is managed so efficiently that nobody would like to turn them out, they take no risks of losing a position that they find so profitable'.[16] He continued by claiming that, 'the amount of money that is misappropriated will seldom be as much as would be muddled away by honest, inefficient men'.

Non-economists who hold views like Torr's believe that the effects are not fatal because corruption helps to find ways around regulations that would otherwise hamper economic expansion. They take this opinion to the extreme of claiming benefits for political life, asserting in the British case that trafficking in peerages assimilates members of emergent elites, thereby stabilising the political system.[17] At least from the state's viewpoint this is relatively cheap, since potential trouble-makers are satisfied by fancy titles, fancy dress and other non-pecuniary rewards.

The reasoning may be extended to places where monetary rewards are what really count. Perkin points out that in late 20th-century Chicago many judges were gaoled for corrupt practices. Chicago is indeed a corrupt city, as I observed myself when I lived there in the 1970s, yet Perkin says it boasts of being 'the city that works'.[18] I observed this too; the city worked well and as Perkin concludes, 'Chicago made corruption an admirable social success'. The unpalatable conclusion may be that the negative effects of corruption can be exaggerated, though economists will still find it a second-best solution. Maybe corruption is incident to growth: corruption failed to staunch the industrial revolution. Perhaps Mandeville was near the mark when he inverted the traditional association of greed, corruption and decadence: 'Every Part was full of Vice, Yet the whole Mass a Paradise'.[19]

Accordingly we have four hypotheses. First is the standard view that corruption distorts economic activity and reduces its overall level. Second, corruption may be merely a form of churning which has a trivial distributional effect; some members of elites gain and others lose, but this is of little systemic importance. Third, corruption may be actively beneficial, helping to neutralise growth-reducing regulations, conceivably with diffuse political advantages as well. Fourth, corruption may be damaging but in the period we are considering was neutralised by unexpectedly strong forces for growth. Late pre-industrial growth must surely have been stronger than it seems. Outrageous corruption failed to stem it. This returns us to searching for the hidden sources of growth.

The Enlightenment Once More

Although the outlines of the Enlightenment are well known, they have not been integrated into economic history, which focuses on material factors. Porter's comprehensive account, *Enlightenment*, published in 2000, failed to alter this, probably because it was not aimed at economic change. The field of study most concerned, the History of Economic Thought, has not succeeded either, being over-concerned with the arcana of opinion and the hagiography of economists from more recent centuries. The fact that so many historians are determined to find nothing distinctive about Western history may be why they as well as economists have continued to downplay the influence of ideas. Fortunately, the presidential address by Joel Mokyr to the American Economic History Association in 2004 and Deirdre McCloskey's work pointedly entitled, *Bourgeois Dignity: Why Economics Can't Explain the Industrial Revolution*, may help to broaden attitudes.[20] They show that the economist's aversion to studying thought reaches a check with the Enlightenment.

Mokyr traces Enlightenment thinking to the commercial capitalism of the late Middle Ages and the 16th century. He finds the beginnings of the systemisation of useful knowledge in the Baconian programme for early 17th-century science. The aim was to control nature, enabling the Baconian programme to be incorporated in the subsequent Enlightenment. This, Mokyr proposes, blossomed in the atmosphere of political stability encouraged by fading Puritan hopes for the Millennium or arose from the increase in writings by artisans about the mechanical arts. In these sources he detects the genesis of an Industrial Enlightenment.

The Enlightenment was associated with — or defined by — the rise of a cultural belief in improvement. Knowledge was more readily transferred, helped by declining costs of access and by institutions designed to diffuse information. For all the evanescence of thought, Mokyr therefore argues that with the Enlightenment randomness cohered and became directed at the encouragement of action. 'Cultural belief' may seem an insubstantial input to economic change; where is the term for it in a Cobb-Douglas production function? Yet those who have read the contemporary literature will hesitate to scoff.

The alternative is to ignore the possibility that opinion may influence behaviour, along the lines by which purists deny a role for institutions, because they believe that inefficient ones will be eliminated in a quasi-Darwinian struggle for the survival of the fittest. This over-extension of evolutionary analogy rests on assumptions of rational maximising and open competition, in this case competition in the market place for ideas. Its corollary is that institutions, and by extension ideas, are facades behind which the grinding of the economic machine is driven solely by changes in relative prices. The resultant price signals are assumed to be faithful representations of material factors, such as discoveries of physical resources, fluctuations in population and novelties in technology. But this takes us round in a circle, since these are part of what needs to be explained.

What is required is room for an autonomous role for ideas. This has been sidelined since the collapse of a theological framework for political economy in the mid-19th century.[21] 18th-century intellectuals took no such materialistic view. Despite David Hume's emphasis on theodicity, Adam Smith and his circle grounded their work in natural theology, in interpretations of the natural world rather than the revealed theology of the scriptures. The invisible hand was the Providence intended by the Creator; individual actions unintentionally summed to benevolence. 18th-century debate became more thoughtful and less strident. The appeal to natural theology precluded the schism, or chasm, between religion and science which the Victorians were to experience after Darwin.

The Enlightenment may have been, in Porter's view, as much a language as a programme; if so, it was a singularly optimistic one. There was a sense that earthly problems were the ones worth addressing, that this was not contrary to religion, and controversies were open to orderly solution. Optimism about an orderly cosmos and about human sociability already permeated Shaftesbury's writings at the start of the 18th century. Granted this, the difficulty lies in connecting the Enlightenment specifically with the industrial revolution.

Mokyr raises the question of an anterior connection between the Glorious Revolution, to which the Enlightenment is traceable, and the industrial revolution. Those who think of 1688 as *fons et origo* of economic advance find one of the benefits in improved borrowing conditions for the government, but Mokyr wonders how this could have led to technological breakthroughs half a century later.[22] On the face of it, the gap between Enlightenment thought and industrialisation is even more troubling, since changes in attitudes are less concrete than activity in the capital market.

Diffuse the Enlightenment may have been, and not responsible for specific investment decisions, but it did inspire and justify an array of changes en route to industrialisation. Consider the counter-factual: without optimism and open competition among ideas, the economic outcome seems improbable. Industrialisation would be reduced to clockwork — there would be no ghost in the machine. Something would be lacking. A remark by Goethe seems appropriate: 'having all the pieces in his hand but lacking, alas, the inner band'.

Those who think the Enlightenment was responsible for economic change therefore urge that industrialisation would not, maybe could not, have taken place without appropriate 'cultural beliefs'. The term 'cultural' adds little to understanding but a role for optimism is credible. It was unlikely to have been sustained, nevertheless, without supportive institutions and promising politico-economic conditions. Producing an image of the industrial revolution needs both positive and negative: a suitable economic matrix and appropriate attitudes, acting reciprocally.

During the relevant period, economic circumstances were set reasonably fair, even allowing for depression during the second quarter of the 18th century. Between 1680 and 1725 the standard of living rose. Demand swelled for doctors, lawyers, military men and bureaucrats and much of the political stability of the period has been attributed to the social stability this rise of the bourgeoisie produced.[23] Incentives to disturb the peace or wrangle about religion were converted into strivings for a respectable living.

Fruitful investment actually preceded the Glorious Revolution. From 1680 or earlier, prosperity was being signalled by the rebuilding of small provincial towns in brick, reducing fire disasters, followed by street improvements such as paving and lighting.[24] In the market towns, and in county towns and cathedral cities, Enlightenment attitudes were promoted, reinforced and sustained by evident signs of betterment. The expanding professions had a civilising and modernising influence.[25] The consumption of culture in the form of the arts went up and towns became known for genteel activities such as flower festivals.

Opportunities for making money continued to grow. No longer did it seem urgent to flaunt politico-religious disagreements, for which solutions had proved so elusive. Behaviour changed in the warm sun of what Adam Smith called, 'the happiest and most fortunate period of them all', between 1660 and 1760.[26] Business became a subject of interest and not merely a daily chore. It became acceptable to show off earthly riches in a bourgeois, almost Dutch, fashion.

Exactly how far this moulded the philosophical ideas that came into prominence — I almost wrote out of the closet, since they had been latent in the debates of earlier times — is not easy to be sure. The great thinkers of any period may be capable of spinning ideas out of their imaginations without being seduced by comfort or derailed by discomfort. What prosperity did was release the next tier of people, less known to posterity but not insignificant in their localities and their day, to engage in cerebral activities. Their ruminations meant the leaders were kept on their toes, since few people really spend a lifetime isolated from audiences or circles of critics.

The concept of cognitive dissonance helps us understand the diffusion of Enlightenment attitudes. Without such an explanation we cannot account for the spread of benign thinking. Values adjusted, since clinging to the old adversarial views created mental unease by clashing with the rise of prosperity. Fresh values meant approving a world in which economics tended, if not wholly to oust politics and religion, then at least to replace the old anxieties and occupy a larger share of everyday life. The age was characterised by a steady devotion to trade, investment, and scientific and technological enquiry, together with mannered forms of consumption.

This shift in attitudes occurred as a population difference, not involving everyone but affecting a larger proportion of society than before. Some did turn to fox-hunting or dissipation, or both, but these were displacement activities engaged in by Tory squires whom the Whig Ascendancy had edged out of national politics. The abiding feature was the substitution of a society primarily devoted to accumulation for one obsessed by ideological disagreements.

Was something more needed to ensure the perpetuation of the Enlightenment? Montesquieu and Voltaire both thought that liberty and the security of property may have been instigated by values but could be preserved only by law and institutions.[27] Even then the laws must not rest on the statute books as testimonies to pious intentions, they must be enforced. Here there came an ambiguity in practice. Postlethwayt noted in 1776 that England had good laws but these were, 'shamefully neglected in their execution'.[28] More than that, private property — supposedly sacred — was held conditionally. The central government gave private turnpike, river improvement and canal companies the right to oblige landowners to sell them land, introducing the concept of eminent domain. As Szostak has it, this alone made it possible to construct, or impose, the transport system of the late 18th century.[29] The rule of law held firm but its construction was more equivocal than this sounds. In the last analysis a sense of procedural order was as instrumental as the law in fostering economic growth.

The Glorious Revolution

'There is an element of myth in common notions about the peculiar British capacity to settle their political and economic differences through peaceable, fair, and democratic processes', wrote Barrington Moore, 'Such notions are a partial truth rather than a myth'.[30] One antidote among others to pacific versions of English history is Peter Levi's revelation of the country's endlessly blood-soaked landscape.[31] The 17th century had seen a series of disorders: Civil War, Monmouth's Rebellion, the ousting of James II and scares such as the one that led Samuel Pepys's father to bury Pepys's wealth in the garden (and forget where). Subsequent decades offered more certainty. This took time to sink in, 30 years or thereabouts; Stuart pretenders continued to lurk in the wings but only occasionally became a heart-stopping threat. The Glorious Revolution and the political settlement involved had dampened down the disturbances.

William III's accession is presented as the result of a pact between two elites, Whig and Tory, who carried with them, or imposed themselves on, the remainder of the populace.[32] Before formally inviting William to take the throne, Parliament debated the Revolution Settlement. By this it set limits to the sovereign's power and arranged to discipline him by withholding funds if he overstepped the mark. To achieve this, they had to compromise and since William needed money to fight France, he in turn had to assent. Agreement was reached, although as Wellington said in another context, it was, 'a damn near-run thing, the nearest-run thing you ever saw'. The agreement featured a division of labour: the Crown was to make foreign policy and project England's commercial interests abroad, while domestic government was reserved for landed families and the oligarchs in the boroughs.

The categorisation of 1688 as an elite settlement may seem to have a soft centre, since restraint on opportunism by all parties remained less than wholly secure. '[L]imits become self-enforcing', states the leading theorist of constitutions generated like this, 'when citizens hold these limits in high enough esteem that they are willing to defend them by withdrawing support from the sovereign when he attempts to violate these limits. To survive, a constitution must have more than philosophical or logical appeal; citizens must be willing to defend it'.[33] We cannot tell, however, whether citizens approve or disapprove unless they are driven to the extreme of mounting a defence, at which point they approve by definition. This circularity makes economists' impatience with political science almost as understandable as their slighting of the history of thought.

As with ideology, no partisan slumber followed. Political contention persisted at a fairly high level for 30 or 40 years, but disputes were confined within the system and the constitutional framework held. In a variant of mutually assured destruction, neither Whigs nor Tories were eager to extend the power of central government, each aware they might be in opposition one day.[34] The main recent authority proclaims that pacts must make all sides feel they have more to lose by withholding concurrence than by agreeing, but gives no details just at the point where details are needed.[35] The settlement worked, but this was not guaranteed.

James II had managed to curb Whig representation in Parliament while retaining Tory support, but once he was successful he turned on the Tories as well. They therefore felt they had little to lose by combining with the Whigs to restrict royal power. Divine right and support for royal prerogatives constituted baggage the Tories were prepared to jettison when their interests were no longer served. They did not go willing, however, and continued to hanker after the hereditary right of kings. Only on James II's death in 1701, when Louis XIV recognised his son as 'James III', rightful king of England, did they finally feel embarrassed by the presence of Jacobites in their midst.[36]

Hence the Glorious Revolution was a grubbier affair, a result of everyday politics more than the shining rebirth or abstract model since portrayed. A turning point did come in 1688 but it was not the only one and there were aftershocks in the American colonies.[37] The judgement of its outstanding importance contains a measure of retrospection. History is invariably a continuum. As to the Enlightenment, scholarly investigation had been shimmering in the social depths for generations, and although the way it became formalised after 1660 (but before 1688) is celebrated as a metropolitan achievement, it was wider than that. A strong interest in history and topography was signalled by the publication of Dugdale's *Monasticon* in 1665. Robert Plot published his natural history of Oxfordshire in 1677, the year when Elias Ashmole gave his museum to Oxford. Ashmole's collection was essentially the work of the Tradescants, father and son, who had worked even earlier in the 17th century.

Yet, to escape an infinite regress, the Glorious Revolution makes the most reasonable dividing line; it crystallised emergent trends. Part of its role was to symbolise the new-found security which thereafter characterised England, but there was more to it than symbolism. It had a decisive impact on the investment environment. Studies that reject this try to show that taxes were higher under England's constitutional monarchy than under the Absolutist rulers of Europe, and that borrowing by the English state came at higher rates of interest than on the continent. This should have forced up interest rates on the private market, too, the implication being that investment in England was dampened overall.

It was not. Taxes were relatively neutral and did not press too heavily on the economy.[38] Adam Smith observed that the country was resilient, indeed continued to grow, despite a succession of physical disasters. During the 100 years from 1660 to 1760 there were seven wars, three rebellions, the Great Fire and the Plague, yet all together they did not halt, 'the progress of England towards opulence'.[39] The wealth of the period was marked by innumerable new buildings and the late 17th century may have been the true era of W. G. Hoskins' Great Rebuilding. People had to have been willing to finance this.

Nor is it acceptable to dismiss the building spree solely as consumption. Leaving aside mansions set in spacious parks, tens of thousands of solid, comfortable middle-class houses were erected in towns and villages — England became Holland without the canals. Like Holland, the country was increasingly clad in brick. Many of the houses survive. They were residences when they were built but at the time tended also to be flanked by workshops and storerooms, since dismantled or turned into garages. In the towns there were shops on the ground floor while the family lived upstairs. The houses were, in other words, appurtenances of an England which still worked for its living while becoming more comfortable in the process. Rather than dispute rates of tax and interest and perhaps end up thinking that the climate for investment in England must have been dire, one might aim a kick at a wall of Georgian brick and say, like Samuel Johnson kicking the stone, 'I refute it thus'.[40]

The late Stephan Epstein, making a resolute argument for decoupling modes of governance and economic performance, introduced an ingenious twist.[41] Urging that England steered clear of continental wars and the financial reforms entailed by having to pay for them, his claim was that when interest rates normed on continental ones after 1700, they had actually to rise to do so. Unfortunately his case is entwined with disparagement of representative government and of negative freedoms (freedoms from interference and control). In rejoinder, we might observe that negative freedoms are consumption goods in themselves. People desire them for their own sakes as well as for the freedom of action they confer.

The landowners and great merchants who had a say in the polity after 1688 were unlikely to debauch the system by encouraging excessive borrowing by the crown. The revolutionary settlement was aimed at curbing such excesses. Constitutional guarantees mean that the citizens of a democracy, even the limited democracy which is the other face of limited monarchy, are more willing to lend to the state than are the citizens of autocracies.[42] The alternative would be to agree with Epstein that constitutions and governance are irrelevant when it comes to accounting for economic growth.

On the face of it Epstein does seem to have brought a promising line of enquiry about England's advantages to a stop. But more recent studies consider what actually happened to investment rather than what taxation and interest levels may theoretically imply. They come to positive conclusions. Fluctuations in the price of capital have been investigated for the spells of threatened Jacobite invasion, with the conclusion that the growth of the capital market and decline of mercantilism were indeed by-products of institutional changes from 1688.[43] The evidence of investment in roads and rivers has been scrutinised, with the conclusion that it went up; after the Glorious Revolution promoters and investors did respond to the greater likelihood that their rights would not be abrogated.[44] This argument is carried further by demonstrating that about 1700, Parliament established a forum in which rights to land and resources could be reorganised. The advance in market security and flexibility is also indicated by Hoppit's conclusions about the deployment of personal Acts of Parliament.[45]

The implication of these studies is that there was a pent-up demand for productive changes which turned from a stream to a spate through greater security and more appropriate institutions, in short that institutional quality did matter. This is not to claim that post-1688 constitutionalism was designed to protect the weak. It was the result of a wary concord among the powerful, meant to aid co-operation and decision making among them.[46] Disputes certainly continued: there were winners and losers from every decision to run a canal or turnpike here rather than there, or to enclose open fields with many owners, but the rules of the game were grumbled at, not overthrown.

Promoters of schemes had to face down local opposition. Town merchants and consumers tended to favour schemes of river navigation but farmers opposed them.[47] This shows up in figures of the relative participation by commercial interests and farmers in transport investments as a whole.[48] Import-competing farmers were prepared to see local markets overstocked in years of plenty in order to hold a local monopoly against the years of bad harvest, when — demand for food being inelastic — prices would soar. They tended not to prevail, especially when big landowners were among the investors. Landowners had an interest in the prosperity of their tenants but they or their agents could see further ahead and usually commanded enough resources to wait for a better return on their money.

Consider as a single example the Basingstoke Canal, begun 1788, completed 1794. This was designed to link the market town of Basingstoke with the Wey Navigation and hence the London market.[49] The main investors were landowners, among whom one major individual, Lord Tylney, objected. Although he cited other reasons, Tylney probably had amenity considerations in mind. He did not want the canal to pass close to his house, a preference for seclusion that was typical of the well-to-do. Instead, the promoters had to agree to tunnel under Greywell Hill, whereupon Tylney withdrew his objection. Presumably it was cheaper to indulge him than to chase him through the courts. Further objections came from people who thought they stood to lose trade through competition with goods traffic along the Thames. The principal inhabitants of nearby Farnham, on the other hand, petitioned in favour of the canal. As people in their position saw the issues, one either joined in investing, sacrificing neighbours who could not face import competition, or missed out on the prospects of the age.

Overall, conflict did become comparatively subdued, while larger-scale political disagreement was subsumed in the rise of party politics. During the 18th century investment decisions were easier than before, though Pareto optimality could scarcely be expected. Had it been insisted on, innumerable decisions among multiple claimants would never have been concluded. Despite some recurrent forms of opposition, for instance the characteristic obduracy of farmers, change in general was not blocked. The interests of the poor may have been formally recognised, as with enclosures, but in practice they were often ridden over roughshod. The holders of mere customary rights were losers; as far as they were concerned, enclosure was asset-stripping at their expense. Chapter and verse can be cited to support the proposition that plebeian voices were being 'inhibited by structures of social inequality' well before 1615.[50] Rightly or wrongly, what was most likely to hamper enclosure or new transport links was conflict among the well-to-do.

A framework to contain these observations would be helpful and North and his collaborators oblige by dividing polities into limited and open-access orders.[51] In the latter, political, legal and economic access become open to competitive entry by all. 'All' may mean as few as 33 per cent of the population, but to reach even this level from the rent-seeking world which previously existed, a bridge must be crossed. Dominant groups have to agree to compete rather than persist in extracting rents. They have to believe their individual rights will be respected. While insisting that no single break in the trend of political history was utterly decisive, nor any step taken that could not in principle have been reversed, the Glorious Revolution — treated as an elite settlement — remains the best candidate.

Market Ideology

Enlightenment thinking carried its signature mood of reasonableness, from high-flown philosophy and science to down-to-earth economic policy. Free trade, infrastructural improvement, commercial law and, Mokyr adds, less distorting taxes were among the policies it encouraged. Although the usual suspects of mercantilism, economic rivalry and political hostility continued to tip sand into the machine they were continually oiled away. Accordingly, the Enlightenment, together with the not quite adamantine security of property and other developments in the political and constitutional spheres, were vital to the age. Yet this is still not a full explanation of growing market friendliness.

Market ideology, pro-competition, had been accepted in some circles for a long time, seeking always to dissuade protectionism, monopoly, oligopoly, rent-seeking and the remainder of that piratical crew from boarding the ship-of-state. The judges removed some restrictions very early, in 1599 for instance declaring illegal the confiscation of goods during raids by guilds. They were however somewhat inconsistent, being jealous of their autonomy as a profession and as individuals. They asserted their independence by reintroducing restrictions from time to time.

Little more may be said, given how little is known about policy formation, than to agree with O'Brien, Griffiths and Hunt in warning that, 'mercantilist regulation and pressure group politics has been rather "crowded out" by economic analysis, concerned to bring demand and supply, prices and costs to the foreground'.[52] After the Glorious Revolution, pressure groups turned to working through Parliament, which is another reason for thinking the event significant.[53] Parliament was however only theoretically supreme; it is best thought of as *primus inter pares*, with the crown and the judges as its rivals.

Although the central tendency was towards the freeing of markets, the path resembled a corkscrew more than a poker and recent work has eroded the certainty that historians were wont to find. Indeed, Weber long since argued that the procedural and institutional structures of the common law were more significant than its unclear and sometimes unhelpful content.[54] The 'unwieldy and uncertain' features of English private law were not wholly offset, on readings of this type, by the success of 1688. The Glorious Revolution enshrined judicial independence in several Acts of Parliament.[55] Judges secured lifetime appointment at the Act of Settlement in 1701 and could interpret contracts by following wherever the logic of argument took them, without reference to the public interest. Appellate courts could make legal rules separately from Parliament. Modern students of legal history come no closer to the relationship between law and the economy than to point out that, while the law may not have been as decisively responsible for economic change as many have thought, it did not check growth on balance and may have diverted it only a little.

A balder narrative might say that the judges and Parliament together increasingly overlooked, rejected or struck down local protectionist measures.

'It is not more than fifty years ago', wrote Adam Smith in 1776, 'that some of the counties in the neighbourhood of London petitioned the Parliament against the extension of the turnpike roads into the remoter counties'.[56] They pretended that farming close in to the capital would be ruined by low-cost competition, but the opposite happened and farming on the metropolitan fringe switched to more intensive cropping. The judges, on the whole, wanted ordinances to be 'consonant with reason'. This was reflected in their preponderant embracing of competitive ideology, though the precise inception remains obscure. In any case, small towns could not afford to bring many expensive law suits to protect their manufacturers.[57] Agricultural producers in some districts, who tried to have bans placed on new crops such as clover because they gave the advantage to farmers elsewhere, likewise failed to secure support in either the courts or Parliament.[58]

The decline of the guilds was an aspect of rising individualism which proceeded throughout the 18th century, its main phase having perhaps come even earlier — differences from place to place and trade to trade make it hard to generalise. In London, which remained the leading manufacturing centre although the small size of its firms obscures the fact, a member of one trade guild was entitled to take up any other trade.[59] This implies an unexpected measure of flexibility. Moreover, as early as 1680 a majority of the population and most manufacturing had located on London's fringes, and thus commonly eluded guild control.

London's population had been dispersing for over a century, aided by occasional shocks that displaced tradesmen, such as the Great Fire of 1666 when 'the marring of the City was the making of the suburbs'.[60] The City was where the guilds chiefly reigned, having a right of search for 10 miles out and continuing to prosecute violators, but only as late as 1650. Shopkeepers avoided the retailing guilds by moving to the suburbs, despite official bans on the building of shops there.[61] But a picture of secular decline in the London guilds would be too simple, since much depended on the craft. Guild studies, long ignored in economic history, have returned and reached a level of complexity which for the moment precludes generalisation.

A tentative conclusion from examining industrial regulation in some towns in the South of England is that enforcement tended to revive during trade depressions but dwindled when business was good. The guilds therefore represented a secondary rather than a front-rank impediment, sometimes delaying adjustment to market conditions but not invariably halting it. One interpretation of guild function is that the aim was to secure from the political authorities charters granting members exclusive privileges, i.e. the purpose was rent-seeking.[62] If so, it was not very successful in preserving the rents against competition, especially as the rules were often ignored. One example previously mentioned was that during the early 17th century 30 per cent of members of the London Stationers' Company broke its ordinances. A general claim that, because they lasted so long guilds must have been efficient, signals little more than a belief that facts can be deduced from theory. The name and form of the guild institution may have survived but this tells us little about its practical force.

The temptations of profit progressively overcame incentives to enforce regulations. The general mood turned against protectionism. In Lancashire a lack of restraint on trade and industry by corporations and guilds had always promoted flexibility; the absence of guilds in the West Riding is credited with encouraging technological innovation; and in the West Midlands corporate control, rarely strong, was dissolving in the 1690s.[63] With exceptions such as Coventry and Lichfield, few towns in the last-named region were hampered by guild regulation. A majority of towns in parts of England where industry thickened in the 18th century had by then accepted market competition.

Non-market elements remained more obvious in the countryside, partly as a perverse outcome of the investment in estates of money acquired in the capital. The advantages for the whole economy of competing jurisdictions were reduced in rural England by the class interest of landowners. They formed a growth-impairing coalition, monopolising resources and reducing access to the market; they were interested in the level of rents their tenants could pay but not so interested that they encouraged maximum production. They nudged part of the economy a little way back towards a command system. Side by side with this, elements of a customary economy persisted in the form of common fields, and lot meads where rights to take the hay were drawn for annually.

Possibly members of the landed class did not recognise the contradictions in spending out on landscaping and blood sports while simultaneously investing in agriculture. Some, with great extra-agricultural wealth, did not much care: to them, profit was secondary to the maximising of status and consumption that the ownership of estates permitted. The landowners in Wiltshire and Gloucestershire, who had been prominent in national politics in the early 17th century, seem to have withdrawn to the countryside after the Civil Wars, preferring estate life, rustic consumption and local power.

A paper by Mokyr and Nye describes the adoption of the ideology of the market.[64] They attribute it to the post-1688 Whigs — a coalition of big merchants and big landowners who could override the conservatism of the smaller Tory landowners. In reality not every part of England was equally capable of benefiting. The century it took for protectionist rent-seeking to be demolished was a time when southern towns prospered from their trading functions but were ineffective at defending their manufacturing, meaning that London and the north gained the industrial advantage.

In his discussion of railway investment in the immediately following period, Casson finds that competition between towns led to duplicated facilities and wasted resources.[65] Despite the fact that the elite in many towns were divided by religion or party, any town was likely to present a fairly united front when investment opportunities arose. In the early 18th century the common interests of members of the professions were already helping to heal the breach between Anglicans and dissenters.[66] There were disputes between towns, but pragmatism meant that the contest between Whig and Tory assumed no clear spatial pattern.[67] The south-north industrial pattern that emerged seems to have been the *ex post* outcome of the competition induced by market unification rather than of *ex ante* political distributions.

Endnotes

1. E.g. W. McCarthy, *Anna Letitia Barbauld: Voice of the Enlightenment* (Baltimore: Johns Hopkins University Press, 2009).

2. M. M. Postan, Investment in medieval agriculture, *J. Econ. Hist.* **XXVII**: 576–587, 1967.

3. J. O. Appleby, *Economic Thought and Ideology in Seventeenth-Century England* (Princeton: Princeton University Press, 1978), pp. ix, 9, 245.

4. D. Stanciu, *Shaftesbury's 'Characteristics' — A Socratic Programme of the Eighteenth Century* (Bucharest: Editura Universitatii din Bucuresti, 2004), p. 211.

5. E. Calamy, *The Nonconformist's Memorial*, second edition, edited by Samuel Palmer (London: Sutton and Son and T. Hurst, 1802).

6. M. L. G. Pallares-Burke, *The New History: Confessions and Conversations* (Cambridge: Polity 2002), p. 87.

7. R. Porter, *Enlightenment: Britain and the Creation of the Modern World* (London: Allen Lane The Penguin Press, 2000), p. 127.

8. I am grateful for the example to Mr. Alan Albery, who is working on the Herriard estate papers.

9. C. Berkvens-Stevelinck *et al.* (eds.), *The Emergence of Tolerance in the Dutch Republic* (Leiden: Brill, 1997), pp. 155, 171.

10. R. Porter, *Enlightenment*, pp. 30, 243. Porter acknowledges Margaret Jacobs as his authority on the Enlightenment's beginnings.

11. See M. G. Heller, *Capitalism, Institutions, and Economic Development* (London: Routledge, 2009), p. 179.

12. R. Davis, The rise of protection in England, 1689–1786, *Econ. Hist. Rev. N.S.* **19**(2): 306, 1966.

13. W. D. Rubinstein, The end of the "Old Corruption" in Britain 1780–1860, *Past & Present* **101**: 55–86, 1983.

14. P. Harling, *The Waning of the 'Old Corruption': The Politics of Economical Reform in Britain, 1779–1846* (Oxford: Clarendon Press, 1996).

15. K. M. Murphy *et al.*, Why is rent-seeking so costly to growth? *Am. Econ. Rev., Pap. & Proc.* **LXXXIII**: 409–414, 1993.

16. C. Torr, *Small Talk at Wreyland III* (Oxford: Oxford, 1979), p. 92.

17. G. R. Searle, *Corruption in British Politics, 1895–1930* (Oxford: Clarendon Press, 1987), p. 436.

18. H. Perkin, *The Making of a Social Historian* (London: Athena Press, 2002), p. 238.

19. A. Bick, Bernard Mandeville and the "economy" of the Dutch, *Erasmus J. Philos. Econ.* **1**(1): 91, 2008.

20. J. Mokyr, The intellectual origins of modern economic growth, *J. Econ. Hist.* **65**(2): 285–351, 2005; D. N. McCloskey, *Bourgeois Dignity: Why Economics Can't Explain the Industrial Revolution* (MS., McCloskey's website, 2009).

21. P. Oslington, Recovering the theological roots of economics, *Debate* **4**: 22–25, 2009.

22. J. Mokyr, The institutional origins of the industrial revolution, MS., Northwestern University, January 2008, pp. 28–29, 33.

23. G. Holmes, The achievement of stability: the social context of politics from the 1680s to the age of Walpole, in J. Cannon (ed.), *The Whig Ascendancy: Colloquies on Hanoverian England* (London: Edward Arnold, 1981), pp. 16–17.

24. For an excellent example of the sequence of improvements (in Chichester), see F. W. Steer (ed.), *The Memoirs of James Spershott* (Chichester: City Council, 1962).

25. A. Everitt, *Change in the Provinces: The Seventeenth Century* (Leicester; Leicester University Press, 1969), pp. 44–45.

26. A. Smith, *An Inquiry into the Nature and Causes of the Wealth of Nations* (New York: Modern Library, 1937), pp. 328–329.

27. E. L. Jones, *Cultures Merging: A Historical and Economic Critique of Culture* (Princeton: Princeton University Press, 2006), p. 110.

28. Quoted in A. Greif, The impact of administrative power on political and economic development, SSRN: http: ssrrn.com/abstract = 1004394.

29. R. Szostak, *The Role of Transportation in the Industrial Revolution* (Montreal and Kingston: McGill-Queen's University Press, 1991), p. 44.

30. B. Moore, Jr., *Social Origins of Dictatorship and Democracy* (London: Allen Lane The Penguin Press, 1967), p. 4.

31. P. Levi, *The Flutes of Autumn* (London: Harvill Press, 1983), pp. 93–94.

32. B. R. Weingast, The political foundations of democracy and the rule of law, *Am. Polit. Sci. Rev.* **91**(2): 245–263, 1997.

33. B. R. Weingast, Political foundations, p. 251 and n. 10.

34. S. E. Prall, *The Bloodless Revolution: England 1688* (Madison: University of Wisconsin Press, 1985), pp. 243, 251, 292.

35. B. R. Weingast, Political foundations, p. 252 n. 17.

36. W. Speck, Britain and the Dutch Republic, in K. Davids and J. Lucassen (eds.), *A Miracle Mirrored: The Dutch Republic in European Perspective* (Cambridge: Cambridge University Press, 1995), p. 192.

37. D. S. Lovejoy, *The Glorious Revolution in America* (New York: Harper & Row, 1974).

38. Mokyr, Institutional Origins, p. 33.

39. Smith, *Wealth of Nations*, pp. 328–329.

40. Negative views of England's situation concerning tax and interest are not usually persuasive. See E. Jones, *The European Miracle* (Cambridge: Cambridge University Press, 2003), third edition, pp. 245–247.

41. S. Epstein, *Freedom and Growth: The Rise of States and Markets in Europe, 1300–1750* (London: Routledge, 2000).

42. J. Macdonald, *A Free Nation Deep in Debt: The Financial Roots of Democracy* (Princeton: Princeton University Press, 2006).

43. J. Wells and D. Wills, Revolution, restoration, and debt repudiation: the Jacobite threat to England's institutions and economic growth, *J. Econ. Hist.* **60**: 418–441, 2000.

44. D. Bogart, Did the Glorious Revolution contribute to the transport revolution? Evidence from investment in roads and rivers, Working Paper, Dan Bogart's website, University of California, Irvine, 2009.

45. D. Bogart and G. Richardson, Adaptable property rights: Britain's property system before the industrial revolution, Dan Bogart's website, University of California, Irvine, 2009; J. Hoppit, Patterns of parliamentary legislation, 1660–1800, *Histor. J.* **39**(1): 122–123, 1996.

46. Greif, The Impact of Administrative Power, p. 34.

47. T. S. Willan, *River Navigation in England 1600–1750* (New York: Augustus M. Kelley, 1964).
48. G. R. Hawke and J. P. P. Higgins, Transport and social overhead capital, in R. C. Floud and D. N. McCloskey (eds.), *The Economic History of England since 1700* (Cambridge: Cambridge University Press, 1981), p. 233.
49. G. Crocker, *The History of the Basingstoke Canal* (Surrey and Hampshire Canal Society, 1977).
50. A. Wood, Subordination, solidarity and the limits of popular agency, *Past & Present* **193**: 172, 2006.
51. D. C. North *et al.*, Limited access order in the developing world: a new approach to the problem of development. World Bank Policy Research Working Paper No. 4359 (2007). Ron Harris, Law, Finance and the First Corporations (Prepared for World Justice Forum, Vienna, 2–5 July 2008) agrees that the Northian analysis is correct in identifying credible commitment as a precondition for the rise of a government bond market, and the Glorious Revolution as the source of that commitment in the English case.
52. P. K. O'Brien, T. Griffiths and P. Hunt, Political components of the industrial revolution: Parliament and the English cotton textile industry, 1660–1774, *Econ. Hist. Rev.* **XLIV**: 396, 1991.
53. Elsewhere O'Brien diminishes the role of the Glorious Revolution in favour of the consensus about taxation and property rights forged among the elite during the Civil War and Interregnum. P. K. O'Brien, Fiscal exceptionalism: great Britain and its European rivals from Civil War to triumphant Trafalgar and Waterloo, in D. Winch and P. K. O'Brien (eds.), *The Political Economy of British Historical Experience, 1688–1914* (Oxford: Oxford University Press/British Academy, 2002), p. 263.
54. J. Getzler, Theories of property and economic development, *J. Interdiscip. Hist.* **26**(4): 639–669, 1996.
55. R. La Porta *et al.*, The economic consequences of legal origins, *J. Econ. Lit.* **46**(2): 303, 306, 2008.
56. Smith, *Wealth of Nations*, I, p. 134.
57. P. Langford, *A Polite and Commercial People: England 1727–1783* (Oxford: Clarendon Press, 1989).
58. E. L. Jones, English and European agricultural development 1650–1750, in R. M. Hartwell (ed.), *The Industrial Revolution* (Oxford: Basil Blackwell, 1970), p. 60.
59. A. L. Beier and R. Finlay, *London 1500–1700: The Making of the Metropolis* (London: Longman, 1980), pp. 143–157.
60. Quoted by C. Wilson, *England's Apprenticeship 1603–1763* (London: Longman, 1965), p. 177.

61. J. R. Kellett, The breakdown of gild and corporation control over the handicraft and retail trades in London, *Econ. Hist. Rev.* **10**: 381–394, 1958.

62. S. Ogilvie, Can we rehabilitate the guilds? A sceptical reappraisal, CWPE 0745 (September 2007), on Google Scholar.

63. Walton, 1987; Rowlands, 1977; Ogilvie, Rehabilitate the guilds?, p. 35.

64. J. Mokyr and J. Nye, Distributional coalitions, the industrial revolution, and the origins of economic growth in Britain', *South. Econ. J.* **74**: 50–70, 2007.

65. M. C. Casson, The efficiency of the Victorian British railway network: a counterfactual analysis, MS., University of Reading, 2007.

66. Holmes, Achievement of Stability, p. 20.

67. See e.g. A. Cossons, The Tewkesbury and Cheltenham roads, *Glo. Soc. Ind. Archaeol. J.* 42, 1998.

CHAPTER 9

TRANSPORT AND MARKETING

The decay of crafts was in fact due, not only to the growth of foreign commerce, but still more perhaps to the concentration of English industries in localities specially adapted to them.

George Unwin, 1904

Studies of turnpikes, canals and railways tend to sweep under the carpet the transport improvements that preceded them. They seldom ask what advances these had made on even earlier innovations — advances that maybe resulted in equivalent social savings. Incremental gains, organisational changes and more intensive maintenance receive short shrift. Base-weighting in early times, historically more appropriate, is needed to correct the assumption that big innovations, bursting on the scene in the late 18th and 19th centuries, transformed a communications system that had been languishing unchanged. On the contrary, Yrjo Kaukianinen shows that as late as the years between 1820 and 1860, small organisational changes saved more days on shipping and overland routes than the adoption of the electric telegraph.[1] Better arranged mail-coach connections (and on North Atlantic routes, sailing packets) were contributing gains until the late 1830s. Only afterwards did the railways start to shrink time and distance drastically.

The attraction of the statistical data available for novel modes of transport and communications means that dawn's early light is traded away for a bright view of mid-morning. Eric Pawson has complained of 'source domination' in historical geography, as a result of which individually small and scattered experiences find themselves neglected.[2] The dynamism of the early modern economy is missed. Joan Thirsk, a scholar who used none of the formal concepts of economics, spot-lighted this by adding up thousands of mentions of tiny consumer items trawled from primary sources. She extended the procedure to uncover the aggregate importance of minor crops.[3] Those of us who were seduced by the grand silhouettes of agricultural change had failed to appreciate this dense body of detail.

A rare counterpoint to the impression of abrupt change comes in one of Pawson's studies of the diffusion of turnpikes.[4] He notes that the costs of maintaining the pre-existing roads had fallen on some parishes more than others, because of differences in terrain, and on some parishioners more than others, since not every individual made the same use of the roads. To reduce the inequities, the parish system was strengthened in the 17th century, the amendments being made permanent by an Act of 1691 which empowered parishes to levy a highway rate. Extensive use was made of this: for instance Marylebone, then on the outskirts of London, levied 13 rates from 1705 before it secured a turnpike Act.

A second means of shoring up the parish system was additional private repair, paid for by subscription. Pawson says this should not be underestimated. Yet neither method internalised the externalities created by the absence of full user-pays arrangements. Efforts were accordingly made to spot the categories of users who harmed the road surfaces most, and levy them for costs proportionate to the loads they carried. The Wealden Acts of the late 16th century, which charged ironmasters for their heavy wagons, had started along these lines. There was a subsequent swelling of regulation to curb harmful usage, culminating in two Acts of 1773. Restrictions were placed on the weight of loads, the number of wheels on road wagons and the size of the horse teams pulling them, and on the width of treads on wheels. Endless complaints about damage are often taken to mean that communications were in a hopeless condition, whereas in reality the roads were suffering because trade was expanding.

Usage was hard to monitor. Tolls promised the most elegant solution, calibrated to the harm particular types of use might be expected to cause and its frequency on any given stretch of road. The outcome was the turnpike trust, embracing local farmers, landowners and tradesmen who were made collectively responsible for maintenance and empowered to levy tolls to pay for it. This obliged users to internalise the cost of using the roads. A small stream of trusts began to operate from as early as 1696. Dan Bogart has shown that in both 1800 and 1820 turnpikes accounted for a social saving of at least 0.5 per cent.[5] This was part of the improvement of communications that distinguished England from other countries, except perhaps the United Provinces. The achievement of the turnpike system should nevertheless be set in context. Not only do turnpikes conceal other road improvements, they exaggerate the growth of traffic in their own day, omitting, for instance, the movement of animals along ancient droves where tolls were not levied. In similar fashion, canalised rivers were the predecessors of canals. Too single-minded a focus on turnpikes or canals blurs the evolution of communications.

Traffic on roads left few lasting signs and was only faintly recorded in official sources. This is hardly surprising when so many goods were being smuggled along the green lanes. In the mid-18th century, 3,000 horse-loads of contraband regularly arrived at Sussex ports and were distributed via well-established inland centres.[6] Marlborough was a major staging post on thoroughfares from the Dorset and Hampshire coasts to customers in Oxfordshire, Warwickshire and Worcestershire. Yet smuggling leaves little trace other than cellars and secret passageways that may or may not have been used for this purpose. As for legal traffic, road wagons (as opposed to farm wagons) are rare to non-existent in museums, while herds of cattle or flocks of sheep driven long distances on the hoof have not now been seen for decades. Road usage before the turnpikes is therefore obscure and easily brushed aside.

Transport Developments

Factors common to the whole country are seldom persuasive in explaining change because they cannot account for regional divergences. National averages are statistical artefacts and may accurately reflect no component region. Transport was an exception, operating widely and intensifying regional specialisation. Better communications knitted the market together and unveiled comparative advantage. This allowed farming, or rather crop growing, to separate increasingly from manufacturing, to which it had been joined in the form of part-time cottage industry, ever since medieval merchants had escaped the jurisdiction of urban guilds by seeking cheaper labour in the countryside.

Improvements began before the Civil Wars (the Upper Thames was made navigable then) and showed renewed energy after 1660. The story is known in detail and only an outline is needed here. The stock of navigable rivers was doubled by 1750. Artificial canals followed, although the network may not have been completed until the first decade of the 19th century. While it is unclear how far the most enthusiastic accounts allow for stoppages through the freezing of canals in the frequent frosts of the era, or through shoals in the rivers in times of drought, waterborne carriage was far cheaper than parallel overland transit.

Road carriage nevertheless retained an overall advantage because there was less of a topographical constraint on roads; they could service areas no waterway could reach. This may however conceal fluctuations in relative efficiency about which little seems to be known: a study of the Basingstoke canal reports that in 1810 wagon carriage was twice as dear as carriage by barge but by 1822 the difference was slight, because wagons had become quicker and could travel from door to door.[7] George Sturt's grandfather, a potter, complained that the packing of barges was extraordinarily difficult.

Meanwhile road beds and surfaces were improved and are said to have been important sources of increased transport productivity, well before the main phase of turnpike construction.[8] Productivity rose two-and-a-half or three times between 1658 and 1820. A regular, professional system of long-distance carriage was in being before 1700. The delays imposed on goods traffic by deep winter mud had been reduced or abolished. The number of horses used for transport (as opposed to field work) expanded comparatively late in time, but increased further when needed to pull barges and carry goods to and from the wharves.[9] For Gloucestershire the calculation has been made that in any given year during the 18th century the population of horses was 10,000, their feed requiring four per cent of the county's total area (not merely the farmed area).[10]

Early transport improvements involved little by way of technological change. Flash and pound locks on canalised rivers may have been something of an exception, but otherwise developments comprised more intensive routines of maintenance, the better delineation of routes, inscribing of road maps, and placing of milestones. Part of the transport system remained rough and ready for a long time; the neat maps and orderly tables of turnpikes, canals and postal services convey too regular an impression. Until the first two or three decades of the 19th century it was customary for riders to set out in a general direction over unenclosed heaths, wolds and downs, asking shepherds the way as they went. On some of his *Rural Rides* as late as the 1820s, Cobbett proceeded in this ad hoc fashion. The father of the painter, Sir Thomas Lawrence, who kept The Bear at Devizes, set up poles to guide potential customers across Salisbury Plain.

A negative opinion of road improvements has been voiced by Harrison in a thorough study of bridge building.[11] Harrison believes that the increase in road transport from the 16th to 18th centuries, though real, has been exaggerated. This is too harsh. Change may look slight compared with what was to come but is substantial when benchmarked against what existed before. Any study of the physical artefacts of communication systems is likely to under-rate 'soft' gains through organisational improvements, which are hard to identify.

Away from London's surrounds, Harrison finds little more than the building of minor new bridges between 1540 and 1770, and most of them late in the period. The question is did a restricted number of crossing points, via smallish bridges, imply that domestic trade remained flat? There is little evidence that the bridging points were impossibly congested. The Middle Ages had left a lasting stock of bridges, enough to accommodate a sizeable growth in traffic. As with the medieval duplication of churches, over-servicing and redundancy in bridge-building cannot be ruled out. Bridges were often charitable works too. There was no call for them to be nicely adjusted to existing volumes of traffic. Besides, plenty of routes involved no river crossings.

As for vehicles, whereas the wealthiest yeomen of Oxfordshire might not own a wagon at the Restoration, hardly a yeoman did not possess at least one by the reign of George I.[12] In Wiltshire, Richard Jefferies records that the first wagon was seen at Draycott Foliat about the middle of the 18th century, but so clumsily constructed that a whole field was needed to turn it.[13] Nevertheless any wagon was better than alternatives like the wheel-less sleds used to carry home the hay. Farmers who owned wagons sometimes became part-time hauliers. After turnpikes came in, specialised hauliers appeared, though the farm wagons were still at times more reliable. The clothiers of Mere, Wiltshire, continued to send their cloth a great distance to the River Kennet at Newbury (for the London market), hiring farmers' wagons en route at Andover fair.[14] The introduction of stage coaches, coach baskets, pannier baskets, larger road wagons and fly vans came relatively late and were largely responses to increased volumes of traffic.

Information Markets

The coalescence of information markets was an important feature of late pre-industrial England. A biographer of William Tyndale (1494–1536) remarks that he had been in small towns in North America cut off from a view of the larger world because all their news media are local.[15] The Gloucestershire in which Tyndale was born was not like that; every northern European current flowed there. Alan Everitt notes that in Elizabeth's reign the Familists spread their doctrines by travelling round as basket-makers.[16] They would have spread news and gossip too. More formal postal services were integrated early. In 1629, Thomas Hutchins of Crewkerne, Somerset, established the first private letter post service. This was between London and Plymouth and within 20 miles of the route. All letters were originally sent to London to be redistributed, but the rapidly growing volume of mail meant that cross-posts had to be added.[17]

Ostlers passed on what they heard from coachmen while, away from main routes, all manner of people filtered news through the countryside. During the 18th century, information about popular entertainment was being diffused: in 1741 the church bells were rung at Upton, near Slough, to announce that the final instalment of Richardson's *Pamela* had reached the local bookshop.[18] Other such events followed and were not necessarily trivial: the power of soap operas to alter lifestyles is well understood today.[19] Clearly the information market was less perfect than now but modern works make too much of past isolation, endlessly citing Cobbett's tale about the poor young woman marooned at Tangley, Hampshire. Although men were far more likely to travel than women, the news did come in and both sexes could glean much of what they wanted to hear.

Sir John Hawkins, in his life of Johnson published in 1787, gave the 'instant' spread of fashion as one of the main changes over the preceding 50 years. He mentioned particularly the cap of the farmer's wife: 'The convenience of turnpike roads', he wrote, 'has destroyed the distinction between town and country manners and the maid of honour and the farmer's wife put on a cap of the latest form almost at the same instant'.[20] Ceaselessly repeated down the ages though this objection to social change was, at least Hawkins explained how fashionable change occurred. News of fashions excited the aspirations of consumers and increased their willingness to work harder in order to share in novel forms of consumption: the Industrious Revolution.[21]

With respect to more substantial commodities, wheat markets may have coalesced as early as the 1690s. Price data certainly show integration by 1770–1794, earlier than in China or mainland Western Europe.[22] This had followed the emergence of specialist carriers and was achieved despite the incomplete physical meshing of the road system. The problem of incompatible gauges, commonly mentioned in railways histories, was older than that, since traffic by road wagon also necessitated trans-shipments; Suffolk wagons, for instance, were too broad for the ruts worn by those from Gloucestershire.

Relocations

Entrepreneurs raising capital for transport schemes were obliged to finesse the contradictory ambitions of investors. The landed interest wished to see farm produce shipped further afield, with backloads of inputs such as rags for fertiliser and coal for burning lime. No doubt shopkeepers anticipated bringing in more cheaply the goods they sold. Manufacturers were potentially threatened by import substitution, although whether they recognised this at first is unclear. Some would be forced out of business when industrial goods came in from elsewhere at prices too low for them to match, even if they did acquire cheaper raw materials too.

Poorly differentiated proto-industrial regions had existed side by side, separated by the high cost of exchanging goods. By 1670 some patches of cottage industry were thickening and others were thinning out. A majority of market towns had grown but some had ossified or were in decline. Competition had already begun to concentrate industries, including punctiform industries as well as rural domestic ones. 'The overriding reason for the concentration of various industries in particular regions during the 18th century was the drop in transport costs', Szostak concludes, 'indeed, it would be an incredible coincidence were the same process to be observed in many branches of the textile, iron, pottery, and other industries without there being some common cause'.[23]

The woollen trades of the Upper Thames valley and some parts of East Anglia had been outclassed as early as the third quarter of the 17th century. During the next century the cloth industry of Wiltshire retreated to Trowbridge and that of Gloucestershire to Stroud, while by the early 19th century east and north-east Dorset and parts of Worcestershire had ceased to be clothing country altogether.[24] After the middle of the 18th century, when many places had become well linked, further groupings disappeared. They were regions that lacked a varied industrial base which could offer complementarities among different trades and provide insurance against a downturn in any one of them.[25]

Rural domestic industries, though sometimes established to exploit female labour in arable districts, were typically located in districts that were not good for crop growing. Such areas specialised on livestock farming. Pastoral-cum-proto industrial districts were commonest in the north, where soils were poorest and rainfall highest. Farms in Lancashire were subdivided on inheritance into units so small that petty industrial work was needed to supplement agricultural earnings — if families were to be able to stay together in their homes on the land.[26] By the start of the 19th century the flightiness of capital was evident: 'manufactories are, by nature, perpetually fluctuating', wrote *The Leominster Guide* in 1808, 'disdaining restriction, they will unavoidably fly to those places wherein provisions and coal are plentiful and cheap'.[27]

Rural areas in the south were increasingly exposed to competition from London, which is often overlooked as the home of workshops as well as consumers. Even the concentration of rural domestic industries was a sign that merchants from the local towns were organising them into clusters. And when south and north were linked to the same markets, southern industries became vulnerable to competition from areas where industries as a whole were particularly dense. The process underlying the decline of southern industry and rise first of London and then of the north was the competition made real by an increasingly linked network of communications. This was what began the re-ordering of economic distributions. The fact is seldom underlined, though Donald Coleman referred to it with respect to the paper industry.[28]

These points are necessarily general and assume that the comparative advantage of the north did not lie in crop growing. Nor can it be dismissed that the developments overlapped, evolved over time and, given the limitations of the sources, must for ever remain indistinct. It scarcely needs to be added that south and north were not hermetically sealed; resources, trade and occasionally labour and enterprise flowed between them, and not exclusively in one direction. Yorkshire and East Anglia were closely linked; they petitioned Parliament jointly in the interest of worsted production and there were partnerships between clothiers in the West Riding and Norwich.[29] In the 1780s cotton was spun around Reading, Berkshire, the finer grades being sent to London en route for the distant Manchester trade.[30] In 1806 yarn for the north was spun in East Anglia and Gloucestershire. It was sought because weaving had been mechanised but not yet spinning; the spinners of Yorkshire on their own could not keep up with demand from the weavers.

Urban Improvement

A corollary of expansion in transport and trade was the improvement of the market towns, already noted. Building and rebuilding in brick, with tile roofs, accelerated during the period 1660–1730 and continued to increase afterwards.[31] Non-flammable materials reduced the loss of capital from settlement fires, which had swept through every generation or so: if even a small proportion of dwellings was built of brick and tile this could act as a firebreak. The gain was partly a consequence of changes in architectural fashion, influenced by builders' pattern books which spread the styles imposed in London after the Great Fire of 1666. Contemporaries were happy to be fashionable but were also well aware of the value of building to minimise fire losses.

Explicit urban betterment was brought about by the Parliamentary Improvement Acts of the 18th century. The market towns widened their roads, strengthened their bridges, and expanded their commercial facilities. Many saw a substantial increase of population. The larger ones pulled down walls and demolished or by-passed their medieval gates. The growth which encouraged these things was not primarily a response to industrialisation — manufacturing towns were in a minority.[32] It was a virtuous circle responding to, and contributing to, the expansion of domestic trade and agriculture.

The example of Warminster, Wiltshire, illustrates some of the procedures.[33] In 1759 the road out of town towards Westbury was widened by pulling down old houses and throwing gardens into thoroughfares, so that the road became 'fairly passable'. A new road to the common was cut and the old narrow, deep, winding lane abandoned. The hollow channel in Pound Street was filled in and, as a foretaste of the future, a turnpike to Salisbury was proposed. Turnpikes involved new and powerful institutional arrangements but can blind us to the civic energies which were already active. In this respect Warminster was by no means alone. Similar changes were taking place across the country. Improvement Acts and the appointment of Improvement Commissioners became almost general after about 1750, although at that date the north lagged. All the same, 1750 was not the most conspicuous break of trend in urban environments, which had come as early as 1680.[34] The majority adopter phase for reconstructing the market towns in brick was from 1650 to 1750.

Paving improvements often date from the 1680s, when many towns paid companies to put up the new oil-burning street lamps. Quite early in the 18th century the responsibility for lighting was often taken over by local authorities and made a charge on the rates. Finally, the coincidence of Improvement Acts with road and navigation developments, not to mention the increase of traffic, was noticeable. This marked out the first half of the 18th century, however much more evident it became during the second half.

The common impression that market towns were little fiefdoms sunk in backwardness may have originated during the arable depression of the late 19th century. Their service functions were then curtailed, their growth slowed; some have grown little ever since. Although their populations had risen they were still small enough to be dominated by cabals of dullards and petty tyrants who lacked the energy to leave and clung to the doubtful security of the small businesses they had inherited. Improvement had once been initiated by local tradesmen but now came at the behest of national or county governments. Market towns had not always been so passive, but it is hard to peer through the Victorian veil and discern their former vigour.

Competition among Settlements

Patterns of settlement altered as a result of competition among towns and would-be towns, brought about by greater opportunities for offering their goods in markets that had previously been the preserve of a single place. This was not new, merely speeded up, but many of the minuscule fluctuations in business went unrecorded and can scarcely be glimpsed in retrospect. The consequences are more evident than the process: the number of settlements that functioned as markets shrank and some which had obtained their charters during the Middle Ages were sidelined.

Examples come from the Vale of White Horse, Berkshire (now Oxfordshire), where Baulking, Shrivenham and Stanford-in-the-Vale secured market charters during the expansionary period of the early 13th century but have been mere villages for centuries now. Their former status is revealed by layouts (spacious greens) and archaeological remains (house platforms on the green at Baulking).[35] Three other settlements in the Vale of White Horse, Faringdon, Abingdon and Wantage, are the ones that grew into the market towns of recent centuries. During the 16th century the Berkshire woollen industry was settling in Newbury, Reading and Abingdon, having more or less quit the villages of Padworth and Shrivenham.[36]

A pattern of rising and falling localities has been discerned nationally by comparing tax records of the 1520s with those of about 1670.[37] Regionalisation was still not strongly marked at the latter date, but some concentrations of wealth had appeared in the West Midlands and the counties close to the west side of London. To contemporaries the way settlements responded to the slow merging of markets seemed to be ad hoc. At the start of the 18th century, Defoe was definite about the changes but could offer little by way of a common explanation: 'the fate of things gives a new face to things, produces changes in low life, and innumerable incidents; plants and supplants families, raises and sinks towns, removes manufactures, and trades; great towns decay, and small towns rise; new towns, new palaces, new seats are built every day ...'[38] Exogenous alterations in coastal physiography, the silting up of one estuary here, the scouring open of another elsewhere, were all he could suggest. Given that most settlements lay inland this explanation was decidedly incomplete.

Away from the coast Defoe could cite only happenstance, though the happenings were becoming frequent enough. When the industries of towns and large villages were run by a small handful of employers, it is not surprising that the forces eliminating some of them might appear random. For the trade of a town to dwindle, it may have been sufficient that the head of one or two households died at an inopportune time for his business. If firms in neighbouring towns were efficient they might seize the market and penetrate the borough itself. This depended on communications good enough to permit wares to be diffused over what, in early cases, was probably only a few miles.

Regional self-sufficiency was never absolute. Wilfred Smith observed that at least from the late 15th century generalised manufactures were giving way to industries producing a narrower range of commodities in localities with special advantages.[39] These advantages pertained to 'the qualities of the regional geographical environment'. Smith was probably thinking in terms of natural endowments. More plausibly, he noted the propensity of certain industries to turn out goods, 'beyond the capacity of the local market to absorb their production'. He quoted Defoe on the increase in trade, navigation, wealth and population in towns that turned to specialised manufactures, 'while their Neighbours Decay'.

Market areas had usually been small in medieval times. Going to market meant withdrawing labour from the fields for several hours, possibly the whole day, which was a serious loss for tiny communities with low productivity. At sensitive stages of the agricultural cycle it could not be afforded. Nor could diverting much land to grow hay for draft animals be afforded. By the end of the Middle Ages, however, an upward shift in the area served by certain market towns becomes evident, giving rise to hierarchies of settlements like those in Berkshire. According to Pawson there had been 2,000 or so functioning markets in England in the early 14th century.[40] By the mid-17th century there were approximately 800 towns with markets, 300 of them specialised by commodity and able to attract buyers from a distance. Numerical shrinkage continued; there were only some 520 markets in 1770. Better roads to the bigger markets undermined the lesser ones, though the exact details of the fortunes of individual towns remain questions for local historians.

Trinder takes stock of the manufacturing in market towns about Defoe's time. He reports 40 or 50 towns in England with populations of 2,000 to 5,000, and about 30 with over 5,000 inhabitants, the latter all selling goods beyond their own hinterlands.[41] In London and the chief provincial centres there were sophisticated industries like tin-ware production, besides brewing and malting on an expanded scale. This hierarchy emerged in an integrated market before the days of turnpikes and canals. Admittedly the risk exists of observational equivalence. Similar prices and price movements may not signify genuine integration, since weather shocks, currency changes or foreign wars may lead prices to converge. The physical evidence is more conclusive. The scale of the areas over which a town's products began to be sold, the range of goods involved and the different fates of towns all indicate that the circles of market access were growing, overlapping, overtaking and merging.

The turnpikes sealed the dominance of one town over another, and reduced the prominent roles of others, but inter-urban competition had been evident much earlier. Rollison demonstrated the degrees of early specialisation on manufacturing in Gloucestershire by calculating occupations on the muster role of 1608.[42] He compared the total male population with the number of occupations, reasoning that the higher a town's ratio, the more it would have been a centre manufacturing for non-local markets. The most specialised towns lay in the Stroudwater valley, which doubled in population between 1551 and 1676 and doubled again by 1779. The district grew twice as fast as Gloucestershire as a whole. Stroudwater was nationally important for the making of woollen cloth, though destined to fade from the late 1820s.

Increased activity and improved routes started to become conspicuous in the late 17th century, when hamlets emerged specifically to service road transport: a few cottages, an inn or two, a blacksmith's forge and a wheelwright's shop. One grew up in the 1680s on the strategic climb over the Cotswold Edge at Birdlip. The corn badgers supplying grain to the Stroudwater industrial area clustered there, as did the carriers of cloth and cheese, receiving from local producers goods that had been carried up the escarpment on donkeys.

An effect, and sometimes a cause, of spatial competition was product specialisation, as with buttons at Shaftesbury, steel jewellery at Woodstock, boots at Cookham, and so forth. These products were light; some were sold at the post-harvest fairs or hawked from place to place. Nor was specialisation the only route to urban success. The opposite might be true in an era of inland trade. In 1608 the least specialised town in Gloucestershire was Cirencester, signalling that it was a place which lived by commerce, despite the fact that before the establishment of turnpikes the road from Gloucester to London by-passed it. Gloucestershire was a prime case where industrial growth, coupled with London's demand, reshaped the network of routes and determined the volume of traffic. Despite the cost of carrying goods or even driving animals over the Cotswold Edge, the east-west orientation came to prevail over the medieval trade route up and down the Severn valley. In the 1830s cloth from the Stroud area was still being sent to London overland, which was more convenient than canal, though dearer.[43] Surprisingly it was carried by coach which, although more expensive, was quicker than by wagon.

Communications and the South-North Shift

The initial character of improvements involved a thousand purely local innovations. All was parochial in early modern industrial history, said Charles Wilson, all was a 'confused patchwork'.[44] Wilson, like Donald Coleman, was less impressed by numerical data than modern scholars. Imperfect evidence, he said, often masquerades as statistics. Historical observations and carefully handled impressions have to be used to pick up changes that came in gradually and were on a small-scale.

The parochial patchwork coalesced into regional units grounded in environmental variety, which translates into differences in production costs.

Without categorising the units, their shifting patterns cannot easily be grasped, though what readers familiar with an area may find straightforward, outsiders are likely to think complex. The classification of regions is parallel to solving history's colligation puzzle, that is to say, deciding where to begin. In both cases the sensible answer is not to impose an *a priori* scheme but to select what best illuminates the class of problems to be tackled.

Geological and topographical variety ensures that nowhere in England can be called typical. Some areas were nevertheless conspicuously out of the mainstream, one of them being the Midland clay plain, despite its location in Lowland England. The Midlands lacked navigable rivers down which grain might be sent to London and as a result their producers gained little from rising demand in the capital. Much of the area remained pastoral, its farmers described as 'lockt up in the Inlands'.[45] The Midlands could not readily share in the inversion whereby grain came to be grown on the drier uplands of southern England instead of in the traditional 'granaries' of the clay vales.[46] No doubt Aubrey's 17th-century remark was not literally true that, 'as ten thousand pounds is gained in the hill barren countrey, so the vale does lose as much, which brings it to an equation'.[47] Yet agricultural innovation reversed land values in southern England, prompting new patterns of traffic.

Linking settlement patterns to transport improvements is difficult. Chronologies are sketchy. In the Middle Ages, the west side of the country from Bristol to Chester had been notably self-contained, its trade running from the south-western to the north-western quarter. At the start of the 18th century Defoe thought this belt ran right from Exeter to Manchester. The change had come between the 16th and 18th centuries, when the proportion of produce from Gloucester going east to London via Cirencester and the booming inland port of Lechlade-on-Thames rose steeply. Only with the growth of Manchester was farm produce pulled north again in any quantity, though when foodstuffs from Herefordshire began to move in that direction they were being switched from the Bristol market rather than London.

Framing questions about the effect of improved communications solely in terms of the rise of industry in the north and its decline in the south would be to misconceive how mutable the late pre-industrial economy was. Consider fluctuations in the relative status of Bristol. In 1668 Pepys described Bristol as 'in every respect another London'.[48] Every respect except size, perhaps, though Bristol grew enough to engross the finishing trades of neighbouring towns: in 1780 it was reported that, 'formerly [Gloucester] had many manufactures but Bristol has since supplanted it: and there is nothing remaining of that kind worthy of observation'.[49] Over much of the 18th century Bristol expanded because of the Atlantic trade, but London reasserted itself, through becoming accessible from the Stroudwater textile district by canal as well as road and being in the opposite direction nicely placed for trade with the Low Countries.

We should envisage a continuum in which firms and industries were relocating, concentrating, shrinking or standing still. Given tiny local markets, many firms were probably marginal once they lost the protection of high transport costs. Nor did guild regulations permanently shield them from external competition. When their defences were breached, they evaporated, mostly unsung. Fairly small cost advantages made a big difference once markets were joined. These effects especially coincided around London. A spider's web of communications was created whereby London's needs could be met and its goods distributed. This was why milling, malting and brewing prospered in market towns along routes for 100 miles around the capital: Abingdon-on-Thames is an example where the wharves and merchants' houses may still be seen. Other industrial regions, as they grew, all needed to be fed and mimicked London's reach by drawing supplies from great distances. The Derbyshire uplands at first drew from Nottinghamshire; the West Riding took its cereals from Lincolnshire and the East Riding; Birmingham from rural Warwickshire; and Lancashire from as far away as Lincolnshire and Ireland.[50]

Wilfred Smith noted competition between London and the remainder of the country as early as the 15th century: felt hats made in London replaced caps made elsewhere.[51] He tabulated turnpike and canal Acts between 1750 and 1830 by blocks of counties, demonstrating concentration in the north, especially of canals.[52] But Smith also recorded competition *within* the north. Among southern producers, the British History Online section on Tiverton, East Devon, cites the way its inhabitants at first attributed their town's decline to competition from elsewhere in the south, not the north. By 1745 they were indicting competition from Norwich stuffs. Later they held that Fox's new manufactory at Wellington, 15 miles away, had caused their woollen industry to decay, obliging them to switch down to net-making.

There were plenty of switches within individual towns. Where little fixed capital was involved, changing occupations needed only resolve on the part of the owners and flexibility from the workers. An unusual example was that of the shalloon 'factory' manufacturing light cloth at Wimborne, Dorset.[53] Most of the congregation of a Presbyterian chapel worked there. The Anglican clergyman at Wimborne Minster managed to have fines levied on any who failed to attend service in the parish church. To avoid this, the works moved to Romsey, Hampshire, in 1673 and most of the 400 employees went as well. For more mundane reasons, Worcester's clothiers migrated to Gloucestershire and Somerset at the start of the 18th century but about 1750 Dr. Wall, whose life is celebrated by displays in the Royal Porcelain Museum, introduced the china industry to take its place.[54] Worcester had not a single resource advantage for making chinaware.

Stocking-knitting nicely illustrates the cross-currents of regional competitiveness out of which the industrial revolution was to emerge. It establishes that, despite the pattern into which industrialisation eventually settled, there was initially no straightforward north-south contest. After the spread of the stocking frame in the late 17th century, David Chambers and other sources tell us that the trade of knitting stockings quit the Norwich area, moving not to the north, but to London.[55] In the 18th century it also disappeared from the Godalming area of Surrey. Yet London's reign did not last long. Between 1732 and 1750 a movement out took place, some 800 frames shifting to Nottinghamshire and others to different parts of the Midlands, leaving only high fashion work in the capital. Labour, food and house rents were cheaper in the Midlands, and in practice the writ of the Company of Framework Knitters did not run outside London.

Costs, though, would surely have been low elsewhere in the provinces. The small but vital centre at Tewkesbury had switched to hosiery during the 16th and 17th centuries, when the traditional woollen production of the Vale of Evesham, for which it was the centre, found itself out-competed by the Stroudwater valleys.[56] Tewkesbury was presumably cheap because it urgently needed to find alternative employment. Few other places outside the East Midlands drew much of the work from London and the trade did not return to Norwich or Godalming. Nor did the move from London boost Towcester, Northamptonshire, where in 1727 there were 150 stockingers, nor Odiham, Hampshire, or Reading, Berkshire, with a total of 100 stockingers between them. It is possible only to surmise that, apart from Tewkesbury, the East Midlands was rock-bottom cheapest among provincial areas.

Table 1   Percentages of the national total of stocking frames in various areas

- **London**

1660	61 per cent
1695	*c.* 19 per cent
1780	2.5 per cent

- **Tewkesbury, Gloucestershire**

1782	*c.* 3.35 per cent
1810	*c.* 2.7 per cent
1830	*c.* 2 per cent
1844	1.9 per cent — of which the majority were idle

- **The Midlands (Nottinghamshire, Leicestershire and Derbyshire)**

1780	85 per cent
1812	87 per cent
1833	86 per cent
1844	91 per cent

- **Nottingham and Nottinghamshire villages (a sub-set of the Midlands)**

1660	15 per cent
1714	5 per cent
1812	32 per cent
1833	32 per cent
1844	34 per cent

Figures exist for the total number of stocking frames in England as a whole and for various regions. They are available at intervals from as early as 1660 but the series, especially the regional part, is incomplete and the figures do not match for all dates. To chart locational shifts, four sets of data may be extracted and rendered as percentages of the national total (Table 1). The absolute number of frames would mean little to the modern reader; suffice it to note that the national totals were 660 frames in 1660, 20,000 in 1780 and 48,482 in 1844.

These shifts were not impelled by technological change, the trade being neither coal-based nor steam-driven. Lee's invention of the stocking frame in 1589 had made knitting 10 or 15 times faster without any engine to drive it. The frame, though, came in gradually and in remote districts knitting by hand survived as a form of sweated labour until the very end of the 18th century.

More on South and North

These effects in a single industry demonstrate the cross-currents, but we must come in the end to north-south competition. Once industrialised, the north generated the bulk of traffic in goods. A summary of volumes carried by canal in the mid-19th century reveals this.[57] The canals of southern England were carrying about two million tons per annum out of a national total of 30 million tons. One-seventh of the country's waterways thus accounted for only one-fifteenth of the total traffic and in 1845 an investment of £5 million in them was producing a return of only two-and-a-half per cent.

The north had established its supremacy, but how? Recent work revives the customary story that coal was king. The direct question is asked, whether cheap coal or lower transport costs were what determined industrial location, but by starting so late (at 1871) the conclusions may not apply to the full history of industrialisation.[58] It is important to distinguish the phases, since the answer altered over time.

Three phases can be identified, though they overlapped. First, the north had advantages that arose from its disadvantages, meaning the lack of comparative advantage in agriculture, or at any rate in growing cereals. Clusters of industry — alternatives to farming — created agglomeration effects. These were based on reputation for quality, the sharing of information where industrialists and merchants worked close enough to meet frequently, and the presence of discrete bodies of workers who could be supervised better than when dispersed. (The last point involves double-counting, since supervision improves quality.) The timing of the north's industrialisation suggests that, before coal made a big difference, the region generated features like these that would help it overhaul the south.

The second phase added coal, but for purposes other than generating steam. Here the north's advantage was smaller than it may seem, since coal was not a major element in costs before the steam age. Coal is reported to have become significant in the woollen industry after 1660 for use in dye-pans and hot-pressing furnaces, and by 1700 imports had rose ten-fold — but all this was in Exeter, where coal was used more and more in the 18th century and was cheap enough between 1741 and 1778 for Exonians to switch from wood for their household grates.[59] In this phase, the expansion of industry in the north still rested on other advantages.

The third phase was when coal became routinely employed on a large scale to fire steam engines used in manufacturing. This was not until the mid- or late 19th century. By then, proximity to the mines was valuable enough to fix manufacturing there and for it not to disperse again even though transport costs continued to fall. But the spatial changes of the earlier phases show we should not be mesmerised by the ultimate scale of coal-based industry. In the early stages competitiveness based on standard business considerations was more decisive. Market integration based on transport improvements enabled the north's competitiveness to express itself over wider and wider areas. As Szostak claims, investigating transportation is, 'the only reasonable way of explaining the Industrial Revolution in terms of something other than shifts in the supply curve due to something like an exogenous increase in the rate of technological innovation'.[60] The concentration of industry in the north was a secondary effect of market integration and only subsequently did the presence of coal become its dominant advantage.

Endnotes

1. Y. Kaukianinen, Shrinking the world: Improvements in the spread of information transmission, c.1820–1870, *Eur. Rev. Econ. Hist.* **5**(1): 1–28, 2001.
2. E. Pawson, *Transport and Economy: The Turnpike Roads of Eighteenth-Century Britain* (London: Academic Press, 1977), p. vii.
3. E. L. Jones, Economics in the history mirror, *J. Interdiscip. Econ.* **3**: 168, 1990.
4. E. Pawson, *The Turnpike Trusts of the Eighteenth Century: A Study of Innovation and Diffusion* (Oxford: School of Geography Research Paper 14, 1975), pp. 10–14.
5. D. Bogart, Turnpike trusts and the transportation revolution in eighteenth-century England, *Explor. Econ. Hist.* **42**: 479–508, 2005.
6. P. Langford, *A Polite and Commercial People: England 1727–1783* (Oxford: Clarendon Press, 1989), p. 634.
7. G. Crocker, *The History of the Basingstoke Canal*, 1977 edition (Surrey and Hampshire Canal Society website).
8. D. Gerhold, Productivity change in road transport before and after Turnpiking, 1690–1840, *Econ. Hist. Rev.* **49**: 491–515, 1996.
9. H. J. Mackinder, *Britain and the British Seas* (Oxford: Clarendon Press, second edition, 1907), p. 325.
10. D. Rollison, *The Local Origins of Modern Society: Gloucestershire 1500–1800* (London: Routledge, 1992), p. 61.
11. D. Harrison, *The Bridges of Medieval England: Transport and Society 400–1800* (Oxford: Oxford University Press, 2004).
12. M. A. Havinden, Agricultural progress in open-field Oxfordshire, in E. L. Jones (ed.), *Agriculture and Economic Growth in England 1650–1815* (London: Methuen, 1967), p. 78.

13. R. Jefferies, *Round about a Great Estate* (Bradford-on-Avon: Ex Libris Press, 1987), p. 73.
14. J. de L. Mann, Documents illustrating the Wiltshire textile trades in the eighteenth century, *Wiltshire Archaeological Society Records Branch XIX* (1964), pp. xxviii–xxix.
15. D. Daniell, *William Tyndall: A Biography* (New Haven: Yale University Press, 2001 edition), p. 392, n. 8.
16. A. Everitt, *Change in the Provinces: The Seventeenth Century* (Leicester: Leicester University Press, 1969), p. 42.
17. G. H. R. Homer-Wooff, *The Postal History of Wantage* (Privately printed, 1988), pp. 3–5.
18. J. Camp, *In Praise of Bells* (London: Robert Hale, 1988), p. 79.
19. Compare the demographic effects of modern Brazilian soap operas, *The Economist*, 14 Mar. 2009.
20. Quoted by A. Buck, *Dress in Eighteenth Century England* (London, 1979), p. 128. I am indebted to Jenny Sargeant for this reference.
21. J. de Vries, *The Industrious Revolution: Consumer Behavior and the Household Economy, 1650 to the Present* (Cambridge: Cambridge University Press, 2008).
22. C. H. Shiue and W. Keller, Markets in China and Europe on the eve of the industrial revolution, *Am. Econ. Rev.* **97**(4): 1189–1216, 2007.
23. R. Szostak, *The Role of Transportation in the Industrial Revolution* (Montreal & Kingston: McGill-Queen's University Press, 1991), p. 13.
24. K. G. Ponting, *A History of the West of England Cloth Industry* (London: Macdonald, 1957), pp. 144–145.
25. P. Hudson, *Regions and Industries: A Perspective on the Industrial Revolution in Britain* (Cambridge: Cambridge University Press, 1989); *The Industrial Revolution* (London: Edward Arnold, 1992).
26. J. K. Walton, *Lancashire: A Social History 1558–1939* (Manchester: Manchester University Press, 1987).
27. Anon., *The Leominster Guide* (Leominster, n.d. [1808]), p. 226.
28. D. C. Coleman, *The British Paper Industry 1495–1860* (Oxford, 1958), p. 220.
29. H. Heaton, *The Yorkshire Woollen and Worsted Industries: From the Earliest Times up to the Industrial Revolution* (Oxford, 1920), pp. 276, 339.
30. R. Valpy, On wool and the woollen manufacture, *Ann. Agric.* **IX**: 524, 1788.
31. E. L. Jones and M. E. Falkus, Urban improvement and the English economy in the seventeenth and eighteenth centuries, *Res. Econ. Hist.* **IV**: 192–233, 1979.
32. Jones and Falkus, Urban improvement.
33. J. J. Daniell, *The History of Warminster* (London: Simpkin, Marshall, 1879), p. 113.

34. Jones and Falkus, Urban improvement.

35. N. Stebbing, *The Vale of White Horse* (Oxfordshire Museum Services, No. 9), pp. 21–22.

36. R. F. Dell, The decline of the clothing industry in Berkshire, *Trans. Newbury Dist. Field Club* X(2): 50–64, 1954.

37. C. Husbands, Regional change in a pre-industrial economy: wealth and population in England in the sixteenth and seventeenth centuries, *J. Hist. Geogr.* **13**(4): 345–359, 1987.

38. D. Defoe, *A Tour through England and Wales* (London: J. M. Dent & Sons, 1928), p. 2.

39. W. Smith, *An Economic Geography of Great Britain* (London: Methuen, 1953), p. 76.

40. Pawson, *Transport and Economy*, pp. 313, 323.

41. B. Trinder, *The Making of the Industrial Landscape* (Gloucester: Alan Sutton, 1987), p. 46.

42. Rollison, *Local Origins*, p. 28, Table 1.1.

43. Charles and A. M. Hadfield (eds.), *The Cotswolds: A New Study* (Newton Abbot: David & Charles, 1973), p. 153.

44. C. Wilson, *England's Apprenticeship 1663–1763* (London: Longmans, 1965) pp. 86–87.

45. Quoted by J. D. Gould, Mr. Beresford and the lost villages, *Agri. Hist. Rev.* **III**: 212, 1955.

46. E. L. Jones, English and European agricultural development,1650–1750, in R. M. Hartwell (ed.), *The Industrial Revolution* (Oxford: Basil Blackwell, 1970), pp. 64, 73.

47. Quoted *ibid.*, p. 65.

48. C. Wilson, *England's Apprenticeship 1603–1763*, p. 179.

49. Quoted by W. E. Minchinton, Bristol – Metropolis of the West in the eighteenth century', *Trans. R. Hist. Soc.*, 5th Series, **4**: 78, 1954.

50. Pollard, *Peaceful Conquest*, p. 11.

51. *Ibid.*, p. 76.

52. Smith, *Economic Geography*, pp. 91 n. 3, 152, 155.

53. A. L. Clegg, *A History of Wimborne Minster and District* (Bournemouth, 1960), pp. 118–119.

54. Victoria county history, *Worcestershire* **II**: 276, 1906.

55. J. D. Chambers, *Nottinghamshire in the Eighteenth Century* (London: P. S. King & Son, 1932), pp. 89–99; British History online, Tewkesbury; and Knitting Together website.

56. T. Rath, The Tewkesbury Hosiery Industry, *Textile Hist.* **7**: 141, 1976.

57. C. Hadfield, *The Canals of Southern England* (London, 1955), p. 333.
58. N. Crafts and A. Mulatu, How did the location of industry respond to falling transport costs in Britain before the First World War? *J. Econ. Hist.* **66**: 575–607, 2006.
59. W. G. Hoskins, *Industry, Trade and People in Exeter 1688–1800* (Manchester: Manchester University Press, 1935), pp. 104–105.
60. Szostak, *Role of Transportation*, p. 40.

CHAPTER 10

THE PACE OF CHANGE

While farm labor took advantage of the higher wages in the cities, it appears that their migration response was nowhere near quick enough to satisfy the excess labor demands associated with the first Industrial Revolution.

Jeffrey G. Williamson, 1994

Economic history does not always deal four-square with the timing of change. The subject is less directly concerned with chronology than with magnitude and process. This is a legacy from economics, which is more interested in defining the forces making for equilibria than in the passages from one to the next. Whole processes are labelled as if they were single events — the industrial revolution, the agricultural revolution and so forth. While it is intuitively obvious that these did not take place overnight, their duration is not ordinarily highlighted.

'Fast' and 'slow' are terms in constant use but what they mean in terms of elapsed time is rarely clear. Occasionally, however, someone asks why industrialisation was so slow or why did it not take place earlier. The issue is raised by Greg Clark, who calls the delay in the Industrial Revolution until 'around 1800' more than a mere 'mystery': he labels it nothing less than, 'the great and enduring puzzle of human history'.[1] An older generation had asked a similar question. In his lectures at Nottingham during the 1950s, David Chambers alluded to the developmental promise of the 1690s and puzzled why there was such a lag before the triumph of the factory system. He knew very well that many ancient impediments had been dissolved before full-blown industrialisation occurred and that, when it did, many constituents of change had long been in place. He was inclined to muse that there seemed a preternaturally protracted delay.

Why Was De-Industrialisation so Slow?

We have traced de-industrialisation to greater competition through market integration and the spatial division of labour which this permitted. This depended on improved communications, which depended in turn on agreements to invest, followed by the practicalities of surveying possible routes and their actual construction. Decisions were hostages to commercial considerations and the engineering tasks of canalising rivers, building canals or laying down better roads. Each stage took time to arrange. Investors who had previously committed funds were prone to protest and drag their feet when fresh proposals threatened to supersede routes or modes of transport in which they had a stake.

We have seen that a landowner objected to the proposed route of the Basingstoke canal. Investors in the Thames & Isis Navigation joined him in objecting, as did the owners of locks and winches along the Thames, who feared loss of trade.[2] This slowed things down and the Basingstoke canal, mooted in 1776, was not completed until 1794. Capital was not always easy to raise, canal mania or no; the proprietors in this case ran out of funds because of the difficult money market during the War of the American Revolution. They were obliged to seek a second Act of Parliament for raising additional capital.

Until new routes were fully operational, the natural protection of distance allowed local businesses to keep going. The owners of firms in small places could rely for a time on the loyalty of customers attached to them by ties of habit and kinship. People were affixed to their communities and the churches, chapels and webs of personal relationships which were all they knew. Their social life was local, from drinking in the pubs with their mates to participating in the venison feasts and flower festivals common in 18th- and 19th-century market towns. The psychic costs of giving up occupations their fathers had followed, and which many may have followed themselves for decades, were high. Rapid abandonment of existing enterprises and ways of life are not to be expected or likely to be well documented. Given that industries succumbed to outside competition at different periods in different places, the picture is full of overlaps made blurry by the lack of precise evidence that always characterises decline.

Thus import competition did not strike home at once and the realisation that local products were being undercut was not immediate. It would be unreasonable to think that outside competitors had it all their own way. Misallocations, easily excluded from accounts of economic growth, had to be corrected: as Pollard observed, the costs of industrialisation in the north were, 'greatly increased by the … misapplication of resources, false starts, errors and rapid obsolescence inevitable in a pioneer economy'.[3] H. I. Dutton and S. R. H. Jones strongly concur that the diffusion of inventions was not cost-less.[4] They stress the uncertainties of the market and the importance of interpersonal relations between contracting parties. These points may seem obvious but Dutton and Jones are responding to positions taken, at least implicitly, by other economic historians. The more sweeping the narrative, the more the impression may be conveyed of smoothly functioning capital markets and frictionless introductions of technology. In close up neither was smooth; the financial markets gave their customary heart-stopping lurches, and inventions took time to bed down in the productive system.

For southern producers, defeat could be put off by cutting costs or trying to copy new fashions. There was no barrier in principle to creating an indus-trial workforce from formerly independent southern weavers, reluctant and unhappy though they were. In his *Brief History of the Weavers of the County of Gloucester* (1838), Thomas Excell said the change had come about during his lifetime and described the displaced weavers, 'as an army defeated and taken prisoner'.[5] This leaves unexplained why so few went elsewhere to better themselves.

During the 1850s the hand-loom weavers hung on at Broughton Gifford, Wiltshire, working long hours at home in their 'shops' for no more money (and suffering worse health) than farm workers.[6] They could no longer afford ponies to take their cloth for sale at Trowbridge and onlookers marvelled they had persisted so long in their trade 'against the steam-power looms of the factory'. Why did they not become farm hands? 'This is easier said than done', wrote a local observer, 'Transplanting full grown trees is an operation attended with very poor success'.

The first response of more organised groups was to decline to meet competition, resorting instead to protectionist measures, hoping to reinforce guild edicts against interlopers. The realisation that pie-slicing, market-sharing measures would merely prolong the decline took time to sink in. By 1792 Newbury, with its once-defensive cloth guild, was reduced to begging 'strangers' to enter its clothing trade, promising no interference and empha-sising the good canal route to the Thames and London.[7] By then it was too late; besides, the canal was what had improved Newbury's role as a collecting centre for farm produce and contributed to its switch from manufacturing. The changes surrounding industrial decline took time to work themselves out. The key point is that producers tended to cling on while they were covering their variable costs. The die-off was delayed. With so many imponderables, shrouded by uncertainty, it is impossible to post-dict just how prolonged decline would prove to be, but there is no doubt about the lags before competition took its toll.

Why Was Enclosure so Slow?

Looking today on a mostly privatised landscape, we may brush aside the difficulties of enclosing. Since only vestiges of communal farming remain, we may conclude that the disadvantages were obviously sufficient for it to be abolished. Nevertheless, privatisation and physical enclosure took centuries to complete. Given the considerable power in the hands of landowners, why were they unable to bring about, if not a general enclosure, at least a more rapid expropriation of the 'inefficient' small farmers of the common fields?

The supposed inefficiencies of communal husbandry led in the 1960s to an emphasis on the 'tragedy of the commons', a concept developed by the biologist, Garrett Hardin, and enthusiastically taken up by the proto-ecologists who emerged during that decade.[8] The idea was that, because individuals have an incentive to overstock a common property resource, *ergo* they must indeed overstock it. A denuded and over-grazed countryside was conjured up out of thin air, consistent with classical economics and insufficiently tempered by primary evidence.

The source of this dismal vision was the work of a political economist at the University of Oxford, William Forster Lloyd. In 1832 Lloyd asked why cattle on the common were so puny and stunted, why the common was so bare-worn and why was it cropped so differently from adjoining enclosures? Lloyd's lectures do not indicate what prompted his surmise but perhaps he was thinking of Port Meadow, to which the 19th-century historian, Freeman, used to take visitors who asked to see the oldest monument in Oxford.[9] Port Meadow was an ancient grazing meadow that had conceivably become over-grazed. The growing number of townsfolk may not have been able to organise well enough to prevent this. At any rate, Lloyd cannot have been thinking of Yarnton Mead or other meadows belonging to villages a very few miles further up the Thames, where rights to the hay were allocated by lot and communal management lasted another 150 years without ruining either the land or the farmers.

Hardin balanced the tragedy of the commons on the head of Lloyd's pin. Although he later came, rather reluctantly, to acknowledge that common-field farmers were able to manage their affairs adequately and exclude individuals without legitimate rights, the intellectual damage was done. A generation of readers swallowed an argument against communal husbandry that exaggerated its admitted weaknesses. Agricultural improvers eventually supplanted the commoners but it took them long years of argument and chicanery to reduce communal systems to the shreds left today.

A widely held view is that institutions are necessarily efficient, the argument being that, were they not, rational people would change them. This is the standard contractual view of property rights.[10] Changes would be prompted by shifts in relative prices deriving in turn from technological changes, meaning in this case innovations in husbandry. At first sight, the enclosure of the common fields appears to fit the thesis. The high cost of negotiating alterations in their cropping or livestock routines seems to explain a willingness to privatise. But this does not account for the timing; taken at face value, privatisation should not have been so long delayed. There were successful efforts to upgrade traditional regimes by inserting new fodder crops into them but the practice was far from universal and far from complete where it did take place.[11] If efficiency gains were so tempting it is hard to explain why extinguishing communal husbandry was so drawn out. The contractual view does not allow for the persistence of inefficiencies, the 'survival of the mediocre'.

Nor does the contractual view fully incorporate the alternative 'tragedy of the anti-commons' identified by Michael Heller, whose model is appropriate here.[12] Whereas Hardin's intention was to explain over-use and supposed ecological damage to the commons by multiple owners, Heller points to under-use arising from the ability of some of those involved to block change. This is termed 'group exclusion', although a single dissenting owner was capable of frustrating an enclosure if he had a large enough share of the land.

Heller's interest in under-use is readily assimilated to our concern with delay. We are not required to decide whether productivity gains actually did follow enclosure. All we are attempting to account for is the protracted nature of the process: why enclosure took so long to accomplish. Neither the abstractions found at the extreme among economists nor the meandering descriptions supplied by historians persuasively explain the duration of change. The approaches need to be fused; the academic tribes ought to trade.

Where landed property was involved, the potential for disputes was always considerable. There were many occasions for contention over routes, for instance. The marketing of a district's produce depended upon the route chosen, while existing investments in communications might be threatened by a new proposal. There were repeated conflicts like the following in 1756: 'our Gloucestershire Gentlemen ... are again very eager after a Turnpike Road from Stratford [-on-Avon] into Gloucestershire: They had a meeting ... when Mr Brighton, who has a little money on a neighb'ring [turnpike] Gate, made strenuous opposition'.[13]

Enclosure was even more divisive than roads, because it touched directly on livelihoods. Those who feared they might become losers would hope to impede reallocations of land or common rights. The resultant delays are usually attributed to the opposition of commoners and small holders. Searches by historians in the tradition of the Hammonds have uncovered occasional striking instances of resistance by humble people, but they were usually forlorn. By definition, the poor had few resources. Only rarely do we come across examples of obduracy on their part like the subscription raised by the paupers of Potterne, Wiltshire, to buy a Burns *Justice* with the avowed intent of baiting the authorities.[14] Potterne's inhabitants were 'a very discontented and turbulent race', known ironically as the 'Potterne lambs', which merely indicates how untypical they were.

Working class protests against their lot, among them the petition carried to George IV at Brighton by farm workers from north Hampshire and the speech that the Wiltshire labourer, Jacob Baker, wished to address to a meeting of the agricultural interest in Swindon, received no sympathetic hearing or no hearing at all. When it came to blocking enclosures, commoners seldom prevailed. Nevertheless their unwillingness to relinquish their rights might raise the costs, since anyone who had a legally demonstrable right had to be bought out. On surpassingly rare occasions a person of property might even stand up for the poor against others of his own class. William Sherborn was actually presented with a painted tea-tray in gratitude for organising the abandonment of a proposal for enclosure in Middlesex. He must have been very eloquent. The inscription on the tray reads:

A witness for William Sherborn, of his abhorrence to robbing the poor by Enclosures, Bedfont, 10th March 1801 on which day the Duke of Northumberland, the Bishop of London, the Governors of Christ's Hospital etc., withdrew their signatures from the petition which they had signed for the Enclosure to their perpetual honour on being informed of the great evil the poor would sustain by it'.[15]

We cannot directly observe how far this sand in the wheels slowed down change. The grumbling of the silent majority is not well documented, nor is it certain when improvers held off because they feared having to buy out the commoners. These were essentially non-events that escaped comment. Wrangling among the improvers themselves, or at any rate among the larger owners, was more significant. Although mentioned from time to time, even this is rarely given its due. A moment's reflection shows that there must have been a great deal of argument where so many individuals possessed overlapping rights to the land. Conflicts of interest were perennial, sometimes becoming embroiled in long-standing feuds between families.[16] While the great aristocrats might expect to get their own way, disputes over ways and means rumbled on among lesser figures. These inserted delays and raised the costs of bringing plans for enclosure to fruition. Consider the experience of Sir Richard Temple during the decade 1678–1687: Temple was engaged in such expensive law suits over enclosures in Oxfordshire that it was a distinct relief when legal costs fell to a mere 10 per cent of his total expenditure.[17]

At a similar period the Verney family was trying to prevent other men enclosing parts of Buckinghamshire because their own rents were falling and they feared that rising output from additional enclosed land would depress them further.[18] When another family proposed to enclose Steeple Claydon, Sir Ralph Verney warned his son that this, 'might not only cloak up your estate in point of hunting, hawking, coursing, riding and other pleasures … but it needs be a great loss to you in letting your grounds'. He complained, too, that a Dr. Busby had negligently omitted to buy land in another hamlet, 'to prevent enclosing'.

Verney instructed his son to discover whether cows' commons might be sold without land, a separation of rights foreshadowing the marketisation of customary rights. Verney subsequently bought one-and-a-half yardlands and one cow's common, 'enough to prevent an enclosure', and by so doing managed for the sum of £60 to defer enclosure for another 120 years. In 1673 the Verneys prevented the division of the common wastes of two further parishes in which they had interests, only to complete the task themselves 70 years later, when they had the effrontery to bill their action as intended for, 'the encouragement of future industry, good Husbandry and Improvement'. They did not start the physical enclosure of East Claydon until 1741.

The delays, distortions and additional expense caused by intra-elite conflict are illustrated by three geographically separated disputes over landed property in Sussex, Berkshire and Dorset. These provide foundations in actual cases to set alongside the hypothetical reasoning prevalent in the property rights approach, which tends to offer abstractions imposed on, rather than anchored in, the evidence. Specific examples have the advantage of letting us glimpse some of the motives at work.

Let us take the cases from east to west. First, Sussex. The author of a study of the enclosure of the Broyle in Sussex about 1770 calculates that only four of approximately 40 opponents fell into the 'peasant' category.[19] Early modern developments had long since stripped most of the cottagers of their *de jure* rights. Although several minor property owners did put in claims for allotments at the enclosure, they possessed no supporting documents and hence had no *locus*, as the lawyers call it. They were ignored. Some were clear losers, for instance the men engaged in making bricks using clay from the Broyle; their trade ceased immediately on the enclosure award and did not resume for 40 years. Others received allotments of tiny strips not worth the expense of fencing and sold out at once for £5 or £10, which was nowhere near the potential of what they had lost.

All who had been accustomed to graze a few animals on the common lost what to all appearances were merely *de facto* rights. The contrary argument is that clear-felling the timber prior to the enclosure created jobs for sawyers — until all the trees were down and the underwood removed, when work of that sort ceased. The argument might also be made that physical enclosure, fencing, ditching and the like, gave work, and that subsequently 50 jobs were created for full-time farm-workers. These jobs meant, however, labouring for a wage at the whim of an employer; no matter how hard-scrabble the commoners' lives had been, they had at least been independent.

Legal rights — legalistic rights depending on desperate searches for Elizabethan and medieval custumals — may actually have been upheld by the formal processes of enclosure. But customary rights were not recognised, the irony being that a 13th-century custumal had guaranteed every cottar on the manor an unstinted right of common. This mysteriously failed to come to light in the 18th century. Effective opposition at the Broyle arose solely from property owners of approximately the same social class as those promoting the enclosure.

'Peasant' resistance was already a thing of the past. Only people whose upbringing had given them a strong sense of self-worth, who were literate, and whose income came from independent sources could afford to mount serious legal challenges — hiring attorneys to present counter-petitions and so forth. At the Broyle, their opposition may have arisen because they were also politically opposed to the pro-enclosure aristocrats and super-rich incomers. Furthermore, the leading opponent had a personal interest in gaining a right-of-way which would have enabled him to avoid the toll road. Tradesmen, innkeepers and the like stayed neutral. Their living depended on local patronage and in a decidedly threatening atmosphere they may have been wise to stand aside.

The second case is that of East Lockinge, Berkshire, which was bought in 1718 by Matthew Wymondsold, a speculator in the South Sea Company.[20] Like a typical new broom, Wymondsold tried to sweep all before him. It is no surprise that he built Lockinge House as his residence and greatly enlarged the park, for this was a standard move on the part of aspiring landowners. He strove to enclose the open fields and, although failing to bring about a complete enclosure, did manage to reduce the number of farmers to a handful of tenants. Each tenant had more land than before and the flexibility to farm as he wished, which was more or less the practical aim of enclosing. Wymondsold also closed some rights of way. It was this that brought him into conflict with the rector, Dr. Niblett, whom he additionally incensed by refusing to pay some of the tithes.

As a clergyman, Wymondsold's adversary belonged to one of the few categories of potentially independent men living in the countryside. This is not to say that an incumbent was independent of the owner of the advowson, but the rector of East Lockinge happened to be none other than the Warden of All Souls College, Oxford, and hence an opponent not lacking in resources. Information concerning his quarrel with Wymondsold ('a man fond of Oppression') comes from a document prepared by the rector in order to solicit advice about bringing a prosecution. As may be imagined, the document has a tendentious tone but there is no reason to disbelieve its factual allegations, among which was that 'Mr Wymondsold also about Three or Four Years ago Stopt up the Footway from Hendred to Lockinge without any writt or Authority and the Foot people are now obliged to go a great Way round about'. Other ways and roads had been closed and at least one — 'the pack and prime Way from Ardington to Lockinge' — had been 'turned', that is walled off and diverted.

A problem for the rector was that Wymondsold had bought so many parcels of land that 'most of the parishioners are become his Tenants and Vassals and it may be difficult to have any prosecution carried on by the parishioners in General'. In the event no prosecution was ever brought and the blocked ways have never been restored. Describing this case, Michael Havinden suggests that Wymondsold's tactics may have been designed to make the rector agree to have the parsonage moved away from the manor house. The old parsonage house was eventually pulled down in 1780 or 1781 and a new rectory was built by agreement between Wymondsold's widow and the rector's successor. The widow may have been pursuing a protracted feud with the church on behalf of her late husband, for she cannot have thought the new rector, Hon. John Tracy, a socially undesirable neighbour. More likely the Wymondsold family shared the intense 18th-century desire for privacy which was displayed, for example, in the insistence on box pews so private their occupants were visible to the preacher but not to the congregation.

The third example is the destruction and relocation of Milton Abbas, Dorset, which is as well known as the previous cases are obscure.[21] At Milton Abbas, the Whig M.P., Joseph Damer, later Earl of Dorchester, undertook what has been called the most audacious act of landscape engineering in the whole 18th century. Damer was in a position to carry this out; he had amassed estates in Ireland and apparently gone in for money-lending there on a large scale, and was extravagantly rich.

Where other landowners had moved villages, Damer shifted a market town of over 100 houses: Middleton, which he renamed Milton Abbas, possessed a market chartered by Athelstan in the 10th century. Damer also enclosed a highway. He moved the settlement into a side valley, out of sight of his Great House, and hired Capability Brown to remodel the park. Yet for all his wealth this cavalier procedure took 20 years from its first planning in the 1760s. Whereas a 15th-century landowner might simply have evicted the inhabitants, the 18th century worked — formally — by the rule of law. By that period men fought, in the words of the poem, by shuffling papers and dare not carry their swords. The rich and powerful could co-opt the law in their own interest but by the same token other members of the elite might, if they were stubborn, use the courts to oppose them.

This was what happened at Milton Abbas. Damer was held at bay by a local lawyer, William Harrison, who refused to relinquish his holdings. This may have been the same Harrison, a Quaker, who had been summonsed in 1766 for the non-payment of rates.[22] The dispute over the properties at Milton Abbas was bitter and in the process Damer made sure that one of Harrison's houses was flooded by the water diverted to fill an ornamental lake. Harrison took Damer to court about this and won. By 1776 the last two houses left standing were owned by Harrison. They were held on three lives, his being the last life. Only when Harrison died in 1786 was Damer able to complete the razing of the town.

The potential for enclosure was part of the *Zeitgeist*. Third parties were constantly snooping around, hoping to promote enclosures for the sake of the fees they might bring: the curate, Gilbert White, author of *The Natural History of Selborne*, was warned by his brother, James, about just such a person who was concerning himself with the prospects at Selborne, Hampshire.[23] By chance their aunt had been an objector at the Broyle. According to James White, a Mr. Fisher, 'a man of meddling disposition', employed by the Lords of the Manor but actually acting in his own interest, had already privately mooted a scheme for an Act to enclose Selborne. If Fisher could find a loophole in a Decree of the Court of Chancery made in their grandfather's time, and now in Gilbert White's possession, he might revive the scheme.

The Decree stated that the wood, commons and other wastes of Selborne belonged to the tenants and not to the Lord. This was an impediment to enclosure, since with a clear title the poor tenants could not be evicted and they might demand a high price to sell or even flatly decline to do so. It was unlucky for Fisher that James White seems to have had an interest in Chalgrove, Oxfordshire, where Fisher had once tried to promote an enclosure that failed because of a similar obstruction. James counseled his brother not to let Fisher see the Selborne document if it were in the least ambiguous.

Disputes over property were endemic within and among landed families, and between parishioners and incumbents over tithes. It is scarcely necessary to cite more than a further representative example or two, such as the protracted litigation in the Court of Chancery among the descendants of the

Duncombe family at Downton, Wiltshire. Their squabbles led to a whole series of contested elections between 1774 and 1790, and even that did not conclude the matter.[24] With respect to eleven cases of contested enclosure bills in Nottinghamshire, W. E. Tate found that five were clearly the result of disputes between aristocrats or where aristocrats were opposed by lords of manors, men to whose name Esquire was affixed.[25]

It may be objected that cases of intra-elite conflict were neither large in total number nor representative of all enclosure. But that was probably not so and is in any case hardly the point. Tate's evidence, for example, refers to objections signaled in Parliamentary committee and cannot reveal earlier stages of foot-dragging, negotiation, or every proposal that was still-born, which is a reason for investigating actual cases. If the principal landowners had been able to have their own way freely, any enclosure might have taken place the moment they thought of it. Scheming was not hard. The pushy young attorney, who volunteered a plan for the Broyle enclosure (it proved to be very like the one adopted), had drawn up his proposal in a single hour's work. Executing an enclosure was, however, seldom as easy as this makes it seem. Given the potential for small numbers of individuals with competing interests to frustrate the dreams of projectors, the wish may have been father to the thought but was rarely father to the deed.

Why Did Rural Labour Leave so Slowly?

The defining feature of economic change in England is nowadays considered to be the exceptionally large, and exceptionally early, movement of labour from agriculture to industry. This interpretation concentrates on the 17th and 18th centuries and is taken as having distinguished England from countries that achieved structural change and industrialisation later. Other things being equal, the exodus would be expected to have raised the real return to farm labour, instead of which by the 19th-century rural poverty had become a notorious problem in the south. The assumptions are that despite a large wage gap between agriculture and industry people were reluctant to migrate, meaning that labour markets were and remained regionally segmented. People did move to London, the northern cities and the colonies, but not fast enough to raise real incomes in the countryside to the levels obtainable elsewhere.

Let us call the reluctance of rural labour to move the 'stifled exodus' problem. It is the subject of two ingenious contributions by Jeffrey

Williamson, which provide an excellent starting point.[26] Williamson makes an effort to determine which questions should be posed and then undertakes appropriate measurements. His conclusion is that although the gap in nominal wages exaggerated the difference in real incomes, and hence the size of the incentive to move, a serious gap did remain. The inadequate transfer of labour meant that industrial wages were higher and farm wages lower than they might have been. This held industrial profits and manufacturing output below what would have been obtainable in a more integrated labour market, and swelled the landed sector excessively. Compared with markets for goods, labour markets thus were, or rather became, oddly sticky.[27] The scale of the outflow needed to equilibrate rural and urban wages was too large for the market to clear.

From having been a landscape of small farmers strewn about with minor industrial premises, the South became almost exclusively rustic and blighted by poverty after 1815. Rural degradation was extreme. As William Cobbett fumed about a Cotswold landowner in the 1820s, he was like a plantation owner and all the people were 'his *slaves* as completely … [as] the blacks are the slaves of the planters in Jamaica, the *farmers* here, acting, in fact, in a capacity corresponding with that of the *negro-drivers* there'.[28] The landowner may even have obtained his fortune as the owner of sugar plantations: plenty of plantation money was laundered, so to speak, through the purchase of estates and was unsurprisingly consistent with oppressive treatment of the English poor.[29] Cobbett's protest was an understandable description of landowner-dominated upland villages, where every resource was stripped from the inhabitants, including access to wood for firing. The concern about trespass which developed, amounting to a phobia, has been called 'landowners' disease'. This was truer of the uplands than the vales, and truer of closed villages than open ones, but the problem was widespread.

Cobbett's views on the subject are well known. Returning to England in 1813 he saw what had happened in the Surrey labourers' cottages: 'The *clock* was gone; the *brass* kettle was gone; the *pewter dishes* were gone; the *warming pan* was gone … All was gone!'[30] There was a market for these items, the better designed ones ending as pretended heirlooms in middle-class house-holds. Hugh Mundy, the Hampshire farmer who later blew the whistle on the Andover Workhouse Scandal, wrote in 1830 that, 'once upon a time I could go into any labourer's cottage and they could give me a glass of ale, always having two or three pigs to fat every year, they used to have decent clothes to wear on Sunday with a change for themselves and their families. They used to keep their cottages as clean and neat as possible. Now that is not the case ...' and he follows with graphic detail.[31] Testimony by Penelope Hind about destitution in Berkshire is similarly graphic.[32]

One response on the part of parish authorities was to subsidise the outflow of pauper, or pauperised, labour. In 1791 three covered wagons had taken 49 boys and girls from Gosport workhouse to be bound apprentice in cotton factories at Manchester, but direct transfers like this seem relatively uncommon.[33] They were mainly noticeable when waves of unemployment suddenly overcame a declining industry. Soon after the textile mills of the upper Stroud valley underwent a severe slump at the end of the 1820s, public emigration was organised by the clergy. In Australia, a descendant of weavers extruded from Nailsworth at this time married a descendant of Jacob Baker, an impoverished farm worker known for his eloquence, thus joining in a far land the rejects of failed southern industry and over-stocked southern agriculture.

Less organised removals took place to London and the northern cities, but the first shifts were into farm work or agriculturally related jobs in the vicinity of the mills. Staying in the district, entering the over-stocked ranks of farm workers, was however no good way to restore one's fortunes. Yet if we look from the viewpoint of households rather than individuals we can see that the threat of a dire future may have been masked by local opportunities for some members of a family, such as domestic service for daughters.

Compared with later industrialisations in other countries, the outflow from rural areas of the south in the 1830s and 1840 was rapid — 'except', as Williamson says, 'in terms of what would be necessary to eliminate the disequilibrium'.[34] For that purpose it was 'nowhere near quick enough'. As economic historians have long believed, there really was labour market failure. Williamson's method is properly comparative, contrasting north and south, town and country. He introduces considerations that have usually been overlooked, in particular the higher all-round costs of urban living. Taking into account the cost of living and environmental disamenities in urban areas reduces but it does not eliminate the south-north gap in earnings.

Nevertheless, the comparisons Williamson makes with later migrations may not be entirely apposite, since transport and flows of information subsequently became better than those prevailing in England during the second quarter of the 19th century. Likewise, although Williamson's second contribution does encompass emigration, he may not give sufficient weight to the improvement in colonial city environments, at least in Australia. For instance, at the period when Williamson argues that English cities were deteriorating environmentally, gold was transforming Melbourne. At first tagged Smellbourne, it was turning into Marvellous Melbourne, while other Victorian towns, such as Sale, were also remarkably well provided with services. The colonies were becoming more attractive. This continues to tax us with explaining labour's reluctance to leave the land of England.

One possibility is that the sheer cost of travel — to northern industrial cities, let alone overseas — may have seemed insuperable to destitute or near-destitute people. Credit markets were unlikely to have remedied this; what collateral did such people possess? Small wonder that migratory journeys within England proceeded only by short stages. By and large, individuals in their thirties or older did not migrate. Younger men may have been more sanguine about urban disamenities, more prepared to share a room than whole families, less troubled by high urban rents, and more inclined to treat migration as an adventure.

Spatial gaps are only part of the story. Chronological gaps, which Williamson does not discuss, may play a role in the explanation. By this I mean the comparisons that southern labour could make with its own lot in previous years. Given the psychic impediments to moving, together with the objective risks and lack of reliable information, any slight improvement in local conditions may have reduced the incentive to migrate. Horrendous though conditions had been in the early 19th century, they very gradually improved after about the middle of the century. Experiencing better conditions on the spot would militate against taking the scarcely calculable risks of leaving. The past may have seemed a more reliable benchmark than promises of a future in some remote place.[35]

Betterment started with the slight reduction in labour supply that drove the rewards for labour upwards, however minimally. Richard Jefferies noted in the 1880s that the health of villagers had improved within memory.[36] Once the railways came in and police forces were established, young men had a chance to improve their lot without moving far; they could hope to join these aristocracies of labour.[37] When rural conditions improved a little after mid-century, emigration to the colonies paused. It picked up again later, but that is hardly surprising since with each passing year more information and better transport became available, reducing the uncertainties associated with leaving.[38]

Poverty made it hard for unassisted families to move. They faced two main types of problem, first the risks, real and perceived, and second the limited quantity and uncertain quality of information about prospects at the destinations. The costs of migrating included loss of contact with relatives, friends and neighbours. Few would see their homes again. Even, or perhaps especially, in conditions of poverty the ties of kinship and friendship were forms of insurance. Neither private markets nor public provision insured adequately against destitution. The workhouses set up under the New Poor Law after 1836 were designed as last resorts, to dissuade people from claiming relief and to be avoided when at all possible. Personal ties were all that were left — 'it's the poor what 'elps the poor'.

To leave voluntarily was to enter the void, to leave involuntarily to be tossed into it. A handful of individuals did return from the colonies in the early part of the 19th century, but only a handful: just four of the rioters transported after 1830 managed to get back, the most famous being the Hampshire villager, Joseph Mason, who wrote affectingly about his experiences.[39] Returnees might be met with scepticism or resentment. Whereas Captain Marriot wrote that Americans lived 10 years longer than the English, because they crammed so much more into their lives, an Oxfordshire farmer smugly remarked that one of his acquaintants who had returned for a visit looked far older than he did. And there is an account in Laurie Lee's *Cider with Rosie* about a man who came back from New Zealand, patronised the young men of the village with drinks in the pub, and told them how stick-in-the-mud they were. They kicked him to death in the snow.

Positive assessments of the colonies did filter back, for example as early as the end of the Napoleonic wars, when seamen were demobilised. They had heard that Governor Macquarie had made Sydney attractive to its inhabitants, so enticing that some gave it as the reason for choosing to be transported rather than remain in the hulks.[40] The Colonial Secretary, Earl Bathurst, was scandalised by this and sent out Thomas Bigge to make a report. Bathurst was eager to change the perception of New South Wales as being even faintly tolerable. Referring to convicts as guilty of the worst crimes, which must have seemed ludicrous even to the hardened sensibilities of the Georgian era, he demanded that Bigge discover what might be done to make transportation thoroughly feared.

Remaining in rural southern England was almost equally fearful, besides colder, hungrier and less open to upward social mobility. Mantraps were set.

Gardens were ringed with spring-guns. The gentry assaulted the free-form pleasures of the poor, their prize-fighting, gambling and alehouses, and tried to forbid large holiday gatherings. An angler, expatiating on the beauty of the Windrush at Swinbrook, was countered by a youth hanging over the bridge who said he hated it and would leave when he could.[41]

What would such a lad be going to? Many reports about distant places must have seemed tall tales. This was especially so regarding the topsy-turvy ecosystems of Australia, described by the country's own leading modern ecologist as more a new planet than a new continent.[42] We come back to the fact that assessing the reports that did filter through was difficult for a population whose education was poor or non-existent. In the early 19th century illiteracy was on the rise. For every self-taught author such as Joseph Mason there were hundreds of poor women who could have had no idea to what strange world they might be taking their children.

Cobbett's questioning of the 'neat, smart, and pretty' woman of about 30 at Tangley, Hampshire, in 1826 is repeatedly cited: she had visited none of the surrounding towns a mere four, six and nine miles off, and 'the utmost of her voyages had been about two and a half miles!'[43] As another instance, the sympathetic Mrs. Haughton reported that a Mrs. Amor, at Pewsey, Wiltshire, unable to answer her young daughters' questions about going down to the sea in ships, despatched them to the Kennet & Avon wharf, to look at the canal and barges, that they be less frightened on shipboard.[44] Interestingly, Mrs. Amor seems to have been a victim of de-industrialisation. She was 'a superior, nice-mannered woman' who had done good business straw-plaiting when bonnets were made to order, until she was put out of work by cheaper ready-made ones in the village shop.

Migration produces a snowball effect in which laudatory messages sent home by early movers induce others to follow them. Nothing could have been more positive than Jacob Baker's letters from South Australia in the 1850s: 'we have a goint of fresh meet on our table everery day ... This is the countrey, my boys'.[45] Baker's letters were published in the *Devizes Gazette*. Yet private letters from overseas often petered out, as Mrs. Haughton's laundry-maid complained about the correspondence from her husband's relatives in Canada.[46] Early on there was no great volume of first-hand testimony to encourage the majority to leap into the unknown.

By the end of the 19th century things had changed. The vast study of Crawley, near Winchester, by the Harvard business historian, Norman Gras, found that cottagers who had left in the late 18th and early 19th centuries 'went without leaving a trace behind them'.[47] Subsequent emigrants were better able to hedge their bets, at least if they possessed some property. Parting with a cottage was often associated with migration, planned or already accomplished. One who had gone to Australia transferred his tenement only later, in 1875, to a banker who was buying up Crawley lock, stock and barrel. Another who had gone to Iowa surrendered his cottage only afterwards, in 1878, to a builder in Winchester. Yet another left his property to a daughter who was living in New South Wales in 1889; 30 years on the right to the tenement was inherited by her son. Only rare snippets throw light on the micro-behaviour of emigrants like these, but for some people at least the circumstances of emigration had ceased to resemble the blind gropings of the early decades of the century.

The workforce in the South was never a uniform, lumpen proletariat. Its bottom tiers were repressed and degraded but others struggled on, stoically, making a virtue of necessity. Poorly paid their work might be, and their pleasures restricted by upper-class repressiveness, but many continued to find life bearable. And despite everything there was voice as well as exit: religion was a quasi-substitute for politics, deployed to set lord and squarson at defiance. Primitive Methodism spread fast in disgust at the way the established church had sided with the squirearchy during the 'last labourers' revolt' of 1830. Chapel-goers formed their own parallel societies, religiously, politically and as far as possible economically.

Why should the inhabitants of the South have left their old homes? Williamson mentions the psychic costs of leaving but does not speculate what they were. Mechanistic interpretations of the labour market avoid the issue, implying that rational workers would leave if the expected returns were higher elsewhere. Treating labour as a factor of production subject to the workings of price theory is essential for some analytical purposes but can fall into a cold rationalism.[48] It is too remote to take full account of motivations, since its logic requires labour to have left and gone on leaving until rural and urban incomes were equated. That did not happen and has not happened today.

Out-migration would have meant quitting a humanised landscape of unsurpassed beauty. Yet this opinion, wrote Mary Gretton, 'is not the actuality of old England; it is what has remained in the sieve when the sand and slush have gone through'.[49] An appreciation of beauty, she insisted, was merely the subjective view of middle-class outsiders and 'to realize this you have only to watch the present tide of emigration, or to talk with the young labourer …' Gretton was right about many people, especially young men, or they might not have paid the price and left, but she was wrong to think she was adumbrating a general rule in concluding that, 'it is useless to expect the peasant to see the land with our eyes'.

Villagers were not taught to appreciate art but it was (uncharacteristically) condescending of Gretton to write as though none savoured the beauties of the world around them. In the worst of times their gardens were not given over entirely to potatoes.

> The cottage gardens in the vale of the Test are a constant delight to the eye. The poor folk, no matter how low wages may be … manage to show a few bright blossoms in their scraps of garden. A line of hollyhocks or sunflowers, a sprinkling of lupines, some lavender, some sweet peas trained against the wall, a cluster of white roses — with these and the like are the gardens of our humble Hampshire folk made gay in summer and early autumn'.[50]

Leaving the southern countryside was not merely an agonising choice, it had elements of capitulation. Migrating meant quitting the district in which one's ancestors had lived further back than memory, it meant abandoning the family graves in the churchyard, it meant leaving friends and relations and everything that was familiar and loved. These considerations raised the threshold price that many would require before agreeing to go. Psychic costs thus seemed large, minor recoveries in wages made the income gap between the south of England and other places appear smaller than it was, and credible information was hard to come by. Small wonder that exodus was stifled.

Endnotes

1. G. Clark, *A Farewell to Alms* (Princeton: Princeton University Press, 2007), p. 208.
2. G. Crocker, *The History of the Basingstoke Canal* (Surrey & Hampshire Canal Society Internet site, 1977 edition).
3. S. Pollard, quoted in C. H. Feinstein, Capital accumulation and the industrial revolution, in R. Floud and D. McCloskey (eds.), *The Economic History of Britain since 1700* (Cambridge: Cambridge University Press, 1981), p. 135.
4. H. I. Dutton and S. R. H. Jones, Invention and innovation in the British pin industry, 1790–1850, *Bus. Hist. Rev.* LVII(2): 193, 1983.

5. Quoted in A. P. Wadsworth and J. de L. Mann, *The Cotton Trade and Industrial Lancashire 1600–1780* (Manchester: Manchester University Press, 1931), p. 393.
6. J. Wilkinson, History of Broughton Gifford, *Wiltshire Archaeol. Mag.* **VI**: 37–38, 1860. The circumstances of the 300,000 weavers in Varanasi, India, in the early twenty-first century are interestingly similar (*The Economist* 10 Jan 2009).
7. W. Money, The guild or fellowship of the cloth-workers of Newbury, *J. Br. Archaeol. Assoc.* 265–266, 1896.
8. G. Hardin, The tragedy of the commons, *Science* **162**: 1243–1248, 1968.
9. W. F. Lloyd, *Two Lectures on the Justice of Poor-Laws, and One Lecture on Rent, Delivered in the University of Oxford in the Michaelmas Term*, 1836.
10. E. Schlicht, *On Custom in the Economy* (Oxford: Clarendon Press, 1998), p. 181 and n. 1.
11. M. A. Havinden, Agricultural progress in open-field Oxfordshire, in E. L. Jones (ed.), *Agriculture and Economic Growth in England 1650–1815* (London: Methuen, 1967), pp. 66–79.
12. M. Heller, *The Gridlock Economy* (New York: Basic Books, 2008), especially pp. 16–22.
13. L. Fox (ed.), *Correspondence of the Rev. Joseph Greene* (London: HMSO: HMC JP8, 1965), p. 76.
14. Victoria County History, *Wiltshire* (London: Oxford University Press, 1973), p. 208.
15. D. Sherborn, *An Inspector Recalls: Saving Our Heritage* (Sussex: The Book Guild, 2003), p. 9.
16. See e.g. the papers of the Rogers of Dowedeswell, Gloucestershire Record Office D269/A or E. P. Thompson, *Customs in Common* (London: Merlin Press, 1991), p. 110. Thompson refers to Church Oakley, Hampshire, where enclosure was delayed from 1742 to 1773 because at the first date, 'all consent to enclose, except one person who in crossness sticks out …'
17. E. F. Gay, Sir Richard Temple: the debt settlement and estate litigation, 1653–1675, *Huntingt. Libr. Q.* **VII**: 255–91, 1943.
18. J. Broad, The Verneys as enclosing landlords, 1660–1800, In J. Chartres and D. Hey (eds.), *English Rural Society, 1500–1800* (Cambridge: Cambridge University Press, 1990), pp. 39–45.
19. J. E. Kay, The Broyle enclosure, 1767–71, *Sussex Archaeol. Collect.* **138**: 165–189, 2000.
20. M. A. Havinden, *Estate Villages: A study of the Berkshire Villages of Ardington and Lockinge* (London: Lund Humphries, 1966), pp. 37–39.

21. M. W. Beresford, *History on the Ground* (London: Methuen, 1957), pp. 198–203.
22. Dorset History Centre (Ref: PE/PL/CW/2/2/1).
23. James White to Gilbert White, February 1793, letter displayed at The Wakes Museum, Selborne.
24. J. Britton, *The Beauties of Wiltshire* II (London, 1801), p. 21.
25. W. E. Tate, Opposition to parliamentary enclosure in eighteenth-century England, *Agric. Hist.* **19**: 139, 1945.
26. J. G. Williamson, Did English factor markets fail during the industrial revolution? *Ox. Econ. Pap.* **39**: 641–678, 1987; and Williamson, Leaving the farm to go to the city: did they leave quickly enough? In J. A. James and M. Thomas (eds.), *Capitalism in Context: Essays on Economic Development and Cultural Change in Honor of R. M. Hartwell* (Chicago: University of Chicago Press, 1994), pp. 159–182.
27. Some labour had been migrating freely from the countryside for centuries, including the widespread movement to London apprenticeships. T. Leunig, How fluid were labour markets in pre-industrial Britain? New evidence from apprenticeship records, Unpublished paper, LSE, 2008, kindly supplied by Dr. Leunig.
28. Quoted by M. Stourton, *The Mill Inn, the Mill House and Withington* (Privately printed, 1972), p. 16.
29. For example, a Fairford, Gloucestershire, attorney who married a Colston of the Bristol slave-trading family took her surname by Act of Parliament in 1755, bought an Oxfordshire estate, and at once began enclosing the common near his house. The commoners several times pulled down his wall but did not prevail.
30. Quoted in N. Crane, *Great British Journeys* (London: Phoenix, 2008), p. 197.
31. D. J. Tempero, *They Simply Stole to Live* (Andover: Andover Advertiser, n.d.), p. 5.
32. S. Markham, *A Testimony of Her Times: Based on Penelope Hind's Diaries and Correspondence 1787–1838* (London: Michael Russell, 1990), passim.
33. L. F. W. White, *The Story of Gosport* (Southsea: Barrell, n.d.), p. 90.
34. Williamson, Leaving the Farm, 1994, p. 164.
35. E. L. Jones, *Agriculture and the Industrial Revolution* (Oxford: Basil Blackwell, 1974), pp. 211–233.
36. R. Jefferies, *Wildlife in a Southern County* (London: Lutterworth Press, 1949), p. 132.
37. Jones, *Agriculture and the Industrial Revolution*, 1974, p. 218.
38. It did not pick up much as a proportion of the population. B. R. Mitchell, *Abstract of British Historical Statistics* (Cambridge: Cambridge University Press, 1962), pp. 50, 59.

39. J. Mason, *Joseph Mason: Assigned Convict 1831–1837* (Melbourne: Melbourne University Press, 1996); N. Townsend, Reconstructed lives: the swing transportees in New South Wales, *Aust. Stud.* **16**(2): 19–39, 2001.

40. Letter from Earl Bathurst to Mr. Commissioner Bigge, Commonwealth of Australia, *Historical Records of Australia,* Series I, **X** (Jan. 1819–1822 (Sydney, N.S.W., 1917), p. 5; copies of Bigge's interrogation on the *John Barry* in 1819 of the Tarrant brothers, transported for theft and poaching in Berkshire (seen by courtesy of Michael Tarrant).

41. M. S. Gretton, *A Corner of the Cotswolds through the Nineteenth Century* (London: Methuen, 1914), p. 205.

42. E. C. Rolls, *More a New Planet than a New Continent* (Canberra: ANU Centre for Resource and Environmental Studies, 1985).

43. W. Cobbett, *Rural Rides* (London: J. M. Dent, 1912), II, p. 30.

44. Mrs. Haughton, *In a Wiltshire Valley* (London: Provost, 1879), pp. 56–57.

45. Quoted in E. L. Jones, The land that Richard Jefferies inherited, *Rural Hist.* **16**(1): 89, 2005.

46. Haughton, *Wiltshire Valley*, 1879, p. 60.

47. N. S. B. and E. C. Gras, *The Economic and Social History of an English Village* (Cambridge, Mass.: Harvard University Press, 1930), pp. 128–129.

48. For an eloquent criticism of the inability of the econometric approach to encompass 'intimate questions of causation in the individual case, and large vaguely perceived phenomena of massive change in social organisation and behavior' see W. N. Parker, quoted in E. L. Jones, Economics in the history mirror, *J. Interdiscipl. Econ.* **3**: 157–172, at 157, 1990.

49. Gretton, *Corner of the Cotswolds*, 1914, p. 205.

50. G. A. B. Dewar, *Hampshire with the Isle of Wight* (London: J. M. Dent, 1900), p. 12.

PART III

INDUSTRIALISATION

CHAPTER 11

NORTH AND SOUTH

Mechanisation in the [cloth] industry was not important until the 1780s at the earliest. The West Riding's supremacy, evident by the 1770s, was achieved without its aid or reliance upon factor advantages which only became crucial once the steam engine and power spinning and weaving became general.

R. G. Wilson, 1973

Why, when and where did the industrial revolution begin? The question 'why' is often tackled by inducement models. The assumption is that actions follow automatically if they pay. But there is always an incentive to improve one's lot, urgently in the case of poor societies. Spirits do not, however, rise out of the vasty deep just because they are called. To refer back to a single example, it is unhistorical to think that although individuals appear to have had an incentive to overstock common land, it was necessarily overstocked. The real puzzle is why individuals do or do not respond to particular incentives. What, then, explains industrialisation, the greatest response in history? It cannot be accounted for by assuming that useful inventions appear if and when they are wanted.

To the question 'when' the usual answer is that economic growth was late and abrupt. This retains an unshakeable grip on the public imagination, as Leigh Shaw-Taylor and E. A. Wrigley lament.[1] The interpretation is fortified by repeated observational biases in the literature which, through relying on statistical sources newly emergent in one sector after another, minimise pre-industrial change and exaggerate the suddenness of growth. In reality change began early and was prolonged. Ann Kussmaul's ingenious work on marriage patterns shows no clear regional differentiation before 1650 but after that date agriculture grew regionally specialised, which she attributes to market integration.[2]

The answer to the question 'where' has several levels. Western Europe was distinct from the remainder of Eurasia in all but the most general respects. And England, which shared some of its heritage with Europe, nevertheless differed from neighbouring countries in various respects. Treating it as a backward area modernised by immigrants from more developed areas is correct only up to a point. Its response to opportunity was unique: industrialisation. This suggests concentrating on internal factors rather than foreign influences or international trade. Despite the effects of trade at the margin, 'it seems unbalanced', as Maarten Prak says, 'to direct 90 per cent of one's attention to what was actually far less than 10 per cent of the economy'.[3] As Rick Szostak points out, although international trade leaves the best records and mercantilists were preoccupied with discussing it, neither fact guarantees that overseas demand dominated English industry.[4] Industrialisation prompted foreign trade, he observes, rather than the reverse.

England's shifting assortment of regional differences means that it is its own laboratory. 'Controls' are more conveniently found within the country than by venturing offshore to others with less compatible institutions, politics or religion. Most explanatory schemes cite national factors, such as policy, the legal system, sets of values and so forth, but these do not pinpoint regional differences or at any rate have not been shown to do so.

The standard answer to the more precise question of 'where' within England is the north, the favoured reason being superior natural resources, including water power and especially coal for steam engines. This acknowledges the north-south divide but does not account for the timing, which tends to be attributed to the invention of manufacturing machinery; this, though vital, was in reality a secondary effect of growing concentrations of industry. Nor is an emphasis on resources a sufficiently general response: it does not deal, for example, with the early industrialisation of Saxony or Switzerland. An alternative approach is to start, as this book has, by asking why the industrial revolution did not evolve in the old industrial areas of southern England.

A central feature of English development was the merging of its domestic market through improved transport and communications. 'The manufactures of England are happily settled in different corners of the kingdom', wrote Daniel Defoe, 'from whence they are conveyed by the circulation of trade to London by wholesale ... and from thence disperse in lesser quantities to the other parts of the kingdom by retail'.[5] He cited many examples, proclaiming that, 'all these send up the gross of their quantity to London and receive each others sorts in retail for their own use' and he especially mourned the removal of stocking knitting from Norwich and weaving from Canterbury: 'these are the effects of transposing manufactures'.

This commercial metabolism was prompted by the safer and relatively speaking more settled climate for investment after 1688. Associated with this was the curiosity and optimism of the Enlightenment, and the somewhat mysterious acceptance by the elite of readier economic competition among themselves in addition to their customary political rent-seeking. Market integration meant that slowly widening circles of producers came into competition with one another, until at last the more distant districts of the north were incorporated and their goods arrived to challenge the southerners.

North and south had been slowly prised apart by asymmetric changes in farming, meaning earlier and more extensive improvement in the south. In the gentler southern environment improvers faced lower costs. Not all southern landowners were interested in farming, but some were, and so were their tenants. They brought in productivity-raising crops and rotations — changes in technology which (in contrast to the technological emphasis of industrial history) are slighted in current writing on agricultural history. The opinion that technological change in farming was minor stems from relying on grossed-up samples of data from the probate inventories, but Margaret Spufford has demonstrated that the legal definitions undermine the suitability of inventories for tracking innovation.[6] The deep scholarship of Mauro Ambrosoli's study of annotations in books on husbandry shows, on the other hand, the extent to which landowners and large farmers did follow recommendations about new methods.[7]

A shift to absolute property under single ownership and away from contingent property (where many individuals had some title) took place over several centuries. Landowners became better able to determine outcomes. They did not need to wait for a demonstration effect, like that which induced 18th-century lairds in the Scottish highlands to demote their kindred from clansmen to rent-paying tenants. The assumption in economics is that transfers bring land into the hands of individuals prepared to put it to the highest use. In principle this should follow, but the existence of an incentive is not evidence of a response. Although enough landowners did undertake, encourage or permit innovation for the agricultural sector to develop, their interest in blood sports meant that few were outright maximisers of agricultural production.

Investment was attracted to the farm sector in the south, or more strictly in Lowland England, because demand was growing and the costs of producing, processing and marketing food were lower than in the north. Much of this advantage derived from superior topographical, soil and climatic conditions but increasingly reflected better access to the London market. The network of routes and its altered modes (navigable rivers, canals and turnpikes) mirrored the capital's growth. London consumed twice as much grain in 1700 as in 1605.[8] The capital's demand tends, nevertheless, to mask that from part- or full-time workers in the provinces who had migrated into manufacturing 'on the spot'. When these people are added in, the number quitting agriculture becomes larger than it seems at first and the sector's early capability the more impressive.

Current thinking treats agriculture as a puppet dangled on the string of expanding urban populations and city-wards trade. Dutch historiography, for instance, is inclined to assert that the countryside of the western Netherlands was made in the town and lacked an independent influence. The urban bias in European history is as artificial as it is palpable: 'the sources almost always force us to take the urban point of view'.[9] Furthermore, it is said that, 'urbanization is indeed a good proxy for development'.[10] This is as if no-one has heard of the tax-eating cities of pre-industrial times or impoverished cities in underdeveloped economies like, say, Naples or Palermo in 1700. In those cities there was plenty of buying and selling but much of it was petty, with no persuasive link to growth. The influx of workers to London kept many teetering on the verge of poverty there too. Colquhoun estimated that 13 per cent of Londoners lived on criminal or immoral earnings: as to the cramped existence of others read Mayhew on London labour and the London poor.[11]

Its vast underclass and supply of cheap labour did not quite displace London's hierarchy or upset its equilibrium.[12] Manufacturing in the capital continually moved up the value chain, relinquishing to the provinces fustians in the 17th century, framework knitting early in the 18th century, silk and handkerchiefs and shoe-making late in the 18th century. They were replaced by higher-value finished goods such as coaches, mathematical instruments and watches.

To assume it was the towns that led agriculture by the nose ignores fluctuations in supply from weather shocks, bad harvests and animal plagues. It amounts almost to believing the weather was uniform over the centuries. Instead, there were plenty of occasions when agriculture's misfortunes made the sector count in the whole economy, and count hard. The towns had then to dance to rustic tunes, as industry did while its raw materials originated from the land.

The landed system was plainly sub-optimal, but this does not mean all improvement was blocked.[13] Conceivably the fostering of the selective breeding of cattle and sheep by landowners spilled over from the line breeding of dogs and horses for sport. But French landowners cherished their dogs and horses too, without becoming such ardent agricultural improvers, and we have to fall back on fashion, non-pecuniary competition, and the optimism prevailing in the Enlightenment, to explain the English improvers.

Withdrawing or reserving agricultural acres for blood sports, and distorting rotations for the purpose, must have raised food prices and made farming on the remaining land more profitable. High prices were more the goal than maximum output. Trying to bolster prices politically was a rational allocation of landowner effort. As Byron wrote:

> The *Landed Interest* – (you may understand
> The phrase much better leaving out the *land*) –
> The land self-interest groans from shore to shore,
> For fear that plenty should attain the poor'.[14]

The English Sequence Amplified

Ordinarily we might expect that economic growth would be spurred by market freedoms but there are problems with this line of argument. A number of the outcomes do not seem to have been stable. Free-market preferences within the judicial system were inconsistent, since the judges reverted to precedent when it suited them — not that every law was enforced. Protective duties were raised precisely when 'a modest flow of works' was starting to extol the virtues of free trade.[15] Nor was corruption decisively reduced until some way into the 19th century. Other factors that once seemed promising appear to have been supplementary at best or impediments to growth at worst, so modern work claims. It is hinted, for example, that dismal trends in literacy denoted a pause in the deepening of human capital during the early stages of industrialisation.[16] If these things were negative, stronger but less evident forces must have swamped them.

Despite the awkwardness of resorting to general history, where everything is narrated but little explained, the solution to the puzzle of English industrialisation lies where material conditions intersected with religious-cum-intellectual-cum-political history. The threat of violent politics no longer dissuaded investors and, unlike the United Provinces, England avoided becoming hostage to international violence. Looked at more closely, nevertheless, there is ambiguity here too, with scares about invasion and threats of a return by the Stuarts persisting to the middle of the 18th century. The balance of probability does lie with more benign politics and a more reassuring climate for investment, but it was a balancing act rather than a dead certainty.

The problem in history of where to begin is best solved pragmatically. The 16th-century revival of commerce looks possible. In Elizabeth's reign the economy was commercialised and monetised: take as an example Walter Money, *A Perfect Booke,* which is a purveyance of the Royal Household for the north of Hampshire in 1575.[17] Landowners are listed, even small ones, stating the type of holding and what each would have to supply. Many compounded instead of supplying provisions in kind, which reveals the extent of Elizabethan commercialisation. Thereafter economic expansion never ceased, though it was disturbed by Civil War.

In 1688 England acquired a king who agreed to a limitation of his powers in a settlement with the Whig grandees and London merchants. Politics began to calm down and religion became a less vexing public issue. A marked upturn in growth may thus be attributed to more favourable conditions after the elite settlement. The stage had of course been set much earlier with the emergence of a large middle class who favoured political stability and depended on market activity. Useless to try to date the origins of the bourgeoisie; its definition is problematical and its rise was continual, though presumably not exactly continuous. What was needed was a polity capable of advancing bourgeois interests.

Two related points may be made. The first is that the length of time afterwards taken for markets to merge is a common objection to accepting the economic significance of 1688. The lag before the advent of powered machines housed in factories seems a long one. Yet what was to be expected? No-one was aiming teleologically at an industrial revolution. They were investing in their little businesses and in communications which promised to increase trade. They can have had no conception of the ends to which inter-regional competition would eventually grope its way; they were flying blind. Many would later become appalled at the import competition with which the opening of routes saddled their own towns and districts.

The second point is the more positive one that attending to the politico-intellectual background avoids economic determinism. A single-minded concern with material factors over-extends the economic calculus. Models are not meant to map reality, yet the economist's professional urge is to go too far down this track, to see how far any model will run. It then becomes an exercise, not a history. It is all *wahrheit* and no *dichtung* — no poetry, conveying a stunted version of human behaviour.[18] This seems methodologically outmoded now that the cutting edge of the discipline lies in evolutionary and behavioural economics. Economics is a generalising subject which has always incorporated time poorly and preferred to skip from one equilibrium point to the next. There has been little room for events that cannot be fixed in the standard analytical scheme. To those in other disciplines, attributing industrialisation to a unique combination of predominantly extra-economic events may nevertheless seem an act of rescue rather than an evasion.

Had the Enlightenment idea of progress not influenced practical affairs, England might have become a normal country, in the terms of the period, content with a quietly prosperous but not forcefully progressive economy — like the United Provinces or Tokugawa Japan or Venice. Living standards would have been well ahead of Stone Age affluence but stalled on a plateau of bucolic prosperity, the potential for growth meandering away in a Venetian twilight.[19]

An element of happenstance remains. Remain agnostic, Stephan Epstein said, because different sets of institutions may have been optimal in different settings.[20] Some may have maximised welfare, subject to current constraints and technology, without being effective at stimulating additional technological change. There is no determinate solution to the puzzle of why the industrial revolution took place, and where and when it did so. All that can be achieved is a narrowing of the range of possible mixes. It is easier said than done to assert that an optimality band existed within which the material and non-material factors acted in concert. But it comes close to the truth which this book has tried to express.

An Output Gap

One of the standard criteria for assessing the performance of an economy is full resource exploitation. Capacity utilisation in the engineering sense refers to the total volume that can be physically produced with the existing capital stock. The economic definition conceives it as the ratio of output, measured at market value, to the level at which the average cost of production starts to climb. By both definitions, the difference between actual and potential gross domestic product measures the slack in the economy and is called the 'output gap'.

The concept of an output gap therefore varies. We may adapt it, in an even looser sense, to assess the England of 1688. At that date (1588 might be better still) production and consumption were more localised than at any time thereafter. In average harvest years, bulky farm produce seldom moved far and grain for export came almost exclusively from eastern coastal districts. Local and regional economies were closer to self-sufficiency than is implied by the 'brand names' which Defoe was so keen to attach to one town or another.

The product specialisation which he remarked shows the competitive advantage of one place over others long before manufacturing was mechanised. Admittedly, agglomeration economies in the early modern period are more readily deduced than demonstrated, for two reasons: thin source materials and the tilt of industrial histories towards better documented periods. Product specialisation did however keep inching forwards through time.

Strictly, or as strictly as a relaxed definition permits, the output gap takes account of this. Full resource mobilisation is, as it were, indexed to the level of trade possible given existing communications. We cannot assume communications so perfect they would have permitted all resources to be combined in such a way as to maximise output. Yet, as an experiment, consider the following counterfactual: the economy of 1688 with the communications network of 1788. A higher level of resource mobilisation would undoubtedly have been possible in the superior trading framework — Lilliputian by the standards of what was to come, but that is not the point. The hypothesised transport improvements would have increased trade, raised competition, heightened product specialisation, and permitted output in the late 17th century to approach the level of a century later.

The real 1688 may therefore be said to have suffered from a species of output gap because its poorer transport services kept many enterprises apart. They were not brought into competition. J. S. Mill thought that registering amazement at how fast economies recover from disasters is a 'sterile astonishment'. The same may be said of surprise at the distributional changes brought about by better transport links. Sometimes the individual effects could be rapid but as they unfolded they were piecemeal. Defoe recognised only a kaleidoscope of change and it is not surprising that the directional or cumulative impact was only slowly understood. The domestic trade unleashed was no less potent for that.

North and South Revisited

The transformation of the north astonishes. In the mid-17th century, Lancashire's largest town had been ranked 82nd in Britain by population. About 1700 the county still held fewer people than Norfolk and barely more than Somerset (all were similar in area) and was one of the very poorest.[21] By 1800, though, Lancashire had emerged as the third wealthiest county and one of the most densely populated, with some of the fastest growing towns, the major staple industry, one of the most productive coalfields, one of the densest networks of inland waterways, some of the largest industrial plant and some of the richest people in the country.

At its full extent, northern economic ascendancy, symbolised and more than symbolised by Manchester, was an affair of early and mid-Victorian times. Until the mid-point of the 19th century, the share of national income produced by the northern industrial districts rose rapidly.[22] London's share fell. By 1900 the capital's share had recovered, though in the interim its shrinkage had been enough to alarm Londoners. They felt islanded in the agricultural south.

North and south are short-hands for the more cumbersome terms Highland Zone and Lowland Zone, which may confuse because on the eastern side of the country the Lowland Zone stretches well to the north. The distinction can in any case be overdrawn.[23] Earlier chapters have recognised that firms and industries rose and fell in spatial patterns related to very intricate differences of fortune. Yet anyone can complicate matters by drawing extra distinctions or, come to that, by claiming there is none of importance.

Available interpretations of regional fortunes are paradoxically both numerous and incomplete. What, then, may clarify northern growth and southern decline without plunging unhelpfully into a 'thicket of causes'?[24] There is an understandable tendency to seek positive features that may explain the industrialisation of the north (including the West Midlands, which were part of the Highland Zone). The possession of water power and coal is usually held to have been pivotal yet coal's significance has been strongly challenged.[25] The argument here is not that natural resources had no effect but that they exerted most of their influence late in time, only then decisively reinforcing the pattern of activity familiar to us ever since the industrial revolution.

Northern entrepreneurs sought raw materials and sources of energy where they could find them, sometimes from places that southern industrialists might potentially have tapped too. Consider the production of tools and cutlery, for which the Sheffield district, with 596 smithies, had achieved a leading reputation as early as 1672.[26] The industry did have coal for its hearths, millstone grit for grindstones, and streams to power the hammers and bellows. But local resources were insufficient: Swedish and Russian iron ore had to be brought in via tributaries of the Humber. Similarly the area around Birmingham was sourcing materials from overseas well before 1700.

Individual villages and craftsmen around Sheffield and Birmingham specialised in making particular types of tools from early dates. Intensive division of labour and concentrated expertise were what really made the reputation of their localities. Output in Sheffield expanded during the 18th century without benefit of machinery and it was not until the 1850s that large steel works were built there. Sheffield was in any event a special case; its resource advantages cannot be denied but few of them applied to other industries such as textiles. The great coal-mining districts of north-eastern England and Cumberland followed a separate course of development involving investment by landowners. Although some technological change was induced by the needs of deeper and deeper mine shafts, similar improvements occurred in Devon and Cornwall. The north-east coalfield was secured on demand for domestic heating fuel in London.

Yorkshire woollen manufacturers did not rely on local wool, they were scouring the south country for supplies by 1770.[27] Nor was water power the free good it is made to seem, for overbearing landowners existed in the north as well as the south. In 1786 Richard Arkwright had to accept an onerous lease from the Duke of Rutland requiring him to restore a stream to its course, since his cotton mill at Bakewell, Derbyshire, had interrupted the flow to the Duke's corn mill downstream, as well as damaging the trout fishing.[28]

The common features of early manufacturing in the metal-working districts were low entry costs and secure tenures arising from weak manorial control. Indeed, weak regulation applied widely across the Highland Zone, benefiting industries at large. Freedom from regulation was not universal but was very widespread. Guilds and closed corporations were few. In the West Midlands many inhibitions on change disappeared during the final decade of the 17th century.[29] Mere copyholds, despite their insubstantial title, could be used as security for mortgages. The lack of restraint on rural trade is also emphasised in histories of Lancashire.[30] Non-corporate settlements such as Bolton, Bury, Rochdale, Blackburn and Colne developed small textile work-shops early. Free Manchester grew faster than any of them. The corporation of Liverpool consisted of enterprising merchants and that in Preston, though conservative, was not strong enough to prevent the emergence of a linen industry in the late 17th century.[31] Wigan and Lancaster were corporate towns tightly run by guildsmen and office holders but places where this mattered were in the minority.

The York worsted industry had weak guilds but competition maintained product quality, and the parts of the West Riding which were free of guilds positively encouraged technological innovation.[32] Otherwise the degree of regulation fluctuated, tightening in hard times. The same was true of the rigour with which the Poor Law was enforced in Lancashire. As in the south, enforcement tended to be relaxed when business picked up but went out of the window in boom times. Weak or vacillating regulation clearly aided enterprise but by itself was insufficiently distinctive to account for northern mastery. Assertions that there were fewer restraints on building cottages in the uplands of the textile districts than in counties such as Norfolk, Wiltshire or Devon, where land was more valuable for farming and dominated by landowners, are also partly correct but never complete: squatters took the opportunity to settle on many an infertile heath in the south.[33]

It is difficult to decide on the earliest significant developments. Which acorns would grow into oaks, which thriving trees desiccate and die?

Mistaking changes once they were under way for initial causes is all too likely. Local histories report successive stages of development but offer only tiny nuggets of information about the first decisions. There is an understandable but confusing tendency to describe the early pages of success stories yet leave the very earliest blurred.

The most thoughtful treatment of comparative issues is R. G. Wilson, 'The supremacy of the Yorkshire Cloth Industry in the 18th Century'.[34] This compares the fortunes of the West Country, East Anglia and the West Riding. By 1775 the last-named had outstripped the former two; thereafter they were stagnant or collapsing, though taking an unconscionable time about it. Conventionally, their disadvantages have been cited as unfavourable location, poor factor endowments, hesitant mechanisation, and the failure of their entrepreneurs to react to threats and opportunities as vigorously as Yorkshiremen.

These drawbacks, Wilson points out, applied only in the 19th century, not to the inception or root causes of decline. Yorkshire, he notes, started with few natural advantages. It possessed none in transport, raw materials or the price of labour, while during the 18th century coal and iron were unimportant to the cloth industry. Before the adoption of steam, Yorkshire was far behind the south in know-how and in the effective use of coal, which was confined to dyeing and finishing. Only well into the 19th century did superior access to running water, coal and iron enable the West Riding to 'exterminate' the industry in Norwich.

Having dismissed resource-based explanations, Wilson turns to explanation by residual. This method defines the answer as the factor that has been omitted and is always troublesome because the answer may be something that has not come to mind. He rejects entrepreneurship or differences in industrial organisation on the dubious grounds that they cannot be measured. Similarly he dismisses special initiative on the part of Yorkshiremen, pointing out that enterprise was not lacking in Norwich or Gloucestershire even after the 1770s. Gloucestershire clothiers were close behind Yorkshire in introducing spinning machines and coped as well as they did with the introduction of finishing machinery between 1793 and 1815.

Therefore — Wilson concludes — the key must have lain in better organisation of production and sales. The Yorkshire industry had low entry costs and large numbers of small clothiers, who sold to local merchants, not to the oligopolistic group of factors at Blackwell Hall in London. Yorkshire triumphalism creeps back with the statement that all the West Riding's energies were recruited whereas the West Country was a conservative place; W. G. Hoskins is quoted as saying that Exeter clung to 'ideas preserved like heirlooms until at last the trade died of it'. Yet Wilson turns again at this point, saying that differences in industrial organisation are exaggerated and were in any case evident by 1700, meaning they cannot account for 18th-century changes.

His final suggestion is different sales procedures. Yorkshire sold on the English market and its travellers went round calling on retailers, whereas Gloucestershire and Norfolk favoured export markets which they could not directly penetrate. By 1700 merchants in Leeds, Wakefield and Exeter dominated the Northern European market but only men in the first two involved themselves closely with the trade. They concentrated on cheap goods and also captured North American sales, keeping out the West Country and Norwich, which specialised on high-quality goods of narrower appeal. Finally, Wilson adds in agglomeration effects, observing that the other industries close to the West Riding cloth industry spurred it to respond to change, whereas no encouragement arose from the agricultural districts surrounding southern industries. Agglomeration effects may be important in explaining further growth once a cluster of trades is in existence but do not indicate why they spring up alongside one another in the first place.

Wilson's chapter is valuable for eliminating most of the supposed production advantages of the north. Once the structure of English industry was set, back in the 16th or 17th centuries, the regional trajectories are made to follow, as it were naturally. Too much is made of the fact that small northern producers sold to local merchants and unlike southern clothiers were not at the mercy of the London factors. Presumably the heart of the advantage was competition within the Yorkshire merchant community but this leaves unresolved questions about the south's reluctance or inability to behave likewise. Wilson accepts that southern clothiers were no sluggards with respect to mechanisation. Why, then, were they unwilling or incapable of altering their minds about product range, markets and salesmanship? Learning-by-doing may be an acceptable characterisation of northern development but the south's failure to learn remains perplexing.

The line of reasoning relies ultimately on unexplained, asymmetrical characteristics of human capital. The thesis is strongly path-dependent, deriving from early structural choices and the subsequent inflexibility of some aspects of southern decision making — though not of others. It is unlikely that this can be generalised to cover decline in all southern manufactures. Regional unwillingness to attend to marketing does not fit: we do not observe a population of hobbyist producers unconcerned to sell what they made, any more than we find that bourgeois values were abnormally lacking in the south.

A better answer is a slow shift in comparative advantage, driven by prolonged agricultural improvement in the south, which attracted investment into farming and processing as manufacturing ceased to do so. The redistribution of economic activity was possible because improved communications permitted market integration. The merging of markets gave environmentally based differences their bite. It accounts for the consolidation of economic activity throughout the country, starting with the concentration of manufacturing in the larger towns of the south before and during its eventual retreat to the north.[35]

In agriculture the south increasingly had the edge. It may be objected that some northern districts did develop intensive farming, for instance around the mining districts of Northumberland and Durham during the first half of the 18th century.[36] This supplied local demand for foodstuffs. In Yorkshire, when Leeds expanded cloth production in the 17th and 18th centuries, Wakefield turned to becoming a market for grain, cattle, leather and wool from eastern England, supplying south Lancashire and the West Riding industrial areas.[37] But other districts developed only much later: whereas agriculture improved in southern England in the 17th and early 18th centuries, this did not occur in Cumbria until the second half of the 18th century at the earliest.[38] Given the high costs of transporting bulky produce, it is neither surprising nor especially relevant that towns and industries drew food supplies from their surrounds, nor that crop growing and large estates appeared on the lower rather than higher elevations in the north. None of this is a sign that the region's comparative advantage lay in farming.

Northern farmers who moved towards full factory industrialisation had often been part-time weavers or other petty manufacturers. Now they tended to switch right out of farming. This is illustrated by Michael Nevell's study of the Pennine Uplands around Manchester, where (to mention only one late phase) tenant farmers, long involved in the domestic spinning of textiles, took during the 1780s to building houses for hand-loom weavers.[39] They also converted barns and put up new buildings to house hand-powered spinning jennies, water-frames and mule spinning machines. There was investment by merchant capital, too, but industrialisation was strongly yeoman-driven. Similarly, at Bramley, near Leeds, scribbling mills sprang up during the first decade of the 19th century in a scatter of little crofts right across the open landscape.[40] At Bradford the shift of smallholders from domestic industry into full-time factories was apparent; their small parcels of land were suitable for housing development by small builders. The boundaries are traceable in the lay-out of modern streets, as they are in Clitheroe.[41]

Technology as Response

New manufacturing technologies have the rhetorical merit of seeming clear-cut. Few scholars of any persuasion are in doubt about their eventual effects. What is less acknowledged is how far the most striking early examples — iron-puddling and cotton-spinning machinery — were the culminations of long processes of trial-and-error, nested in a broad history of experimentation and economic growth. This deserves better than to be taken for granted but the fact that discontinuous advances occurred within it is a matter for gratification more than surprise. A technological focus rather than an economic one means that the rise in productivity is portrayed as starting only during the last years of the 18th century. This obscures the previous expansion of the market, which shows that the industrialisation of the north was more culmination than inception.

The objections to emphasising pre-mechanised manufacturing are the absence of the increasing returns that powered machinery was to bring, the supposition that population would have expanded to eat away the gains of incremental growth, and the overmastering scale of the subsequent industrialisation. The earlier gains were allocative, derived not from the application of inanimate energy but from the division of labour. They were doomed to peter out once every last commercial re-arrangement had been made. This dismissal of Smithian growth, though formally correct, is historically beside the point, since gains continued until the mid-19th century via traditional technologies, greater managerial efficiency, and the shift in household behaviour known as the 'industrious revolution'.[42] About 1800 these influences still had a respectable distance to run.

Plant layout, office routines, business management, marketing and other forms of disembodied technology were still improving.[43] Better methods

were spreading by imitation and learning-by-doing. This is hard to demonstrate because organisational advances have attracted few scholarly eyes. They
are not as conspicuous as machinery and are poorly documented through
being diffused across thousands of small enterprises that seldom left
accounts; the positive externalities created by municipal improvements are
even harder to pin down.

Walt Rostow commented that he was inclined to accept a positive vision
of pre-modern economic activity but it does not account for the industrial
revolution: the steam engine arrives in it, he protested, by 'immaculate
conception'. Yet the steam engine had a history before it was applied to
manufacturing on any scale; it represented no single breakthrough but was
an accumulation of solutions to engineering problems aimed at a variety of
tasks. Newcomen, at Dartmouth, Devon, built his engine in the early
18th century to pump water out of mines and this was a usage which
continued.

The history of technology celebrates the grand developments, but all were
graded along a cline, inspired by emulation and not invariably by the hope
of monetary reward. The sheer fluidity of the technological response is better
grasped when inventive failures are also taken into consideration. There was
endless tinkering from which something hopeful might be expected. The
search for one true, almost magical, upturn in production is forlorn. It is
misleading as far as history goes because the share of output contributed by
the new technologies took some time to surpass the old ones. Meanwhile
competition spurred active development in traditional methods: the sailing-
ship syndrome.

The awe felt about mechanisation is placed too heavily on one side of the
account. Not every act of invention was equally easy, indeed few were at all
easy, but economists should reserve most of their sense of awe for the effect
on real prices. Innovation and the requisite investment are more to the point
than invention, of which there was enough in the Middle Ages, the Ancient
World and Song or Ming China to suggest that, given broader incentives,
striking new technologies might finally supplant their predecessors. 'It was
clearly industrial growth which produced the steam-engine and the railway,
not the steam-engine and the railways which made possible industrial
growth', is the conclusion of a close study of milling in Cumberland since the
13th century.[44]

The eventual increase in output and the downward pressure on prices of producer and consumer goods were what changed the world. This is best traced from market competition heightened by a combination of Enlightenment thought and a political society that saw fit to add items of civilian use to ones meant merely to bolster power. To understand this, intellectual, political and social changes, summed up in broader attitudes to investment, are what deserve attention.

Endnotes

1. L. Shaw-Taylor and E. A. Wrigley, The occupational structure of England *c.* 1750–1871. A preliminary report, http://www-hpss.geog.cam.ac/research/ projects/occupations/ p. 38.
2. As reported by M. Prak, Regions in early modern Europe, in *Proceedings, Eleventh International Economic History Congress*, Milan, 1994, p. 47.
3. Prak, Regions, p. 20.
4. R. Szostak, *The Role of Transportation in the Industrial Revolution* (Montreal & Kingston: McGill-Queen's University Press, 1991), pp. 44–45.
5. D. Defoe, Giving Alms no charity, in E. W. Martin (ed.), *Country Life in England* (London: Country Book Club, 1967), p. 102.
6. M. Spufford, The limitations of the probate inventory, in J. Chartres and D. Hey (eds.), *English Rural Society, 1500–1800* (Cambridge: Cambridge University Press, 1990), pp. 139–174.
7. M. Ambrosoli, *The Wild and the Sown: Botany and Agriculture in Western Europe, 1350–1850* (Cambridge: Cambridge University Press, 1997). Ambrosoli is well aware of the observation bias inherent in surviving annotated works, which favour later rather than earlier sources.
8. J. Chartres, Food consumption and internal trade, in A. L. Beier and R. Finlay (eds.), *London 1500–1700: The Making of the Metropolis* (London: Longman, 1986), especially Table 21.
9. Prak, Regions, p. 32.
10. D. Acemoglu *et al.*, From ancient regime to capitalism: the spread of the French Revolution as a natural experiment, Ts. MIT, 2007–2008, p. 6.
11. J. R. T. Hughes, Henry Mayhew's London, *J. Econ. Hist.* **29**(3): 526–536, 1969; J. Mokyr, The institutional origins of the industrial revolution (MS. Northwestern University, 2008), p. 10 n. Colquhoun's figures, like most such, are unfortunately implausible. Subtract from the clients of the purported 50,000 full-time prostitutes those males who were too young, too old, ill or too

subject to moral scruples, and the ratio of providers to customers reaches the unlikely order of one to four or five.

12. L. D. Schwartz, *London in the Age of Industrialism: Entrepreneurs, Labour Force and Living Conditions, 1700–1850* (Cambridge: Cambridge University Press, 1992), p. 238.

13. A study particularly hostile to the landed interest, S. Wilmot, The business of improvement: agriculture and science culture in Britain, *c.* 1700–*c.* 1870, *Hist. Geogr. Res. Series* **24**: 1990, draws almost all of its material from the post-1770 period.

14. Quoted in E. W. Martin (ed.), *Country Life in England* (London: Country Book Club,1967), p. 124.

15. R. Davis, The rise of protection in England, 1689–1786, *Econ. Hist. Rev. N.S.* **19**(2): 306, 1966.

16. S. Broadberry, Recent developments in the theory of very long run growth: a historical appraisal (Warwick Economics Research Papers No. 818, 2007, p. 12).

17. W. Money, *A Perfect Booke* (Blacket, 1901).

18. W. N. Parker, quoted in E. L. Jones, Economics in the history mirror, *J. Interdiscipl. Econ.* **3**: 157, 1990.

19. E. L. Jones, No stationary state: the world before industrialisation, *Workshop in Economic History*, Department of Economics, University of Chicago, 8283–8289.

20. S. R. Epstein, *Freedom and Growth: The Rise of States and Markets in Europe, 1300–1750* (London: Routledge, 2000), p. 171.

21. E. Royle (ed.), *Issues of Regional Identity* (Manchester: Manchester University Press, 1998), p. 84.

22. D. Smith, *North and South: Britain's Economic, Social and Political Divide* (London: Penguin, 1989), p. 19.

23. J. Styles, Clothing the north: the supply of non-elite clothing in the eighteenth century north of England, *Text. Hist.* **25**(2): 139–166, 1994.

24. C. K. Hyde in a review in the *J. Econ. Hist.* **XLVI**: 528, 1986.

25. G. Clark and D. Jacks, Coal and the industrial revolution, 1700–1869 (UC Davis Working Paper #06–16, April 2006).

26. M. Palmer (ed.), *The Onset of Industrialisation* (Nottingham: Department of Adult Education, n.d. [1977], especially the contributions by D. Hey and M. Rowlands. See also B. Trinder, *The Making of the Industrial Landscape* (Gloucester: Alan Sutton, 1987 edition), p. 25.

27. H. Heaton, *The Yorkshire Woollen and Worsted Industries: From the Earliest Times up to the Industrial Revolution* (Oxford: Clarendon Press, 1920), p. 279. I possess an 1829 account book for Idle, West Riding, in which directions to a

Cirencester, Gloucestershire, wool stapler are carefully noted. Wool staplers' premises are still to be seen in Coxwell Street, Cirencester.

28. M. H. Mackenzie, Bakewell mill and the Arkwrights, *J. Derbyshire Archaeol. Nat. Hist. Soc.* **LXXIX**: 62–64, 1959. The Dukes of Devonshire also resisted the intrusion of industry into the Derbyshire countryside.

29. M. Rowlands, Society and industry in the West Midlands at the end of the seventeenth century, *Midl. Hist.* **IV**(1): 58, 1977.

30. J. K. Walton, *Lancashire: A Social History* (Manchester: Manchester University Press, 1987), p. 67.

31. J. D. Marshall, *Lancashire* (Newton Abbot: David & Charles, 1974), pp. 39–40; A. P. Wadsworth and J. De Lacy Mann, *The Cotton Trade and Industrial Lancashire 1600–1780* (New York: Augustus M. Kelley, 1968), pp. 68–69.

32. S. Ogilvie, Can we rehabilitate the guilds? A sceptical reappraisal, CWPE 0745 (Google Scholar), pp. 17, 36.

33. Trinder, *Industrial Landscape*, p. 17.

34. R. G. Wilson, The supremacy of the Yorkshire cloth industry in the eighteenth century, in N. B. Harte and K. G. Ponting (eds.), *Textile History and Economic History* (Manchester: Manchester University Press, 1973), pp. 225–246.

35. Wilson notes this concentration, *ibid.*, p. 234. For a revealing instance of enterprise outside the north, see A. Everitt, Country, county and town: patterns of regional evolution in England, in P. Borsay (ed.), *The Eighteenth-Century Town* (London: Longman, 1990), p. 108.

36. The 1973 Annual Conference, *Agri. Hist. Rev.* **21**: 110, 139, 1973.

37. W. G. Rimmer, The evolution of Leeds to 1700, *Thoresby Soc. Publ.* **50**(2): 127–128, 1967.

38. W. Rollinson, *A History of Man in the Lake District* (London: J. M. Dent, 1967), p. 1.

39. M. Nevell, Brian Grimsditch and Carolanne King, *Carrbrook: A Textile Village and Its Valley. A Study in the Industrialisation of the Pennine Uplands* (Manchester: Tameside Metropolitan Borough Council, 2006), p. 21.

40. Martin (ed.), *Country Life*, p. 154.

41. M. J. Mortimore, Landownership and urban growth in Bradford and its environs in the West Riding conurbation, 1850–1950, *Trans. Inst. Br. Geogr.* **46**: 105–119, 1969.

42. J. De Vries, *The Industrious Revolution* (Cambridge: Cambridge University Press, 2008).

43. E. L. Jones and M. E. Falkus, Urban improvement and the English economy in the seventeenth and eighteenth centuries, *Res. Econ. Hist.* **4**: 193–233, 1979.

44. D. G. Watts, Water-power and the industrial revolution, *Trans. Cumberland Westmorland Antiq. Archaeol. Soc.* N.S. 67 (1967), p. 205.

GUIDE TO FURTHER READING

The literature on the decline of industries in southern England is immense. Many items are quite minor, however, and serious attempts to explain decline have to be sifted out of the mass. Studies that make more than descriptive use of regional material are also scarce. Regional studies usually depict aspects of an area, often a county, without bringing it into conjunction with others. They seldom directly attack the problem of change in ways that economists would approve, though in fairness economists' own treatments of de-industrialisation with any significant early historical content are rare and not particularly helpful. This blindness to history may cure itself in the future, somewhat like the belated recognition that early financial crises may reveal informative patterns.

Typical studies of de-industrialisation are articles dealing with single industries in one town or county and are aimed at local readerships. The proper term for them is fugitive. Many examples have been pieced together like jigsaws in this book to create general pictures and are referred to in the notes to chapters. But from the explanatory viewpoint the items are so often individually unrewarding there would be little point in directing the reader to them or providing lists. The largest fraction refers to the textile trades, which were widely distributed and undeniably important. Other types of manufacturing are under-represented in existing studies. I draw attention here only to the more complete or respectable sources which tackle, or can be made to bear, on de-industrialisation as a general process.

Should the reader wish to delve more deeply, the places to start are the multi-volume Victoria County Histories of each county. These have been appearing intermittently for over 100 years. Even the more recent volumes are far from analytical but they do gather together descriptive information that is otherwise immensely scattered.

Is all this a covert admission that studying the industrial history of the south is making bricks without straw? To some extent the point must be granted because appropriate business histories are vanishingly rare. Yet the total body of material is so large that some common patterns do become evident. Moreover, occasional economic historians have made professional forays into the subject and rescued it from antiquarianism. They have exposed the underlying processes common to the whole economy but expressed differently in the various parts of the country. Enough such work exists to enable the decline of the south to be presented in undergraduate lectures, tutorials and essays in order to counterpoint studies of northern industrialisation.

What follow can be only suggestions whereby the reader can enter such an enormous literature. I have not keyed the sources strictly to successive chapters, partly because some of them refer to more than one topic, but have made slightly different groupings to emphasise themes and topics.

International Context

Astute remarks about the timing of change occur in K. Inwood, Economic growth and global inequality in long run perspective, *Rev. Income Wealth* **48**(4): 581–593, 2002. The case for similar development across Eurasia appears in V. Lieberman, Transcending east-west dichotomies: state and culture formation in six ostensibly different areas, *Mod. Asian Stud.* **31**: 463–546, 1997; a contrary position is taken by J. M. Bryant, The west and the rest revisited: debating capitalist origins, European colonialism, and the advent of modernity, *Can. J. Sociol.* **31**(4): 403–444, 2006, and J. M. Bryant, A new sociology for a new history? Further critical thoughts on the Eurasian similarity and great divergence theses, *Can. J. Sociol.* **33**(1): 149–167, 2008.

Asian primacy and Chinese superiority are indicated by K. Pomeranz, *The Great Divergence* (Princeton: Princeton University Press, 2000). Different views are expressed by Y. Xue, A "fertilizer revolution": a critical response to Pomeranz's theory of geographic luck, *Mod. China* **33**(2): 195–229, 2007; and T. Roy, Review: an Asian world economy? *Econ. Polit. Weekly* **36**(31): 2937–2942, 2001.

Comments on Europe's advance may be found in P. Crone, *Pre-Industrial Societies: Anatomy of the Pre-Modern World* (Oxford: Basil Blackwell, 1989), and C. Karayalcin, Divided we stand, united we fall: the Hume-North-Jones mechanism for the rise of Europe, *Int. Econ. Rev.* **49**(3): 973–997, 2008. On the Dutch-cum-English 'little divergence' from other European norms, see K. Davids and J. Lucassen (eds.), *A Miracle Mirrored: The Dutch Republic in European Perspective* (Cambridge: Cambridge University Press, 1995).

Regionalisation in England

Starting points are A. Everitt, Country, county and town: patterns of regional evolution in England, in P. Borsay (ed.), *The Eighteenth Century Town: A Reader in English Urban History, 1688–1820* (London: Longman, 1990); C. Husbands, Regional change in a pre-industrial economy: wealth and population in England in the sixteenth and seventeenth centuries, *J. Hist. Geogr.* **13**(4): 345–359, 1987; H. M. Jewell, *The North-South Divide: The Origins of Northern Consciousness in England* (Manchester: Manchester University Press, 1994); M. Prak, Regions in early modern Europe, 11th International Conference, *Debates and Controversies in Economic History: A — Sessions* (Milan, 1994), pp. 19–55; and E. Royle (ed.), *Issues of Regional Identity: In honour of John Marshall* (Manchester: Manchester University Press, 1998), especially the chapter by D. Neave on the East Riding. Neave tempers the north-south division of England with the concept of Highland and Lowland zones, which are visible on the ground and plain to the naturalist's eye; they translate for the economist into relative costs of production. See also the pioneering work of Wilfred Smith, *An Economic Geography of Great Britain* (London: Methuen, second edition, 1953).

De-industrialisation

A general treatment is F. Blackaby (ed.), *De-industrialisation* (London: Heinemann Educational Books, 1978), especially the chapter by A. Cairncross, What is de-industrialisation? As far as economic historians are concerned, fresh life was injected into the topic by S. Pollard, *Peaceful Conquest: The Industrialization of Europe 1760–1970* (Oxford: Oxford University Press, 1981), followed by P. Hudson, *Regions and Industries: A perspective on the Industrial Revolution in Britain* (Cambridge: Cambridge University Press, 1989), which contains an important chapter by B. Short, The de-industrialisation process: a case study of the Weald, 1600–1850. My own contributions include E. L. Jones, The constraints on economic growth in southern England, 1650–1850, *Contributions* V, *Third International Conference of Economic History*, Munich, 1965 (Paris: Mouton, 1974), pp. 423–430, and most recently, Missing out on industrial revolution, *World Econ.* **9**(4): 101–128, 2008.

Useful *Surveys* of early industrialisation are M. Palmer (ed.), *The Onset of Industrialisation* (Nottingham: Department of Adult Education, n.d. [1977], especially the contributions by D. Hey and M. Rowlands; and B. Trinder, *The Making of the Industrial Landscape* (Gloucester: Alan Sutton, 1987 edition).

For specialised studies, see R. P. Beckinsale, The plush industry of Oxfordshire, *Oxoniensia* **XXVIII**: 53–67, 1963; R. F. Dell, The decline of the clothing industry in Berkshire, *Trans. Newbury Dist. Field Club* X(2): 50–64, 1954; H. W. Dickinson, Henry Cort's bicentenary, *Trans. Newcomen Soc.* **XXI**: 31–47, 1940–1941; H. I. Dutton and S. R. H. Jones, Invention and innovation in the British pin industry, 1790–1850, *Bus. Hist. Rev.* **LVII**(2): 175–193, 1983; N. B. Harte and K. G. Ponting (eds.), *Textile History and Economic History* (Manchester: Manchester University Press, 1973); W. G. Hoskins, *Industry, Trade and People in Exeter 1688–1800, with Special Reference to the Serge Industry* (Manchester: Manchester University Press, 1935); G. H. Kenyon, *The Glass Industry of the Weald* (Leicester: Leicester University Press, 1967); J. de L. Mann, Textile industries since 1550, in *Victoria County History, Wiltshire*, IV (1959); E. A. L. Moir, The gentlemen clothiers: a study of the organization of the Gloucestershire cloth industry, 1750–1835, in H. P. R. Finberg (ed.), *Gloucestershire Studies* (Leicester: Leicester University Press, 1957); A. Plummer, *The Witney Blanket Industry* (London: George Routledge & Sons, 1934); T. Rath, The Tewkesbury hosiery industry, *Text. Hist.* 7: 140–153, 1976; H. Symonds, The silk industry in Wessex, *Proc. Dorset Nat. Hist. Antiq. Field Club* **XXXVII**: 66–85, 1916; K. G. Ponting, *The Woollen Industry of Southwest England* (Bath: Adams and Dart, 1971); and A. M. Urdank, Economic decline in the English industrial revolution: the Gloucester wool trade, 1800–1840, *J. Econ. Hist.* **XLV**: 427–433, 1985.

Studies that emphasise *resilient or growing areas* in the south are R. S. Neale, The industries of the city of Bath in the first half of the nineteenth century, *Proc. Somerset Archaeol. Nat. Hist. Soc.* **108**: 132–144, 1964; and D. Ormrod, Industry 1640–1800, in A. Armstrong (ed.), *The Economy of Kent 1640–1914* (Woodbridge: Boydell and Kent County Council, 1995).

Bourgeois Values

This possible explanation of economic growth is put forward by G. Clark, *A Farewell to Alms* (Princeton: Princeton University Press, 2006). Among the many reviews, see D. McCloskey, 'You know, Ernest, the rich are different from you and me': a comment on Clark's *A Farewell to Alms, Eur. Rev. Econ. Hist.* **12**: 138–148, 2008; and R. Solow in *The New York Review*, Nov. 2007. Informed comments about genealogy are made by A. Wagner, *Pedigree and Progress: Essays in the Genealogical Interpretation of History* (London: Phillimore, 1975).

The Landed System

Studies of agricultural improvement and the landed system are staples of economic history and rather than attempt the futile task of selecting particular items, I suggest the reader may find enlightening R. Wilson and A. Mackley, *Creating Paradise: The Building of the English Country House 1660–1880* (London: Hambledon and London, 2000), and the appropriate county volumes of N. Pevsner, *The Buildings of England*, besides when possible visiting houses that are open to the public. Similarly, two books by A. Nicolson counteract the usual dry-as-dust writing on the subject; they are *Earls of Paradise: England and the Dream of Perfection* (London: Harper*Press*, 2008) and *Sissinghurst: An Unfinished History* (London: HarperCollins*Publishers*, 2008).

Politics and Ideas

Foundation sources are J. Mokyr, The intellectual origins of modern economic growth, *J. Econ. Hist.* **65**(2): 285–351, 2005; and J. Mokyr, The institutional origins of the industrial revolution, M.S., Northwestern University, January 2008. On the Enlightenment and related matters, see R. Porter, *Enlightenment: Britain and the Creation of the Modern World* (London: Allen Lane The Penguin Press, 2000), and D. Stanciu, *Shaftesbury's 'Characteristics' — A Socratic Programme of the Eighteenth Century* (Bucharest: Editura Universitatii din Bucuresti, 2004). On other aspects of political change, R. Davis, The rise of protection in England, 1689–1786, *Econ. Hist. Rev.* N.S. **19**(2): 306–317, 1966; B. R. Weingast, The political foundations of democracy and the rule of law, *Am. Polit. Sci. Rev.* **91**(2): 245–263, 1997; and D. C. North *et al.*, Limited access order in the developing world: a new approach to the problem of development, World Bank Policy Research Working Paper No. 4359 (2007). On finance, S. Epstein, *Freedom and Growth: The Rise of States and Markets in*

Europe, 1300–1750 (London: Routledge, 2000); P. K. O'Brien, Fiscal exceptionalism: Great Britain and its European rivals from Civil War to triumphant Trafalgar and Waterloo, in D. Winch and P. K. O'Brien (eds.), *The Political Economy of British Historical Experience, 1688–1914* (Oxford: Oxford University Press/British Academy, 2002); and J. Wells and D. Wills, Revolution, restoration, and debt repudiation: the Jacobite threat to England's institutions and economic growth, *J. Econ. Hist.* **60**: 418–441, 2000; on the legal setting, J. Getzler, Theories of property and economic development, *J. Interdiscipl. Hist.* **26**(4): 639–669, 1996; and R. Harris, Law, finance and the first corporations (Prepared for World Justice Forum, Vienna, 2–5 July 2008); and on corruption, W. D. Rubinstein, The end of the 'Old Corruption' in Britain 1780–1860, *Past & Present* **101**: 55–86, 1983; and P. Harling, *The Waning of the 'Old Corruption': the Politics of Economical Reform in Britain, 1779–1846* (Oxford: Clarendon Press, 1996).

Transport

D. Bogart, Turnpike trusts and the transportation revolution in eighteenth-century England, *Explor. Econ. Hist.* **42**: 479–508, 2005; D. Gerhold, Productivity change in road transport before and after turnpiking, 1690–1840, *Econ. Hist. Rev.* **49**: 491–515, 1996; E. Pawson, *The Turnpike Trusts of the Eighteenth Century: A Study of Innovation and Diffusion* (Oxford: School of Geography Research Paper 14, 1975): and E. Pawson, *Transport and Economy: The Turnpike Roads of Eighteenth-Century Britain* (London: Academic Press, 1977); C. H. Shiue and W. Keller, Markets in China and Europe on the eve of the industrial revolution, *Am. Econ. Rev.* **97**(4): 1189–1216, 2007; and last but not least, R. Szostak, *The Role of Transportation in the Industrial Revolution* (Montreal & Kingston: McGill-Queen's University Press, 1991).

The Pace of Change

Little directly confronts the issue of the speed of change. An exception is J. G. Williamson, Leaving the farm to go to the city: did they leave quickly enough? in J. A. James and M. Thomas (eds.), *Capitalism in Context: Essays on Economic Development and Cultural Change in Honor of R. M. Hartwell* (Chicago: University of Chicago Press, 1994), pp. 159–182.

Northern Industrialisation

H. Heaton, *The Yorkshire Woollen and Worsted Industries: From the Earliest Times up to the Industrial Revolution* (Oxford: Clarendon Press, 1920); J. D. Marshall, *Lancashire* (Newton Abbot: David & Charles, 1974); M. Nevell, Brian Grimsditch and Carolanne King, *Carrbrook: A Textile Village and Its Valley. A Study in the Industrialisation of the Pennine Uplands* (Manchester: Tameside Metropolitan Borough Council, 2006); A. P. Wadsworth and J. De Lacy Mann, *The Cotton Trade and Industrial Lancashire 1600–1780* (New York: Augustus M. Kelley, 1968); J. K. Walton, *Lancashire: A Social History* (Manchester: Manchester University Press, 1987); D. G. Watts, Water-power and the industrial revolution, *Trans. Cumberland Westmorland Antiq. Archaeol. Soc.* N.S. **67**: 199–205, 1967; and another last but not least, R. G. Wilson, The supremacy of the Yorkshire cloth industry in the eighteenth century, in N. B. Harte and K. G. Ponting (eds.), *Textile History and Economic History* (Manchester: Manchester University Press, 1973), pp. 225–246.

INDEX

Acemoglu, D., 28
Abramovitz, M., 48–49
agriculture, 8, 28, 30, 35, 37, 47, 48, 60, 73, 75, 79, chapter 6 *passim*, 148, 159, 160, 186, 201, 210, chapter 10 *passim*, 239, 242, 243, 252
Allen, Ralph, 99
Allen, Robert C., 93, 115
Ambrosoli, M., 241
Arkwright family, 114, 249
Arrow, K., 10
Aubrey, J., 96, 131, 168, 206
Australia *passim*

Baker, J., 220, 228, 231
Banbury, 52, 54, 73, 100, 102, 114
Bateman, Sir J., 151
Bath, 56, 87
Bell, Sir T., 66
Bennet, H., 169
Benson, W., 151
Bentham, S., 99
Beresford, M., 156
Bernholz, P., 26
Betjeman, J., 157
Biddulph, J., 152
Birmingham, 55, 67, 99, 109, 118, 207, 248
blood sports, 12, 16, 150–151, 155, 157, 186, 242, 243
Bogart, D., 194

Boulton & Watt, 57, 58, 98
Bourn, D., 113–114
Braudel, F., 28, 74
bridges, 197, 201
Briggs, A., 58
Bristol, 9, 67, 82, 99, 113, 137, 149, 151, 206, 207
Broadberry, S., 25, 28
Brown, L. ('Capability'), 156, 224
Brunel, M., 98, 99
Bryant, J., 22, 27
Burnett, J., 83
Bull, J., 97, 100
Burroughs, J., 81
Burt, R., 32

Calamy, E., 169
Camp, A., 127
Campbell, B., 37
canals, 75, 108, 148, 180, 182, 193, 195, 196, 204, 207, 210, 216, 242
capital, supplies of, 111–115, 149
Casson, M., 187
Chambers, J. D., 1, 14, 208, 215
Chartres, J., 37
China, 22, 24–27, 29, 34, 74, 95, 111, 139, 172, 198, 208, 254
Cipolla, C., 23
Clapham, Sir J., 52
Clark, C., 28, 84
Clark, G., 7, 78, chapter 6 *passim*, 215